CHRISTOPHER HILL is a Fellow and Tutor in Modern History at Balliol College, Oxford. He is also a graduate of Balliol College and a Fellow of All Souls College. He became a University Lecturer in sixteenth- and seventeenth-century history in 1959 and Ford's Lecturer in 1962. His publications include: *The English Revolution 1640; Two Commonwealths* (under the name K. E. Holme); *Lenin and the Russian Revolution; Economic Problems of the Church; Puritanism and Revolution; Oliver Cromwell; The Century of Revolution;* and numerous articles in professional journals.

THE NORTON LIBRARY HISTORY OF ENGLAND

General Editors

CHRISTOPHER BROOKE
*Professor of History, Westfield College,
University of London*

and

DENIS MACK SMITH
Fellow of All Souls College, Oxford

Already published:

ROMAN BRITAIN AND EARLY ENGLAND, 55 B.C.–A.D 871
Peter Hunter Blair

FROM ALFRED TO HENRY III, 871–1272
Christopher Brooke

THE LATER MIDDLE AGES, 1272–1485
George Holmes

THE CENTURY OF REVOLUTION, 1603–1714
Christopher Hill

FROM CASTLEREAGH TO GLADSTONE, 1815–1885
Derek Beales

MODERN BRITAIN, 1885–1955
Henry Pelling

Forthcoming titles:

THE TUDOR AGE, 1485–1603
Margaret Bowker

THE EIGHTEENTH CENTURY, 1714–1815
John B. Owen

The Century
of Revolution

1603-1714

CHRISTOPHER HILL

The Norton Library
W · W · NORTON & COMPANY · INC ·
NEW YORK

SBN 393 00365 5

First published in the Norton Library 1966 by
arrangement with Thomas Nelson and Sons, Ltd.

BOOKS THAT LIVE

The Norton imprint on a book means that in the publisher's
estimation it is a book not for a single season but for the years.

W. W. NORTON & COMPANY, INC.

Printed in the United States of America
5 6 7 8 9 0

General Editors' Preface

KNOWLEDGE and understanding of English history change and develop so rapidly that a new series needs little apology. The present series was planned in the conviction that a fresh survey of English history was needed, and that the time was ripe for it. It will cover the whole span from Caesar's first invasion in 55 B.C. to 1955, and be completed in eight volumes. The precise scope and scale of each book will inevitably vary according to the special circumstances of its period ; but each will combine a clear narrative with an analysis of many aspects of history —social, economic, religious, cultural and so forth—such as is essential in any approach to English history today.

The special aim of this series is to provide serious and yet challenging books, not buried under a mountain of detail. Each volume is intended to provide a picture and an appreciation of its age, as well as a lucid outline, written by an expert who is keen to make available and alive the findings of modern research. They are intended to be reasonably short—long enough that the reader may feel he has really been shown the ingredients of a period, not so long that he loses appetite for anything further. The series is intended to be a stimulus to wider reading rather than a substitute for it ; and yet to comprise a set of volumes, each, within its limits, complete in itself. Our hope is to provide an introduction to English history which is lively and illuminating, and which makes it at once exciting and more intelligible.

C. N. L. B.
D. M. S.

Author's Preface

THE arrangement of this book calls for a word of explanation. In order to avoid repeating at length what can be found in many textbooks, and to have more space for attempts at explanation, I have, in the narrative chapters, given merely a bald summary of events. The reader should be patient when, for instance, he finds ' the Cokayne Project ' mentioned without explanation on p. 10. It is discussed at length on pp. 35–7. The index indicates where definitions of technical terms are to be found, and gives biographical details of persons not fully identified in the text. Quotations from seventeenth-century sources have been modernised. Dates are given in the Old Style. Seventeenth-century England was ten days behind the New Style used on the Continent. But I have taken the year as beginning on 1st January, not on 25th March as seventeenth-century Englishmen did.

The plan of this series did not allow full documentation. When I have consciously used someone else's idea, or quoted a phrase from a historian not easily identifiable from the context, I hope I have normally given the reference in a footnote. But I have taken so much from Sir G. N. Clark, Professor W. Haller, Professor W. K. Jordan, Mr E. Lipson, Mr David Ogg, and Professor R. H. Tawney, that I can express only my general gratitude here. Extracts from Clarendon's *History of the Rebellion* and his *Life* have been included by kind permission of the Clarendon Press. I have taken advantage of hearing Professor F. J. Fisher talk about the cultivation of forests and waste lands, and of discussions with Dr Eric Hobsbawm, Mr A. L. Morton, and Mr Lionel Munby. Again and again, though this cannot be documented, I am conscious that my ideas are at least less half-baked than they would have been if I had not had to defend them in tutorial discussions with pupils, extending now over twenty-five years.

Dr J. B. Owen, Mr Lawrence Stone, and Mr Angus Walker read this book in typescript, and it has benefited greatly from their searching criticisms. The general editors of the series were encouraging but vigilant, and Mr Denis Mack Smith devoted a great deal of time to helping me to say what I meant. Mr Richard Grassby very kindly read the proofs. My greatest debt, as always, is to my wife.

1960   C. H.

I AM most grateful to Mr R. Barnes, Dr G. R. Elton, Dr H. Koeppler, Professor V. de Sola Pinto, Mrs Menna Prestwich and especially Mr John Cooper for pointing out errors in the first impression. If I have obstinately refused to accept all their good advice the blame is mine alone.

1961   C. H.

I HAVE taken the opportunity of a new impression to correct some slips which reviewers have pointed out. I am particularly grateful for corrections suggested by Professor John Bromley and Mr Ivan Roots. I have also made some corrections arising from Professor Habakkuk's article on Interregnum finance in *Economic History Review*, August 1962.

1962   C. H.

Contents

20   Conclusion, 1660–1714   307

21   Epilogue   312

     Appendices   315

     Books for Further Reading   322

     Index   327

List of Abbreviations

Econ. H.R.	*Economic History Review*
P. and P.	*Past and Present*
H.M.C.	*Historical Manuscripts Commission*
T.R.H.S.	*Transactions of the Royal Historical Society*

List of Plates

between pages 116 and 117

List of Maps

*Acknowledgment is made to the British Museum ; the Central Press
Photos Ltd. ; the Controller of H.M. Stationery Office (Crown copyright
reserved) ; and the Master and Fellows of Magdalene College, Cambridge,
for permission to use photographs reproduced in this book.*

*The photograph of C. Wild's water-colour of the Royal Chapel,
Windsor Castle, is reproduced by gracious permission of Her Majesty
the Queen.*

1 Introductory

But how can I explain, how can I explain to *you*?
You will understand less after I have explained it.
All that I can hope to make you understand
Is only events : not what has happened.
And people to whom nothing has ever happened
Cannot understand the unimportance of events.

T. S. Eliot, *The Family Reunion*

HISTORY is not a narrative of events. The historian's difficult task is to explain what happened. The years between 1603 and 1714 were perhaps the most decisive in English history. The dates are arbitrary, since they relate to the deaths of queens, not to the life of the community. Nevertheless, during the seventeenth century modern English society and a modern state began to take shape, and England's position in the world was transformed. This book tries to penetrate below the familiar events to grasp ' what happened '—to ordinary English men and women as well as to kings and queens or abstractions like ' society ' and ' the state '. What happened in the seventeenth century is still sufficiently part of us today, of our ways of thinking, our prejudices, our hopes, to be worth trying to understand.

It may help if we start with a bird's-eye view of the period. It begins with the accession of King James, who united the crowns of England and Scotland : in 1707 Parliament achieved that more solid union of the two kingdoms which James had failed to bring about. James succeeded by hereditary right, confirmed by Elizabeth's nomination ; in 1714 George I owed his throne to an Act of Parliament which passed over many persons with a better hereditary claim. James, like the Tudors before him, chose ministers and favourites as seemed best to him ; by the early eighteenth century ministers could not

1

govern without a Parliamentary majority. James was still
expected to ' live of his own ', to finance government from
crown lands, feudal dues, and the customs : no distinction was
drawn between the public and private capacity of the King.
Parliament, summoned at the King's absolute discretion,
expected to vote taxes only in an emergency (though here
theory already lagged behind practical necessity). By 1714
Parliament, in almost permanent session, had complete control
of finance. In James's reign members of the landed class
themselves admitted to being absurdly undertaxed ; in Anne's
the gentry paid for Marlborough's wars. By then Parliament
had established a degree of control over the executive and
over all its actions—including foreign policy, which early
Stuart kings had regarded as their private preserve. James and
Charles acted arbitrarily in matters affecting the stability of the
country's economic life—raising or lowering the customs,
granting industrial monopolies, controlling prices, prohibiting
land enclosure. The economy was highly regulated. At the
end of the period economic policy was formulated by Parliament, and *laissez-faire* had succeeded regulation in most
spheres. This made possible the appearance of the Bank of
England, the National Debt, and other modern financial
institutions.

The England of 1603 was a second-class power ; the
Great Britain of 1714 was the greatest world power. Under
James and Charles English colonisation of America was just
beginning ; under Anne England held a large empire in
America, Asia, and Africa, and colonial questions were decisive
when policy was formulated. The East India Company was
formed in 1601 ; a century later it was the most powerful
corporation in the country. At the beginning of our period
men noted as evidence of the topsy-turviness of the times that
some merchants were as rich as peers ; before the end, many
a noble family had salvaged its fortunes by a judicious marriage
in the City. Englishmen's diet was transformed in this century
by the introduction of root crops, which made it possible to have
fresh meat in winter. Potatoes and many new vegetables were
added to it, as were tea, coffee, chocolate, sugar, and tobacco.
Port- and gin-drinking became national habits. Plague was
frequent in the first half of the century, extinct by the end.

The modern arrangement of meals—breakfast, lunch, and dinner—dates from the seventeenth century. So does the modern pattern of male costume—coat, waistcoat, breeches.[1] Calico, linen, and silk came in for clothes ; leather went out. By the end of the century pottery and glass had replaced pewter and wood at table ; many families used knives, forks, mirrors, and pocket handkerchiefs ; at Chatsworth the Duke of Devonshire had installed a bath with hot and cold running water.

In 1603 all English men and women were deemed to be members of the state Church, dissent from which was a punishable offence. Heretics were still burnt at the stake, just as suspected traitors were tortured. By 1714 Protestant dissent was legally tolerated : the Church could no longer burn, the state no longer tortured. Church courts, powerful in all spheres of life since the Middle Ages, lost almost all their functions in this century. Under Charles I Archbishop Laud ruled the country ; under Anne it caused a sensation when, for the last time, a Bishop was appointed to government office.

Under the early Stuarts Justices of the Peace were subjected to direction from Whitehall, and had to answer in Star Chamber for recalcitrance ; by Anne's reign country gentlemen and town oligarchies were virtual dictators of local government, responsible only to men like themselves in Parliament. James I and his son dismissed judges who were too independent of royal wishes ; after 1701 judges could be removed only by address of both Houses of Parliament.

James I preached that kings ruled by Divine Right, and many political writers argued that subjects' property was at the king's disposal. Parliamentarians countered these positions by Biblical texts or medieval precedents. By 1714 politics had become a rational inquiry, discussed in terms of utility, experience, common sense, no longer in terms of Divine Right, texts, and antiquarian research. James wrote a treatise on witches, and was no more credulous than most of his subjects, with whom astrology and alchemy were still in high repute. The second half of the century saw modern science triumphant ; by 1714 fairies, witches, astrology, and alchemy were no longer taken seriously by educated men. The majestic laws of

[1] I owe these points to Miss K. Briggs's *The Anatomy of Puck* (1959), p. 2.

Newton made nonsense of the traditional idea that the earth was the centre of a universe in which God and the Devil intervened continuously. Shakespeare had thought of the universe and of society in terms of degree, hierarchy; by 1714 both society and the universe seemed to consist of competing atoms. A man like Richard Cromwell, who was born under Charles I and lived into the eighteenth century, ' had seen the end of the Middle Ages, the beginnings of the modern world. . . . Between his birth and his death the educated person's conception of nature and of man's place in nature had been transformed.' [1]

So we could go on through every phase of life and thought. During the century occurred what T. S. Eliot called a ' dissociation of sensibility '. For the ' metaphysical poets ', from Donne to Traherne, thoughts were experiences which modified their sensibility. By Dryden's time poets had lost this ability to devour and digest any kind of experience : there were ' poetic ' subjects and there was poetic diction. ' The language became more refined, the feeling became more crude ' as we pass from the tortured doubt of Donne and Shakespeare's tragic period to the superficial certainties of Pope. Prose became less poetic as poetry became more prosaic. At the beginning of our period the fashionable style was scholarly, leisurely, rolled out in the elaborate periods of Richard Hooker or Sir Thomas Browne. When it ends, the plain, straightforward prose of Bunyan, Swift, and Defoe is unmistakably that of modern English. Under James I, Roger North says, ' most sober families ' practised both instrumental and vocal music ; by the end of the period household chamber music was ' utterly confounded ' by public performances of opera, by virtuoso violinists and singers. It was a great century in English musical history ; but by its end native creative talent appears to be dead. On the other hand, the first part of the century saw an increasing dominance of foreign masters and models in painting and architecture, the latter part the re-emergence of a native tradition and styles that were to survive.

The transformation that took place in the seventeenth century is then far more than merely a constitutional or political revolution, or a revolution in economics, religion, or

[1] H. Baker, *The Wars of Truth* (1952), p. 366

taste. It embraces the whole of life. Two conceptions of civilisation were in conflict. One took French absolutism for its model, the other the Dutch Republic. The object of this book is to try to understand the changes which set England on the path of Parliamentary government, economic advance and imperialist foreign policy, of religious toleration and scientific progress.

PART ONE

1603–40

2   Narrative of Events, 1603-40

> The computation of times is not of so great moment, figures are easily mistaken ; the 10 of July and the 6 of August, with a year over or under, makes not a man the wiser in the business then done, which is only that he desires.
>
> Samuel Daniel, *Collection of the History of England* (1612)

QUEEN ELIZABETH died on 24th March 1603, and James VI of Scotland succeeded without opposition. An alleged plot of 1604 to put Arabella Stuart on the throne, for which Lord Cobham was executed and Sir Walter Ralegh imprisoned, was widely suspected to have been manufactured, or at least grossly exaggerated, by Sir Robert Cecil to strengthen his own position. Cecil, later Earl of Salisbury, son of Elizabeth's great minister, Burghley, had been largely responsible for James's peaceful succession, and the King retained him as Secretary, advancing him to the office of Lord Treasurer in 1608.

James had been brought up a Presbyterian, and his accession was greeted hopefully by English Puritans, who sympathised with Presbyterian criticisms of the established Church. They presented him with the Millenary Petition—a very moderate request for changes in ceremonies, which was alleged to have been signed by a thousand ministers. James, however, allied himself with the Bishops, telling the Puritans' representatives at the Hampton Court Conference (1604) that if they did not conform he would ' harry them out of the land '. Many Puritan ministers were deprived of their livings in the years which followed, despite a shortage of preaching clergy. By concluding peace with Spain in 1604 James ended a war which had lasted nineteen years. The revolt in Ireland led by Hugh O'Neill, Earl of Tyrone, which had begun in 1598, was finally suppressed in 1603. So James met his first Parliament with no outstanding financial obligations except a debt of

£100,000 inherited from Elizabeth. Nevertheless, relations were not harmonious. The King's proposal for a legislative union between England and Scotland was rejected. A clash over the right to determine disputed elections led the House of Commons to declare that their privileges were inherited of right, and were not due to the King's grace. The Catholic Guy Fawkes's attempt to blow up King, Lords, and Commons in 1605 caused a reconciliation ; but there were financial quarrels, and James's high view of the royal prerogative aroused opposition. The Commons showed their alarm by attacking *The Interpreter*, a law dictionary published in 1607 by Dr Cowell, Professor of Civil Law at Cambridge : this stated the royalist position in terms of which James probably approved, but which he agreed to condemn.

Parliament was dissolved in 1610, with the financial problem unsolved. Salisbury died in 1612. He had already been succeeded in James's confidence by the conservative family of the Howards (Northampton, Lord Privy Seal and Commissioner for the Treasury, 1612, who was a pensioner of Spain ; Suffolk, whose wife was, too). Allied with the Howards was James's Scottish favourite, Robert Carr, Earl of Somerset. In 1614 the 'Addled Parliament' was dissolved after nine weeks, voting no supplies. The reputation of the government sank low, the Howards being justly suspected of corruption. Somerset was first involved in a divorce scandal, and then was condemned with his wife for poisoning Sir Thomas Overbury. From 1616 onwards the Cokayne Project led to a crisis of over-production and unemployment in the clothing industry, England's major industry. The handsome George Villiers succeeded Somerset as royal favourite, rising rapidly to become Duke of Buckingham, the first non-royal duke in England since 1572.

In 1613 James married his daughter, Elizabeth, to Frederick, Elector Palatine, a leading German Protestant. In 1618 Frederick was invited by Czech Protestants to accept the crown of Bohemia, hitherto almost hereditary in the Catholic Habsburg family. Frederick accepted, and the war which followed lasted for thirty years (1618–48). James disapproved of his son-in-law's action, and tried to mediate between him and the Spanish-Austrian Habsburg alliance. In London and among Protestants all over the country there was strong support for the Elector Palatine, which was expressed in the Parliament of 1621. The Commons were also critical of government economic policy, and impeached Lord Chancellor Bacon for bribery. With his disgrace James lost one of his ablest councillors. The House of Commons tried to make its vote of taxation conditional on a declaration of war on Spain ; and in January 1622 James dissolved Parliament without obtaining supplies.

Then followed the ridiculous expedition of Prince Charles and Buckingham to Madrid in an attempt to negotiate a marriage alliance with the King of Spain's daughter, by which James hoped to bring peace to Europe. After six months of negotiation the scheme broke down humiliatingly, and Charles and Buckingham returned to England determined on war with Spain. In the 1624 Parliament they obtained financial grants in return for allowing the impeachment of Lionel Cranfield, Earl of Middlesex, the merchant financier who had come near to balancing James's budget. They also accepted the Statute of Monopolies, which made illegal all monopolies not granted to corporations.

Buckingham had established himself securely in Charles's favour, and the two had wrested control of the government from the senile James ; so his death in February 1625 made little difference. But the alliance with the Puritans did not last. Buckingham negotiated a marriage for Charles with Henrietta Maria of France, the price of which was English help to Louis XIII in suppressing the Protestant stronghold of La Rochelle, and the granting of liberty of worship to Catholics in England. There was strong opposition to these policies, and the Parliament of 1626, under the leadership of Sir John Eliot, directly attacked Buckingham. It was dissolved without voting supplies—not even the customs dues (tunnage and poundage) normally voted to every king for life at the beginning of his reign. But Charles continued to collect them, and also raised a forced loan. Refusals to pay led to the Five Knights' Case (Darnel's Case), in which the judges reaffirmed the principle laid down in 1591, that the king had the right to commit men to prison without cause shown. This produced the Petition of Right in the Parliament of 1628-9. The

Petition declared illegal both arbitrary imprisonment and the collection of taxes without Parliamentary consent. It also prohibited billeting or martial law, for Buckingham was now engaged in war against France as well as Spain, and the troops levied to relieve besieged La Rochelle were a burden on the southern counties both before and after the disastrous failure of English intervention.

In August 1628 Buckingham was assassinated. But his death altered nothing. Renewed quarrels led to the dissolution of Parliament and eleven years of personal government. Charles's chief minister in this period was William Laud, Bishop of London (Archbishop of Canterbury, 1633), though he never won the King's confidence in the way Buckingham had done. At the beginning of the reign Laud and the Puritan John Preston had competed for Charles's favour. Buckingham at one time appeared to favour Preston. But the King's personal predilection was for Laud, whose emphasis on the more traditionally Catholic ceremonial aspects of worship appealed to Charles no less than did the resolute championing of royal authority by Laud's protégés in the Church. Laud made Juxon, Bishop of London, Lord Treasurer in 1636, and saw that men of his faction were promoted in Church and state. Charles's other outstanding servant was Sir Thomas Wentworth, who became Earl of Strafford in 1640. Wentworth had led a centre party in the Commons in the sixteen-twenties, and his acceptance of office and a peerage in 1628 was regarded as treachery by Pym and the more radical opposition. Wentworth was made President of the Council in the North, in 1632 Lord Deputy of Ireland. ' Black Tom Tyrant ' ruled Ireland with a heavy but efficient hand, reducing the Irish Parliament to submission and building up an army of Papists which aroused apprehension in England.

Charles's government was far from being united. Laud and Wentworth co-operated in working for what they called a policy of ' thorough ' ; they were opposed by a group of courtiers around Lord Treasurer Weston, a Catholic who died in 1635, and later by Lord Cottington and Henrietta Maria. The Queen succeeded Buckingham as Charles's evil genius. Under her protection Catholicism became fashionable at court. The recusancy laws which fined Catholics for not coming to church were not enforced. In 1637 a papal agent was received at Whitehall. The Puritans blamed Laud for this policy, and for England's failure to give any support to the Protestant cause in the Thirty Years' War. Simultaneously critics of the state Church were savagely punished. In 1637 the lawyer William Prynne, the Reverend Henry Burton, and Dr John Bastwick were mutilated, heavily fined, and imprisoned for life.

One reason for the feebleness of Charles's government in foreign affairs was lack of money. Weston effected numerous economies, and a variety of financial expedients was adopted which alienated all sections of the population. It was Ship Money that at last made the government solvent. Originally an occasional tax on port towns in lieu of providing a ship for the royal navy, Ship Money was extended in 1635 to inland towns. Repeated in the next three years, it looked like becoming a regular tax not voted by Parliament. In 1637 John Hampden and Lord Saye and Sele, in concert with a group of opponents of the government, brought a test case. By the narrowest possible margin the judges decided in favour of the legality of Ship Money.

But events in Scotland intervened to thwart Charles. Despite opposition, James had re-established episcopacy there. At the beginning of his reign Charles had tried to recover Church lands from the nobles who had seized them, and so roused hostility : in 1637 he introduced a slightly modified version of the English Prayer Book, and touched off a national resistance movement. In 1638 the National Covenant was signed all over Scotland and an army was raised. Next year war broke out. Charles collected an army to oppose the Scots, but he had no money to pay the reluctant troops. In June 1638 he had to sign the Treaty of Berwick. But he would not agree to abolish episcopacy in Scotland, and negotiations were again broken off. The leaders of the English opposition were already in touch with the Scots, and when Charles at last called a Parliament in April 1640 he found it impossible to appeal to English patriotism against the old enemy. The Short Parliament was dissolved after three weeks. The Earl of Warwick, Lord Saye and Sele, John Hampden, John Pym, and other Parliamentary leaders were arrested. Unprecedentedly,

Convocation, the assembly of the clergy, was continued after Parliament was dissolved. It accepted a series of new canons which ordered the clergy to preach up the Divine Right of Kings, placed restrictions on preaching, and ordered altars to be railed. Convocation also granted the King £20,000 as a 'benevolence' from the clergy. Since Parliament had voted no supply, and the two bodies normally acted together, this demonstrated the Church's subservience to the crown. But it did not solve the government's financial problems. The City of London refused to grant a loan. The army facing the Scots was mutinous. The latter entered England virtually unopposed and occupied Newcastle. Charles attempted to appeal to the peerage by calling a Great Council of peers to York in September 1640. Even they recommended summoning Parliament. Peace was signed at Ripon in October, but Charles had to promise the Scottish army £850 a day until a final settlement was reached. The Scots intended to force him to call Parliament. Petitions from the counties and demonstrations in London made the same demand. The last time for many years that the rack was used in England was on a drummer-boy who had headed a procession to Lambeth to hunt 'William the Fox' (Laud). At last the King had to surrender. The Long Parliament assembled on 3rd November. With intermissions it sat for nearly twenty years.

3 Economics, 1603-40

> *Castruchio* : What an ass is that lord, to borrow money of a citizen !
> *Bellafont* : Nay, God's my pity, what an ass is that citizen to lend money to a lord !
>
> Dekker, *The Honest Whore* (1604), II, i

THE LAND

IT IS not very original to state that Britain is an island. Yet in the sixteenth and seventeenth centuries this fact was of crucial importance. The one hundred and fifty years before the Civil War saw almost constant warfare on the Continent ; in England there was peace. National defence was looked after by the navy ; there was no need for an army. After 1603 the frontier with Scotland no longer needed to be defended. England has excellent water communications, and water transport was in this period far cheaper than land transport. It cost as much to bring goods to London by land from Norwich as by sea from Lisbon. Coastal trade expanded rapidly. In the reign of Charles I the Thames was navigable as far as Oxford ; York, Nottingham, Shrewsbury, Stratford-on-Avon, Peterborough, Hertford, Bedford, and Cambridge were all ports. But government policy and social privilege combined to counteract the advantages which geography had given England. In 1627 the city of Gloucester obtained a charter permitting it to levy tolls on all vessels proceeding up the Severn towards Birmingham ; and ' mighty men ' were able in the next decade to prevent improvements in Severn navigation which were essential for the Midlands industries. The real improvement of communications came after 1640 when aristocratic privilege counted for less.

The century before 1640 was one of inflation. The price of wheat rose six times, and the general price level four or

five times. This favoured those producing in order to sell,
whether in industry or agriculture, provided their own subsistence was ensured by possession or secure tenure of land.
The overwhelming majority of the population lived by agriculture ; those of the propertied class, from peer to yeoman,
who were parsimonious, skilled, or lucky, might get rich
quickly ; the extravagant or unlucky might founder. Many
factors were involved : fortunate geographical location, in a
sheep-farming or clothing area, near a market or cheap water
communications ; the discovery of minerals on one's estate.
For a gentleman or peer, luck might include lucrative office
at court, though no doubt as many gamblers ruined themselves
drawing blanks in that expensive lottery as made fortunes.
Having a successful lawyer or merchant in the family, or
making a judicious marriage with legal or commercial wealth,
might be the turning-point, though not all were as fortunate
as Mr Emmanuel Badd of the Isle of Wight, who ' by God's
blessing and the loss of five wives grew very rich '.

But the safest road to prosperity lay through careful attention to profit and loss, book-keeping, watching markets,
checking and shortening leases, racking rents, through avoid-
ance of unnecessary extravagance. ' To improve land with
profit,' Adam Smith was to say, ' like all other commercial
projects, requires an exact attention to small savings and
small gains, of which a man born to a great fortune, even
though naturally frugal, is very seldom capable. The situation
of such a person naturally disposes him to attend rather to
ornament . . . than to profit.' These *bourgeois* virtues, which
were also those inculcated by Puritanism, were less likely to
be found in aristocratic families, with their traditions of
ostentatious living, their troops of serving men, retainers, and
poor relations, than among lesser gentry and yeomanry or
small farmers. That profits made on great estates went into
the pockets of stewards rather than landlords was a familiar
jest in Jacobean literature. ' For the plough,' wrote Smyth
of Nibley, formerly a steward himself, ' none gaineth thereby
but he that layeth his eye or hand daily upon it.' ' Gentlemen
disdaining traffic and living in idleness,' observed Fynes
Moryson, ' do in this course daily sell their patrimonies. . . .
The buyers are for the most part citizens and vulgar men.'

Nevertheless, though a noble family might take longer to adjust itself than smaller landlords or ' vulgar men ', peers had tremendous reserves of wealth and credit to draw upon when they took in hand reorganisation of estate management. Against the Veres, Earls of Oxford, who virtually went bankrupt in the early seventeenth century, we must set the Herbert and Percy families, who undertook a very profitable reorganisation, or the Russells, whose estates in the outskirts of the expanding City of London proved a gold-mine. In the decades before 1640 land was passing from the crown to the gentry. Historians disagree about whether gentlemen were also benefiting at the expense of the peerage. But in the seventeenth century it was generally believed that an important section of the gentry was rising in economic status ; and these were the men represented in the House of Commons. In 1628 a peer observed, with disapproval at the way times were changing, that the Lower House could buy the Upper House three times over.

This period is traditionally regarded as the golden age of the yeomanry. These small independent farmers caught the eye as the rising class, but we should not exaggerate their significance. At the end of the century (when their numbers had probably declined) Gregory King thought that ' better freeholders ' amounted to less than one per cent of the population, and all freeholders and farmers to five and a half per cent. Freeholders owned their land, so those with capital behind them, or farmers with long leases, might prosper as prices for their products rose : smaller freeholders might keep their heads above water by producing their own food and clothes. The position was different for copyholders, men who held their land merely ' by copy of court roll '. The heir was liable, on succession to a copyhold, to pay an ' entry fine ' normally fixed by custom, but which the landlord might try to raise arbitrarily. Copyhold was thus an insecure tenure, especially for those not rich enough to defend themselves in the law courts. The hunt for minerals endangered any copyholder unlucky enough to have them discovered under his land. The smaller man might also be evicted when the lands of his village were ' enclosed ' ; at least he risked losing his share of the common and waste lands, so essential to provide

fuel and maintain the animals and birds on which his subsistence depended.

' Enclosure ' meant that land held in scattered strips in the
village open fields was consolidated into compact holdings,
which the occupier might hedge about so as to protect them
from other people's cattle. He was then free to experiment
with rotation of crops, or to switch from arable to pasture.
The great age of enclosure for sheep-farming had perhaps come
to an end by the seventeenth century ; but enclosure and
consolidation for improved arable farming, to feed the expanding industrial areas, was proceeding apace. Enclosure had
long been attacked on the ground that it led to eviction of
tenants and so depopulated the countryside. Tudor governments had tried, less and less effectively, to prevent it. 1597
saw the last Act of Parliament against depopulation. A proclamation of 1619 admitted that the laws for the protection
of corn-growing and peasant proprietorship hampered agricultural improvement. They were repealed by Parliament in
1624, and so one obstacle to capital investment in agriculture
was removed. The Parliament of 1621 had seen the first
general bill facilitating enclosure. From 1633 onwards, when
the government was ruling without Parliament, depopulators
were prosecuted. Six hundred persons were fined for enclosure
between 1636 and 1638 : twenty-three out of forty-six members,
returned to the Long Parliament from five Midland counties,
came from families which had suffered. Laud's activities on the
Enclosure Commission were attacked as a breach of the
common law, and contributed not a little to his unpopularity.

As the debates in 1621 showed, enclosure was a complicated
question, affecting more than the profits of individuals. If
the English economy was to continue to expand, a more
specialised division of labour was essential. More food would
have to be grown to feed the industrial areas, food prices must
be lowered, and corn import ended. There were many ways
to increase production. Consolidation of holdings assisted
capital investment in improvements. Introduction of root
crops led to reduction of fallow. Outlying areas of England
still awaited colonisation, as the internal frontier moved north
and west in Lancashire, Yorkshire, Cumberland, and Devon.
But for the really significant extension of the cultivated area

England and Wales, showing places mentioned in the text

that was necessary, there were three main potential sources :
commons, marsh lands, and royal forests.

The combined effects of the sixteenth-century increase in
fuel consumption, the needs of the navy, the importunity of
courtiers, and the demand for cultivable land had led to some
clearance of forests in the Cotswolds, the Chilterns, the Severn
valley, Devon, Wiltshire, Warwickshire. But in the sixteen-
thirties the government's financial extremity caused it to
reassert royal forest rights in order to fine those who had
encroached on them. 'The economic reality behind the
famous battle over the forests,' wrote Professor Tawney, ' was
the struggle between more extensive and more intensive
methods of land utilisation, to which the increased profitable-
ness of capitalist farming lent a new ferocity.' Only after the
collapse of the monarchy did royal forests become fully available
for cultivation. Drainage of the Fens, Sedgmoor, and other
marshes had started ; but it met with much popular resistance,
led in his area by Oliver Cromwell, ' the Lord of the Fens'.
The attack on waste lands also gained fresh momentum after
the Interregnum. Until this break-through in agriculture,
England remained what is now called a backward economy,
with the mass of the population permanently under-employed,
especially in agriculture. Even in industry employment was
often seasonal, because of dependence on water power.[1]

INDUSTRY

The inflationary century before 1640 had seen a considerable
industrial expansion. Its basis was a rapid development of
coal production, from about 200,000 tons a year to 1,500,000
tons. High timber prices created the demand, and England's
excellent water communications provided the means of transport. By 1640 England produced three times as much coal
as the rest of Europe put together. 'Correct your maps :
Newcastle is Peru !' sang John Cleveland : coal was as precious
as silver. It was important as a domestic fuel, especially in
London, whose dependence on coal imports from Newcastle
was demonstrated in the Civil War. But coal was also used in

[1] D. C. Coleman, 'Labour in the English Economy of the Seventeenth
Century', *Econ. H.R.* (2nd Ser.), **8**, 280–95

new industries, like cannon-founding, sugar-refining, paper-making, and for new techniques in old industries, like iron, steel, and copper. Iron production increased five times in the century after the Reformation. Shipbuilding expanded with internal and external trade.

All these new processes called for heavy application of capital. Coal-mining itself, as it advanced beyond the stage of open-cast mining, demanded ever-increasing outlays for digging, draining, and ventilating pits, for haulage above and below ground. So did other extractive industries, iron, tin, copper, and lead. A smelting works at Keswick employed 4,000 men on the eve of the Civil War. Anything up to £1,000 might be spent before a coal seam was reached, a sum which it would take an unskilled worker a hundred years to earn. Use of coal in other industries—brick-making, soap-boiling, glass-blowing, dyeing, salt-refining, and brewing—called for heavy expenditure on furnaces, pans, vats. A London brewery in James I's reign had a capital of £10,000. Industry was ceasing to be primarily the affair of the small master craftsman and the free miner ; the London capitalist and the enterprising landowner played an increasingly important part. Merchant middlemen bought lead, tin, coal in advance from the small miner, or made loans to wire-drawers, pin-makers, nailers. The Lancashire cotton industry was organised on a capitalist basis from the start.

England's most important industry, cloth, was less highly capitalised, and here there were few significant technical advances—apart from the invention of the stocking frame, too expensive for the small master craftsman to buy. But the small producers were being steadily brought under the control of the London merchant or the gentleman clothier from whom (under the ' putting-out system ') they hired looms and obtained raw materials on credit. Clothiers might employ up to a thousand spinners and weavers. The handicraftsman, wrote Thomas Fuller, ' seldom attaineth to any very great estate except his trade hath some outlets and excursions into wholesale and merchandise ; otherwise mere artificers cannot heap up much wealth '.

London profited most of all from these developments. Thanks to the Tudor peace, to the establishment of law and order and standard weights and measures, to good internal communications, the home market expanded steadily, though we have no statistics to measure it and so are apt to attach excessive importance to foreign trade. By 1600 London handled seven-eighths of English trade ; and its exports (excluding short-cloths) increased five times over in the next forty years. London merchants slowly penetrated into spheres hitherto monopolised by local trading oligarchies. They competed with Leeds merchants for the purchase of cloths from the West Riding, with Shrewsbury and Oswestry merchants for Welsh cloth. Jealousy of London and its trading companies was shown in the ' free-trade ' debate in Parliament in 1604 ; it may underlie the conflicts between ' Presbyterians ' and ' Independents ' in the sixteen-forties. The privateering industry, which earlier in Elizabeth's reign had been run advantageously for themselves by the gentlemen sea-dogs of Devon and Cornwall, was from the fifteen-nineties passing under the control of London capitalists who never went to sea at all.[1] London furnished most of the capital for industrial development ; its rapidly expanding population offered a vast market for goods from the rest of England. The Midlands light industries, the west Midlands slitting mills, the nail-making and sword and dagger industry of the Birmingham area, producing a class of small capitalists, catered largely for the London market. London's consumption of corn more than doubled between 1605 and 1661 ; its demand stimulated a rapid development of market- and dairy-farming in the Home Counties. By 1640 most of the richest men in the land were City men. London's economic dominance of the country was unique in Europe.

During the Civil War Charles I tried to develop both Bristol and Exeter as rival export centres. But London's pull proved too strong, and clothiers in the south and west preferred to risk sending their cloths across the fighting lines to the capital. The City's economic dominance was accompanied (part cause, part effect) by political dominance. (The Levellers later complained, exaggeratedly, that the Merchant Adventurers of London controlled elections in all ports.) The

<hr />

[1] Ed. K. R. Andrews, *English Privateering Voyages to the West Indies, 1588–95* (Hakluyt Soc.), pp. 19–22

royal court was ceasing to wander round the country, and settled for most of the year at Whitehall ; the expanding administrative departments also remained there permanently. London's printing presses served the whole kingdom. London merchants established grammar schools and scholarships, or endowed preaching, in the counties where they had been born, and so helped to raise the intellectual and cultural level of outlying areas to that of the City. Richard Baxter noted of the handloom weavers of Kidderminster that ' their constant converse and traffic with London doth much promote civility and piety among tradesmen '. More and more men looked to London and Westminster for capital, for a market, for exotic imports from the East and West Indies, for political ideas and intellectual stimulus.

The internal market for the products of the new industries came not only from the towns but also from increased expenditure by gentlemen, thriving yeomen, and craftsmen. A large part of England was rebuilt in the early seventeenth century as yeomen expanded their houses, and as others lower in the social scale replaced mud huts and wooden hovels with brick and stone cottages. From their wills we can see a separate kitchen appear ; the ground-floor rooms are boarded over to create bedrooms ; permanent stairs replace ladders ; glass appears in windows. Glass and crockery replace wood and pewter in the household equipment, chairs replace benches, knives and forks become necessities rather than luxuries.[1]

THE POOR

We have no reliable statistics about population. Some have suggested that an increase during the sixteenth century was slowing down in the early seventeenth century—i.e. that the population curve moved roughly parallel to the price curve. If this could be proved, it would have important consequences for our interpretation of the economic life of the period. But the arguments by which it is defended are not entirely convincing, and it is probably safest to assume a steady expansion throughout the seventeenth century. This led to pressure

[1] W. G. Hoskins, *The Midland Peasant*, pp. 285-93 ; ' The Rebuilding of Rural England, 1570-1640 ', *P. and P.*, 4

on the means of subsistence which could only have been met by an expansion of industrial production, and of the cultivated area, commensurate with the increase in population. Against this, as we shall see, early Stuart governments set their faces. So we can be quite certain that in this period England was *relatively* overpopulated—that the population was greater than the economy as then organised could absorb. But to contemporaries, struck by poverty and vagabondage, the overpopulation seemed absolute. Emigration to North America won land and freedom for those who survived the hardships of colonisation. In England attempts were made to establish workhouses in which the poor could be set to work. The Puritans, for their part, emphasised the duty of working hard, and the need for ' discipline '. For in a backward economy it was easy for the idle, the ' debauched ', the ' profane ' to take things easy, to work by fits and starts, observing every saint's day as a holiday. There was little incentive to earn when there were so few consumer goods within the purchasing power of the lower classes. Only the lucky few appeared to be helped by God to help themselves. This explains Puritan approval of the Poor Law's sharp distinction between deserving poor and those who would not work. Poor Law and ministers were very harsh against ' sturdy rogues ', whose existence menaced the social stability necessary for industrial expansion. Far-sighted men, like Francis Bacon, could already see here the possibility of abolishing poverty altogether, for the first time in human history.

Wage labourers did not share in the profits of industrial expansion. As prices rose during the sixteenth century, the purchasing power of wages had fallen by something like two-thirds. Since the numbers of those permanently dependent on wages was increasing, the number of those on the margin of starvation was increasing too. This fall in real wages was catastrophic for those who sold or were evicted from their plots of land and became entirely dependent on earnings. The real earnings of a worker born in 1580 would never exceed half of what his great-grandfather had enjoyed. Real wages reached their lowest point in James's reign, after which they began to rise, very slowly. Ironically enough, much of the expanding internal demand for food and manufactured goods came from landless wage labourers, who though absolutely poorer had to purchase more because they no longer produced for themselves.

'Flatter not yourselves with the thoughts of long life,' Baxter warned poor husbandmen. Bad harvests were frequent, as were famine, pestilence, and sudden death. There was no insurance. Prices were unstable ; taxation, lay and ecclesiastical, fell heavily on the poor. Rye bread was the normal food of the lower classes, though for the very poor, and for others in famine years like 1631, bread was made from barley. Average expectation of life was not more than thirty-five years, and less for the poor ; it is twice as much today. The percentage of the population under fifteen was nearly double what it is today. Labouring life was short. The Devon Justices of the Peace fixed wages for women between the ages of eighteen and thirty only, as though no woman over thirty was likely to be capable of working in the fields.[1] When so many families lived on the verge of starvation it was essential that their children should work in agriculture or domestic industry or both. The absolute paternal authority on which all seventeenth-century moralists insisted corresponded to the economic necessities of the average home.

Seventeenth-century labourers had no organisations to protect them. Employers had : wages were fixed by Justices of the Peace, themselves members of the employing class. Official wage rates were not always observed, and government intervention may have helped to keep wages up in years of famine, though in the long run it probably held back industrial expansion. But normal industrial wages hardly sufficed to maintain life. Robert Reyce said of Suffolk in 1618 that ' where the clothiers do dwell or have dwelt, there are found the greatest number of the poor'. The existence of a system of poor relief encouraged Justices of the Peace to fix wages at the lowest possible rates. This helped employers, since where relief was necessary all other ratepayers were taxed to provide it. In 1637 the owner of a paper-mill at Horton, John Milton's village, expected the ratepayers to produce £7 5s 0d a week to supplement the wages of his workers. Hence ratepayers often fiercely opposed the setting up of an industry in a new

[1] W. G. Hoskins and H. P. R. Finberg, *Devonshire Studies* (1952), p. 424

area. Since there was a wage freeze in a period of price rise, the distinction between ' the poor ' and the rest of the population was growing sharper, and the numbers of the former were increasing.

The harsh Poor Law was breaking up the bands of roaming vagabonds which had terrorised Elizabethan England ; but it could not prevent London attracting an underworld of casual labourers, unemployables, beggars, and criminals. The prescribed penalty of whipping home unlicensed beggars checked freedom of movement, and detained a surplus of cheap labour in many rural areas. Fear of the social disorder to which vagrancy might lead, and the consequent emphasis on confining men to their own parish, meant that the real solution— absorption in expanding industry—was prevented. The Statute of 1563, which limited apprenticeship to sons of forty-shilling freeholders, excluded three-quarters of the rural population from the major English industry, clothing. A further Act of 1621 tried to prohibit the propertyless from coming ' to any city or town to dwell '. In some areas Justices of the Peace refused to work the relevant clause of the Statute of Apprentices : in Suffolk it was reported in 1622 that two-thirds of the textile employees had not been apprenticed, and in Yorkshire and Lancashire the figure was probably higher. The poor were treated as utterly rightless. In 1618 a hundred ' young boys and girls that lay starving in the streets ' of London were shipped off to Virginia. In 1625 the monopolist Sir Hugh Middleton was authorised to conscript labourers from any part of the kingdom for his Cardiganshire mines ; and other monopolists received similar rights.

In the Middle Ages relief of the poor had been a matter for charity, dispensed through the Church. The state, which took over so many of the Church's functions at the Reformation, was reluctant to assume this one. The Poor Law was a minimum framework aimed at providing sufficient employment to prevent disorder : but relief of poverty was left mainly to private initiative. The charitable, in this period, were overwhelmingly merchants (especially of London) and the Puritan section of the gentry. So governments, by failing to cope with the problem of poverty in any positive way, encouraged merchants and Puritan gentry to step in and

remould society along the lines which seemed best to them—
by establishing schools, alms-houses, credit for apprentices,
etc.[1]

Since the Poor Law placed the propertied classes in complete
control of those who produced their wealth, they viewed with
grave suspicion any government attempt to upset their local
dominance. The Stuart policy of ' social justice ' aimed at
preserving stability, at reducing eviction from small holdings,
for this meant loss of taxpayers, of trained men for the militia,
and of tithe-payers for the Church ; and it created the possibility of riots and unrest. But even Laud never effectively
helped the lower classes. When the government fined an
enclosing landlord, he then presumably raised the money by
grinding the faces of his tenants harder still. A great deal of
nonsense has been talked about the good done to the poorer
classes by Charles I and his ministers, whereas in fact the
Poor Law was most efficiently administered in areas which
were to support Parliament in the Civil War. Wentworth
had no scruples about selling his corn dear in time of shortage.
The crown enclosed, and a great peer like the Earl of Worcester
could obtain permission to enclose Wentwood Chase in return
for a loan to the King, however loudly the inhabitants protested. In the sixteen-forties, when the Levellers attacked the
Parliamentary governments on many counts, they sometimes
said things had been merrier in England before the Reformation ; they never, so far as I am aware, said the poor had been
better off economically under Charles I.

So, although it would be wrong to think of any body of
organised discontent, there is a permanent background of
potential unrest throughout these decades. Given a crisis—
a famine, large-scale unemployment, a breakdown of government—disorder might occur, as it did in 1607, when there were
' Levellers ' in Northamptonshire and ' Diggers ' in Warwickshire. In 1622 Gloucestershire unemployed went in groups
to houses of the rich, demanding money and seizing provisions.
There were minor revolts in the south-western counties in
1628-31, and anti-enclosure riots over large areas of England
in 1640-3. There was no police force in Stuart England, no
standing army. In normal times law and order were preserved

[1] W. K. Jordan, *Philanthropy in England, 1480–1660, passim*

by depriving the mass of the population of arms. Those entitled to bear arms—the *armigeri*—were the landed class. The gentry, said Sir Walter Ralegh, ' are the garrisons of good order throughout the realm '. A naked basis of force underlay social relations. The prevention of peasant revolt was the monarchy's job ; in this it had the support of the propertied class. Problems arose only when royal policy hit the pockets of those on whose behalf law and order were being maintained, as in the case of restraints on enclosure.

So there was a steady undercurrent of fear of ' the many-headed monster '. He might be led in revolt by a God-sent leader like Captain Pouch of 1607 ; he might be misguided by a clergyman like the Reverend Peter Simon, who in 1631 preached the equality of all mankind in the Forest of Dean. Fear of possible seduction of the lower orders into social and political heresy underlay the paranoiac opposition to religious toleration in the sixteen-forties. Both Charles I and the Parliamentary leaders expected this social anxiety to bring the other side to accept their terms in the Civil War. We shall often misinterpret men's thoughts and actions if we do not continually remind ourselves of this background of potential unrest.

GOVERNMENT ECONOMIC POLICY

The attitude of governments towards the new economic developments was ambiguous. Since they needed armaments and ships, they encouraged expansion of the metallurgical and gunpowder industries, and of shipbuilding. Some industries were protected as being of especial advantage to the nation, like the alum industry which freed England from dependence on a papal monopoly. Since all early seventeenth-century governments needed money, attempts were made to establish claims to royalties in the extractive industries, and to sell monopoly rights of new industrial processes. But in general the official attitude towards industrial advance was hostile, or at best indifferent. It was suspicious of social change and social mobility, of the rapid enrichment of capitalists, afraid of the fluctuations of the market and of unemployment, of vagabondage and social unrest. ' The Elizabethan code,' wrote Sir G. N. Clark, ' aimed at stabilising the existing class structure, the location of industry and the flow of labour supply by granting privileges, and by putting hindrances in the way of mobility and freedom of contract. . . . Noblemen, gentlemen and others, as employers in their households, were left quite free.' The Reverend William Lee, who invented the stocking frame, was positively discouraged by governments, and died in poverty in 1610. Laud disliked profiteering : ' This last year's famine was made by man, and not by God,' he said in the Star Chamber, when enclosers were being heavily fined. Throughout the early Stuart period, governments thought it their duty to regulate industry, wages, and working conditions. In times of dearth they ordered Justices of the Peace to buy up corn and sell it below cost price ; they forbade employers to lay off workers whose products they could not sell. Star Chamber, the prerogative court which had been developed by the Tudors against subjects too mighty to be dealt with in the common-law courts, was used by Stuart governments to enforce economic regulations whose interference with property rights neither Parliament nor common-law courts would have approved.

In so far as Stuart governments had anything which could be described as an economic policy, it was to support the monopoly London export companies against interlopers, to slow down industrial development and control it through gilds and monopolies, to suppress middlemen. The local monopolies of the trading oligarchies of Shrewsbury and Oswestry drapers were supported against intruding London merchants trying to deal direct with Welsh cloth-makers. The gentlemen who had defended Shrewsbury's privileges in the sixteen-twenties were Royalists in the Civil War. The Chester Companies of Shoe-makers and Glovers were supported by the Privy Council in their attempt to suppress unapprenticed rivals outside the city. Chester was one of the few Royalist cities in the Civil War. On the other hand, the success of the metallurgical industries around Birmingham was due to the fact that their craftsmen were not organised in gilds (which regulated output and quality) and that newcomers to the industry did not have to serve the regular seven years' apprenticeship. During the Civil War the region produced sword blades and volunteers for Parliament only. The only branch of the clothing industry which prospered in the twenties and thirties was the New Draperies.[1] The manufacture of these lighter cloths flourished in East Anglia ; and in Lancashire, thanks to lack of gild regulation. East Anglia was Parliamentarian in the Civil War : the clothing area was the only part of Lancashire except the port of Liverpool which supported Parliament. Preston and Wigan, corporate towns which had long opposed the growth of rural trade and industry, were Royalist.

The first half of the century saw intensified rivalries within London companies. As a small group of merchants grew richer, they began to squeeze the small masters out of control ; the latter tried to force recognition for themselves. The journeymen (wage labourers) had become so economically depressed, as real wages fell, that they had sunk to ' a mere appendage to the yeomanry of the small masters '. The yeomanry of small masters wanted to throw off the control of mercantile capital and to obtain independent incorporation in new industrial companies. Charles I's government was pre-pared—for a price—to support them. The thirties saw ' the high watermark of the attempt of the small masters to secure economic independence through separate incorporation '.[2] But—as with so much else under Charles I—the social purposes of the government were perverted by fiscal needs. It was not the mass of the rank-and-file producers who benefited. In 1638 Charles I set up a new Company of Beaver-makers, separated from the felt-makers, with a monopoly of making beaver hats. But the monopoly was dominated by eight capitalists, and within a year the small master beaver-makers were complaining that they were ruined by the new company which they were forced to join. The great majority of them must have been delighted when the monopoly was overthrown by the Long Parliament. There is no sign that the craftsmen of London offered Charles I any support in the early sixteen-forties.

The weakness of Stuart governments was that, unlike the French monarchy, they lacked a bureaucracy. Government

[1] F. J. Fisher, ' London's Export Trade in the Early Seventeenth Century ', *Econ. H.R.* (2nd Ser.), **3**
[2] G. Unwin, *Industrial Organisation in the Sixteenth and Seventeenth Centuries* (1904), *passim* ; M. James, *Social Policy during the Puritan Revolution*, p. 194

regulations had to be enforced by professional informers, an unpopular and bribable class, and by unpaid Justices of the Peace, frequently themselves the employers against whom the regulations were directed. Moreover, the complex regulations often defeated their own objects. ' It were better to have fewer laws with better execution,' the merchant Edward Misselden grumbled in 1622. The government itself realised in 1616 that London could not be fed if distributors of dairy products were prosecuted as middlemen ; and admitted in 1622 that manufacturers were ' perplexed and entangled ' by the multitude and contradictions of the laws in force. The right to break regulations was put up to sale like everything else. In 1619 James I established a commission to sell pardons to those who had evaded the obsolete apprenticeship laws. The officials known as the aulnagers were supposed to guarantee maintenance of standards in cloth production ; but under James the elaborate organisation existed only to subsidise the Scottish Duke of Lennox. The aulnager's seals (the stamp of quality) were publicly sold by the bushel, members of Parliament said in 1624.

Government regulation, in so far as it was enforced, rendered the English economy inflexible, less able to react to changes in demand than a free market would have been. In 1631 the Hertfordshire Justices of the Peace protested that ' this strict looking to markets is the reason why the markets are smaller, the corn dearer '. Free trade would produce better results : the Dorset Justices agreed with them. Lancashire Justices refused in 1634 to cause unemployment by enforcing apprenticeship regulations ; nor would they prosecute middlemen whose activities were essential for spinners and weavers of linen, who could not afford time off to go to Preston market to buy flax. In Essex it was ' found by experience that the raising of wages cannot advance the relief of the poor ', since employers would not take men on at the enforced higher wage rates. Much of the resentment against Charles I's personal government sprang from objection to this autocratic and ineffective interference from Whitehall in local affairs.

Monopolies aroused most hostility. Often there were good reasons for protecting new industries by giving them a guaranteed market for a period of years. Mines Royal helped

to make England independent of foreign copper for the manufacture of cannon ; and Bushell, the privileged licensee of some
Welsh mines, prospered sufficiently to furnish the King with
£40,000 in the Civil War.   Other monopolies protected armaments industries, like that in saltpetre on which the fortunes
of the Evelyn family were founded.   But too often selling
monopolies became a means of solving the government's fiscal
problems.   Monopolies were obtainable only by those with
court influence.   Thus the pin-makers, of humble origin, had to
bribe courtiers to get a charter of incorporation.   The courtiers
in consequence acquired real control of the new company.
In 1612 the Earl of Salisbury was receiving £7,000 a year from
the silk monopoly, the Earl of Suffolk £5,000 from currants,
the Earl of Northampton £4,500 from starch.[1]   On a humbler
scale, Sir Edmund Verney had a share in one monopoly for
inspecting tobacco, in another for hackney coaches and in a
third ' for sealing woollen yarn before it was sold or wrought
into cloth '.   He also had pensions worth £200 a year, and
used his position at court to speculate in Irish lands and the
drainage of the Fens.   When Sir Edmund said he must support
the King in the Civil War because he had eaten his bread and
served him near thirty years, the statement was literally true ;
but his reasons for thus helping ' to preserve and defend those
things which are against my conscience to preserve and defend '
were perhaps less purely idealistic than those who quote the
passage sometimes appear to think.

In 1601 a member of Parliament asked, when a list of
monopolies was read out, ' Is not bread there ? '   His irony
exaggerated only slightly.   It is difficult for us to picture to
ourselves the life of a man living in a house built with monopoly
bricks, with windows (if any) of monopoly glass ; heated by
monopoly coal (in Ireland monopoly timber), burning in a
grate made of monopoly iron.   His walls were lined with
monopoly tapestries.   He slept on monopoly feathers, did his
hair with monopoly brushes and monopoly combs.   He washed
himself with monopoly soap, his clothes in monopoly starch.
He dressed in monopoly lace, monopoly linen, monopoly
leather, monopoly gold thread.   His hat was of monopoly

[1] L. Stone, ' The Elizabethan Aristocracy : A Restatement ', *Econ.
H.R.* (2nd Ser.), **4**, 312–14

beaver, with a monopoly band. His clothes were held up by monopoly belts, monopoly buttons, monopoly pins. They were dyed with monopoly dyes. He ate monopoly butter, monopoly currants, monopoly red herrings, monopoly salmon and monopoly lobsters. His food was seasoned with monopoly salt, monopoly pepper, monopoly vinegar. Out of monopoly glasses he drank monopoly wines and monopoly spirits ; out of pewter mugs made from monopoly tin he drank monopoly beer made from monopoly hops, kept in monopoly barrels or monopoly bottles, sold in monopoly-licensed ale-houses. He smoked monopoly tobacco in monopoly pipes, played with monopoly dice or monopoly cards, or on monopoly lute-strings. He wrote with monopoly pens, on monopoly writing-paper ; read (through monopoly spectacles, by the light of monopoly candles) monopoly printed books, including monopoly Bibles and monopoly Latin grammars, printed on paper made from monopoly-collected rags, bound in sheepskin dressed in monopoly alum. He shot with monopoly gunpowder made from monopoly saltpetre. He travelled in monopoly sedan chairs or monopoly hackney coaches, drawn by horses fed on monopoly hay. He tipped with monopoly farthings. At sea he was lighted by monopoly lighthouses. When he made his will, he went to a monopolist. (In Ireland one could not be born, married, or die without 6d to a monopolist.) Pedlars were licensed by a monopolist. Mice were caught in monopoly mousetraps. Not all these patents existed at once, but all come from the first four decades of the seventeenth century. In 1621 there were alleged to be 700 of them.

Apart possibly from beer and salt, these were not quite necessities. But monopolies added to the price of just those semi-luxuries which were beginning to come within the reach of yeomen and artisans whose standard of living was rising. They affected the daily life of hundreds of thousands of Englishmen. By the end of the sixteen-thirties they were bringing nearly £100,000 a year to the Exchequer.

Monopolies interfered with the normal channels of trade. Merchants were prohibited from landing their cargoes at the most convenient port whenever a monopolist's right of search chanced to require their unloading elsewhere. By the late sixteen-thirties the economy was beginning to suffer. The clothing industry was hit by increased cost of soap and alum, and by the scarcity of potash caused by suppression of imports. The Greenland Company lacked oil. The salt monopoly embarrassed the Fishing Society. The rise in the price of coal hit nearly all industries. 'No freeman of London,' said a pamphlet of 1640, 'after he hath served his years and set up his trade, can be sure long to enjoy the labour of his trade, but either he is forbidden longer to use it, or is forced at length with the rest of his trade to purchase it as a monopoly, at a dear rate, which they and all the kingdom pay for. Witness the soap business.' [1]

Nor was the objection to monopolies only economic. Buckingham, the great monopoly-monger, had popish connections. The soap monopoly, which promised the King £20,000 a year in the sixteen-thirties, was attacked not only because it doubled the price and its inferior product blistered the hands of washerwomen, but also because the monopolists were Papists. If we think of monopolies simply as a tax, then we can regard them as a crude anticipation of the excise, the indirect levy later developed under Parliament's auspices to tax consumption. The fiscal benefit to the crown from monopolies was considerable, but it could not compare with the injury done to the consumer and industry by the rise in prices. Every 1s charged at the customs brought 10d in to the Exchequer ; but 1s increased cost to consumers by monopolies brought a bare 1½d to the Exchequer : the soap monopoly brought less than ½d. The rest went into the pockets of patentees and courtiers.

Since monopolies were enforced by the royal prerogative and the prerogative courts, they gave rise to constitutional conflicts. Parliament, the representative institution of the men of property, naturally favoured free trade. In 1624 Parliament declared that monopolies were opposed to the 'fundamental laws of this . . . realm'. Because of its invasion of the prerogative, this Statute of Monopolies was described by a contemporary as 'a bill against monarchy'. Charles evaded it by disregarding the common-law courts, and bringing cases

[1] It is significant of the interconnection of religious and economic grievances that the pamphlet from which the quotation is taken was called *Englands Complaint to Jesus Christ against the Bishops Canons*.

affecting monopolies before Star Chamber, on the ground that his prerogative was being questioned. Sale of monopolies was the line of least resistance for governments in financial difficulties, and was extensively used in the sixteen-thirties. The knowledge that their patents would be attacked if a Parliament ever met encouraged monopolists to aim at quick profits. Indeed, the King himself was not above selling the same patent twice over, so no patentee could be squeamish about consumers' interests. It was a vicious circle.

There was thus a threefold objection to monopolies. First, they limited output. Secondly, they did not achieve the social objectives claimed for them : standards of production were not maintained, the interests of consumers and employees were not protected ; on the contrary, insecure speculators used political privileges to get rich quick. Thirdly, the harm done to the economy was balanced by no adequate gain to the Exchequer.

Government industrial intervention could have even more disastrous effects. Take for example the Cokayne Project. This seemed a sensible scheme, aimed at recapturing England's position as dominant cloth exporter to the Baltic from which we had been driven by the Dutch. In the early seventeenth century three-quarters of London's total exports were cloth. All the great companies, except the East India Company, exported cloth ; but by far the greatest exporters were the Merchant Adventurers. They sent unfinished cloth to the Netherlands, to be dyed and dressed there for re-export to Germany and the Baltic. Dyeing was the most profitable process in the industry. It seemed reasonable to insist that all cloths should be dyed and dressed in England before export. In 1614 the Merchant Adventurers' privileges were withdrawn, and a new company, the ' King's Merchant Adventurers ', was founded, licensed to export dressed cloths only. James's object was to bring the whole business of cloth export under royal control. Unfinished cloths came mainly from the rural areas : towns preferred to market their cloth already dressed and dyed. So the scheme had the additional advantage, for the government, that it weakened the areas of freer capitalist industry and strengthened the towns. Sir William Cokayne, to whom the new Company was entrusted, promised £300,000 a year to the crown, over and above the £400,000 profit which he expected to make. The time seemed favourable for a variety of technical reasons : alum for dressing cloth had been discovered in Yorkshire ; indigo for dyeing was being imported by the East India Company.

But the scheme was a total failure. Cokayne was more interested in winning a share in a profitable monopoly than in stimulating English industry. The Dutch at once prohibited the import of *any* English cloths, finished or not, and the ' King's Merchant Adventurers' lacked the shipping for direct export to the Baltic. Nor had they the capital or technical facilities for undertaking the finishing processes at home on anything like the scale required. They soon had to admit defeat and obtain permission to export undyed cloth. Unable to sell abroad, they could not afford to buy at home. There was a crisis of overproduction : 500 bankruptcies were reported. Despite wage cuts and emigration, unemployment soared. There were weavers' riots in Wiltshire and Gloucestershire. The government insisted on cloths being bought by London merchants and on clothiers continuing to employ their weavers ; this intensified overproduction. In September 1616 Cokayne had told his society from James that the King's honour was at stake. Yet within a year the scheme had broken down, the old Merchant Adventurers were restored to their privileges, though it cost them £60–70,000 in bribes—a sum which they recouped by a tax deducted from the price offered to clothiers. Some courtiers were skilful enough to be successively bribed by both the new and old Companies. James had to issue an apologetic proclamation in which he declared, ' We intend not to insist and stay longer upon specious and fair shows, which produce not the fruit our actions do ever aim at, which is the general good of this our state and kingdom.' James recompensed himself for the gain which he had failed to secure from the Cokayne Project. He laid new impositions on exported cloth, known as the ' pretermitted customs ', which by 1640 were bringing in £36,512 a year.

The defeat of the ' King's Merchant Adventurers' was a great blow to royal prestige. The outbreak of the Thirty Years' War meant that English cloth exports never again before 1640 reached the level of 1614. Dutch cloth exports expanded, and there was a boom in the Silesian clothing industry. The Cokayne fiasco was one of the reasons for angry criticisms of government economic and foreign policy when Parliament finally met in 1621. Already the English economy was too delicate a mechanism to be left to the well-meaning mercies of the royal amateur and his self-interested associates.[1]

' If such a system could have been maintained,' Mr Unwin wrote of Stuart economic regulation in general, ' the Industrial Revolution would never have happened.' The inefficient administration of the system produced a confusion and dislocation which, in Professor Nef's view, was ' perhaps nearly as dangerous to industrial progress as the successful enforcement of the laws would have been '. During the general slump of the early twenties ' England was left saddled with a rigid, oligopolistic, high-cost economy, ill-fitted to cope with a competitor [the Dutch] who throve on low costs, adaptability and up-to-dateness.' [2] The slump shook the whole English economy, and recovery was slow. Difficulty in collecting rents helps to explain the extreme reluctance of the gentry to pay taxes, and so the breach between King and Parliament. Unrest among the lower classes, leading up to the revolts of 1628-31, partly accounts for the more active policy of state economic intervention in the sixteen-thirties, which intensified friction between government and men of property.

TRADE AND FOREIGN POLICY

Long-term government policy preferred to concentrate trade in the hands of a few rich merchants. Trading in companies was agreeable to monarchy, said Francis Bacon; free trade to a republic. Companies were easy to control; they could be made to accept royal nominees on their governing bodies, with which governments frequently interfered. In 1604 a ' free-trade' bill supported by other ports against London companies failed : but in 1606 Parliament dissolved the Spanish Company, and declared all subjects free to trade with France,

[1] For the three preceding paragraphs see A. Friis, *Alderman Cockayne's Project and the Cloth Trade* (Copenhagen, 1927) ; B. E. Supple, *Commercial Crisis and Change in England, 1600-42* (1959)

[2] J. D. Gould, ' The Trade Depression of the Early 1620's ', *Econ. H.R.* (2nd Ser.), **7**, 87

Spain, and Portugal. In 1624 Parliament threw the export of dyed and dressed cloth open to all ; the Merchant Adventurers were not able to buy their monopoly back until 1634, under the King's personal government.

Companies performed an essential function so long as the market for English cloth was restricted. They limited output, maintained standards of quality, and so kept prices high. But as the market widened, in Europe and beyond, so the rival possibility appeared of selling larger quantities of lower-quality goods—as the Dutch had begun to do. In a competitive world the future lay with the lighter and cheaper New Draperies, produced in relatively free conditions, and so far more adaptable to changing market demand. Yet companies were still needed in the early seventeenth century. They supplied convoys and ambassadors. Convoys were necessary until the seas were policed by a navy : collective trading until English foreign policy was conducted by governments which regarded the lowering of tariffs against English goods and the ensuring of personal security abroad as part of their normal function. It was the fleets of Blake and William III that rendered most of the companies obsolete.

But the companies were also exploited and plundered by early Stuart governments. The Venetian Ambassador summed up the situation in 1622 when he said that ' although favoured by various privileges, the companies are declining owing to the charges laid upon them by sovereigns . . . and because to maintain themselves they are compelled to disburse great sums to the favourites, the lords of the Council and other ministers. . . . Thus *burdened* and *protected* they are *enabled* and *compelled* to tyrannize over the sellers without and the buyers within the kingdom.' [1] So the richer merchants were left restive whilst prospering ; all others hated the system. There were big profits to be made in overseas trade. In 1611 and 1612 the Russia Company paid a dividend of ninety per cent ; in 1607 the East India Company made a profit of five hundred per cent. But such profits were highly speculative, and they were restricted to a narrow circle. The entrance fee for the East India Company was £50, £66 for a shopkeeper, and ' such terms as they thought fit ' for gentlemen. For the

[1] My italics

Merchant Adventurers the fee rose at one time to £200. By 1640 not only were some London merchants richer than peers, but many merchants in provincial towns like Exeter were better off than the surrounding gentry who despised them. Tension naturally resulted.

Governments saw trade primarily as a source of revenue. There was no concerted policy of actively forwarding the expansion of English commerce, nor even of protecting it. In 1612 Barbary pirates inflicted £40,000 damage on the Newfoundland fishing fleet. There was continual interruption to coastwise shipping, and on many occasions London's coal imports from Newcastle were endangered. 'The pirates grow so powerful,' wrote Secretary Winwood in 1617, ' that if present order be not taken to suppress them, our trade must cease in the Mediterranean Sea.' Present order was not taken, because the Lord Admiral, Nottingham (a Howard), was bribed by English pirates. His successor, Buckingham, was no more active against piracy. Parliament's reluctance to vote tunnage and poundage arose in part from the consideration that these customary dues had been traditionally granted to the King for securing the sovereignty of the narrow seas and the safety of merchants ; and now the navy had been allowed to decay. Defence against pirates was one of the pretexts for Ship Money. But the Grand Remonstrance, after referring to tunnage and poundage, impositions, Ship Money, added, ' and yet the merchants have been left so naked to the violence of the Turkish pirates that many great ships of value and thousands of His Majesty's subjects have been taken by them and do still remain in miserable slavery.'

So though initially the peace which James I concluded in 1604 with Spain brought prosperity to England, there were soon complaints that in the struggle for markets England was being out-traded. The French held the leading position in Mediterranean trade ; Dutch merchants gained control of the carrying trade to the Baltic, and even with English colonies in North America and the West Indies. The government of the Dutch Republic enthusiastically supported its merchants, whilst James I felt it beneath his dignity to do more than mediate in squabbles between English and Dutch merchants. Englishmen were virtually excluded from the East

India trade, and the massacre of Amboyna (1623) went unavenged. In 1604, 1617, and 1635 the crown licensed rival traders to the East Indies, in defiance of the charter which the King himself had originally sold to the East India Company. In the sixteen-thirties, in consequence of lack of government support, the Company's profits were declining so catastrophically that it seriously considered withdrawing. Only merchants selling New Draperies took advantage of the peace of 1604 to develop export to Spain and to penetrate the eastern Mediterranean. The fact that this was an area of relatively unregulated trade probably facilitated expansion. Those who profited by this trade were among the few who looked with approval on the government's policy of peace with Spain. But the presence of English merchants in the Mediterranean in increasing numbers created demands for naval protection there which early Stuart governments could not meet.

From the time of Hakluyt and Ralegh onwards many saw America as the future market for English cloth exports, or as a market for slaves bought in Africa with cloth. A memorandum of 1623 included the following ' Reasons showing the benefit of planting in New England ' : it would offer employment for the starving unemployed and so rid England of the expense of maintaining them ; it would create a market for cloths and other exports ' now unvendible ' ; and it would give bankrupt gentlemen a chance to recover their fortunes.[1] Plunder-war with Spain was a policy on which merchants could join hands with gentlemen anxious, with Sir Walter Ralegh, ' to seek new worlds for gold, for praise, for glory '. James's peace with Spain had accepted the exclusion of English traders from the American market. For the next forty years governments tried to retain friendly relations with Spain, whilst the opposition clamoured for war. In 1617 James furnished Spain with full information about the size and destination of Ralegh's fleet bound for Guiana, and so ensured its defeat ; Ralegh's execution in 1618 was the final act of appeasement of Spain which made his name a legend among the commercial and Puritan party.

English colonies on the mainland of North America were founded by private enterprise, without significant government

[1] *City of Exeter MSS (H.M.C.)*, pp. 167–9

support or encouragement. Charles I tried to prevent colonies being run by merchant companies, and to subordinate them to courtiers in feudal dependence on the crown. But the actual financing of colonies still depended on merchants. The King often intervened in disputes over rival colonial patents, which ought to have been tried by the common-law judges. Thus on behalf of his favourite Carlisle, in 1629, Charles simply expropriated rival claimants to the West Indies. Similarly Laud's Commission for Plantations (i.e. colonies) decreed many forfeitures between 1634 and 1637. Colonial enterprises brought together the opposition leaders—Southampton and Sandys under James, Warwick, Saye and Sele, Pym under Charles.

In the sixteen-thirties the Providence Island Company was founded with the object of challenging the Spanish monopoly in the West Indies. Its treasurer was John Pym, and its personnel reads like a nominal roll of the Parliamentary opposition. It acted in fact as a cover-organisation for this opposition: Hampden's resistance to Ship Money was planned by Providence Island Adventurers. Meanwhile the government of Charles I had entered into a secret treaty with Spain, and so wished to discourage plans for settling America. The policy of Hakluyt, Ralegh, and the Providence Island Company was not carried out until after the overthrow of the monarchy.

Throughout the seventeenth century the Parliamentary opposition was ambivalent in its attitude towards the Dutch. The economic and political benefits which the Dutch had won through their Republic were specifically mentioned in the Act of 21st March 1649 declaring England a Commonwealth. Good Protestants and allies against Spain or France, and a model of economic organisation, Dutch merchants were yet our most dangerous rivals. It was said in the Commons in 1624 that English merchants were ' beaten out of trade by the Low-Country men ' because the Dutch government could borrow money at six or seven per cent interest, the English only at ten per cent. Parliament reduced the English rate to eight per cent. It was only after three naval wars and the financial and military exhaustion of the Netherlands in William III's wars against Louis XIV that the Dutch accepted the position of junior partners.

So there were many economic reasons for opposing the government. Industrialists, merchants, and corn-growers wanted freer trade, less government regulation, no monopolies ; gentlemen wanted to escape from the burdens of wardship, feudal tenures,[1] and forest laws ; and to be given a freer hand to enclose and bring fresh land under cultivation. The existence of monopolies and exclusive trading companies, together with the social prestige attached to land, distorted the economy by diverting capital from productive investment into the purchase of real estate. Since the days of Elizabeth there had been many advocates of a larger and more powerful navy, which would police the seas, protect and forward the interests of English trade, fishing, and colonisation ; and in performing these nationally useful functions would give work to the unemployed.

The spokesman of the propertied class on these economic issues, as on all others, came to be the House of Commons.

[1] See below, pp. 49-50

4 Politics and the Constitution 1603-40

> The state of monarchy is the supremest thing on earth ; for kings are not only God's lieutenants on earth, but even by God himself they are called gods.
>
> James I

> A king is a thing men have made for their own sakes, for quietness' sake. Just as in a family one man is appointed to buy the meat. . . .
>
> John Selden

THE LIBERTIES OF THE COMMONS

PARLIAMENT in the seventeenth century represented exclusively the propertied classes. The House of Lords was composed of the biggest landowners, together with Bishops. Under James I and Charles I the peerage was diluted by the barefaced sale of titles ; but this increased rather than reduced the wealth of the Upper House, though it diminished respect for it. We know so much less about the House of Lords than about the Commons in these decades that it is easy to underestimate its importance : contemporaries still regarded it as the more important of the two houses. But the House of Commons also represented the wealth of the country. A county seat was an eagerly coveted social distinction, and the ninety county members were invariably drawn from the leading landed families below the rank of peer. The county electoral franchise, restricted to men having freehold land worth forty shillings a year, excluded smaller freeholders, copyholders, cottagers, leaseholders, and paupers, who probably formed eighty to ninety per cent of the rural population ; and many lesser forty-shilling freeholders, voting by show of hands in open court, Richard Baxter said, ' ordinarily choose such as their landlords do desire them to choose'. In towns the franchise was more varied : it might be vested in the corporation, in holders of certain properties, in all the freemen, in all rate-payers, or, in one or two cities like Westminster, in all male inhabitants. But in most towns the propertied minority had the decisive voice. By the seventeenth century even a borough seat in the Commons conferred social prestige ; more towns were represented by gentlemen than by their own inhabitants. Since gentlemen also represented all the counties, Parliament represented a unified class. The divisions which marked the beginning of the Civil War were not between gentlemen and townsfolk but within this ruling class. Disputed elections were usually not concerned with political issues, but with rivalries for power between local families, though these rivalries might acquire a political flavour as one family attached itself to a court favourite and its rival therefore adopted an opposition standpoint.

The House of Commons, then, represented not the people of England but a small fraction of them—those who mattered in the country, those who effectively controlled local affairs as Justices of the Peace. The Lower House spoke for the prosperous gentry and the richer merchants. ' We be the gentry,' said a member in 1610. Thirty-one years later Sir Thomas Aston equated the gentry with ' the law-givers '. In Parliament, he explained, ' the *Primates*, the *Nobiles*, with the *minores nobiles*, the gentry, consult and dispose the rules of government ; the plebeians submit to and obey them '.[1] The House of Commons represented freeholders in counties, freemen in boroughs.

Note this use of the word ' free '. *Libertas* in medieval Latin conveys the idea of a right to exclude others from your property, your franchise. To be free of something means to enjoy exclusive rights and privileges in relation to it. The freedom of a town is a privilege, to be inherited or bought. So is a freehold estate. Freeholders and freemen are a minority in their communities. The Parliamentary franchise is a privilege attached to particular types of property. The ' liberties of the House of Commons ' were peculiar privileges

[1] Sir Thomas Aston, Bart., *A Remonstrance against Presbytery* (1641), Sig. 1-4*v*

enjoyed by members, such as immunity from arrest, the right to uncensored discussion, etc. 'Our privileges and liberties,' the House told James in 1604, 'are our true right and due inheritance, no less than our lands and goods.' Similarly, when James wrote *The Trew Law of Free Monarchies* he wished to emphasise that kings, like their propertied subjects, had their rights and privileges. The problem of early seventeenth-century politics was to decide where the king's rights and privileges ended and those of his free subjects began : the majority of the population did not come into it. The words which Sir Thomas Smith had written in Elizabeth's reign still remained true : 'Day labourers, poor husbandmen, yea merchants or retailers which have no free land, copyholders and all artificers . . . have no voice nor authority in our commonwealth, and no account is made of them, but only to be ruled.'

The common law was the law of free men. 'He that hath no property in his goods,' said a member of Parliament in 1624, 'is not free.' The gentry were exempt from the servile punishment of flogging. 'No goods : to be whipped' was a frequent decision by Justices of the Peace in quarter sessions. The resentment which the Star Chamber sentences on Prynne, Burton, and Bastwick aroused sprang not so much from their savagery as because this savagery was employed against gentlemen, members of the three learned professions. Any Justice of the Peace daily imposed sentences of flogging and branding on the lower orders, and tried to get confessions from them by means which he abhorred when used by the prerogative courts against his own class. The 'unfree' alone were liable to conscription. It seemed natural to Baxter that 'want of riches' should 'keep men out of freedom in the commonwealth'.

Words are deceptive because their meanings change. When members of Parliament spoke in defence of 'liberty and property' they meant something more like 'privilege and property' than is conveyed by the modern sense of the word liberty. Mr Ogg, who has some wise words on this subject, points out that the Act of 1711 (making substantial landowner-ship a necessary qualification for election to Parliament) was described as an Act for 'securing the liberties of Parliament .

' The fundamental and vital liberties,' Edmund Waller told the Short Parliament, are ' the property of our goods and the freedom of our persons.' Nor were all Englishmen ' freeborn '. ' My birth styles me as freeborn too,' claimed Robert Heath in a poem published in 1650, since ' no peasant blood doth stain or chill my veins.' Lodowick Muggleton called himself ' a freeborn Englishman ' because he was a freeman of London by birth. But in the mouths of Levellers the ' liberties of Englishmen ' came to mean something very different and much more modern ; ' freeborn John ' Lilburne was to make a democratic slogan out of what had been a class distinction. Then Ireton was to assure the Levellers that ' in a general sense liberty cannot be provided for if property be preserved '. But before the Civil War no-one was heard asking for liberty ' in a general sense ', and so the antithesis between liberty and property was obscured.

FINANCIAL AND CONSTITUTIONAL CONFLICTS

The economic developments considered in Chapter 3 had far-reaching political and constitutional consequences. The country and especially the classes represented by Parliament were getting richer ; the government was getting relatively poorer. Like all conservative landowners the King had difficulty in reorganising estate-management to meet the rise in prices. Nor was it necessarily to his advantage to do so. For crown lands were not only a source of revenue : they were also a source of patronage and influence. Leases on favourable terms were a means of rewarding courtiers and royal servants without cost to the Exchequer. So a drastic increase in rents from crown lands, though suggested from time to time, was always unpopular at court, and might have led only to increased expenditure in other directions.

Yet government expenditure was rising rapidly. The court was ceasing to move round the countryside living in part at the expense of the great aristocratic families. Members of those families were more and more reluctant to serve the state at their own expense ; on the contrary, they had their own economic problems, and looked to the crown for financial assistance. ' Bounty,' wrote even a reformer like Cecil,

' is an essential virtue of the King.' James was personally extravagant ; but he also had a duty to distribute largesse to ' well-deserving subjects ', his Council told him ; such liberality would ' multiply and confirm affection and duty '.[1] Unlike his predecessor, James had a wife and children to be provided for in accordance with the lavish standards of the day. The cost of warfare was increasing : ships were getting larger, cannon heavier ; fire-arms were becoming essential for the rank and file of an army. All this involved an increase in paper work at Whitehall, of staffs in the Admiralty and Ordnance Departments. War was becoming a financial disaster. This, rather than Elizabeth's ' parsimony ' or James's ' fear of cold steel ' is the explanation of both sovereigns' sensible desire to remain at peace. To pay for the Spanish and Irish wars at the end of her reign Elizabeth had sold crown lands worth over £800,000 ; she still left James debts to pay. Revenue from lands in James's first year was three-quarters of what it had been a dozen years earlier. The King ended both wars ; but he still had to sell land valued at £775,000, and so income from crown lands fell by another twenty-five per cent between 1603 and 1621, despite improved management. When wars began again in the sixteen-twenties, Charles was forced to sell another £650,000, mostly to the City of London in repayment of loans. In 1639 he could only borrow from the City by offering crown lands as a security. What was left of them was sold by Parliament after 1649 for less than £2 million.

Selling land was living on capital. But it was more than a mere financial disaster. Apropos sale of royal forests in 1623 John Coke had written to Buckingham, ' The crown will necessarily grow less both in honour and power as others grow great.' Lord Treasurer Middlesex, the best financial adviser James ever had, ' told the King that in selling land he did not only sell his rent, as other men did, but sold his sovereignty, for it was a greater tie of obedience to be a tenant to the King than to be his subject '.

Meanwhile the House of Commons increased in confidence as those whom it represented waxed rich and as governments grew more dependent on the taxes it voted, even in time of

[1] R. Ashton, ' Deficit Finance in the Reign of James I ', *Econ. H.R.* (2nd Ser.), **10**, 16

peace. The House was always sensitive to any suggestion that
the King had a right to levy arbitrary taxation. The civil
lawyer Dr Cowell in 1610, the Laudian clergymen Sibthorpe,
Montagu, and Mainwaring in the sixteen-twenties, were all
censured for elevating the royal prerogative in this respect.
' Elected Parliaments,' said a letter-writer in the fifties, ' are
the bulwark of property.' [1]

Revenue from land dropped, but that from customs rose
with the expansion of trade. Customs revenue more than
doubled in the first eighteen years of James's reign, and in
1621 brought in nearly three times as much as crown lands.
But control of the customs was in dispute. In 1608 James
issued a new Book of Rates, cautiously revising the valuation
of certain commodities, and embodying additional duties on
new imports (' impositions '). In an inflationary age periodical
readjustment of customs rates was clearly necessary ; and
trade with the East was bringing new commodities like
currants into the country. The crown's right to make such
adjustments had not hitherto been disputed. But as in so
many spheres, economic developments were changing men's
attitudes towards legal rights. Foreign trade was increasing
in importance, the economic structure of the country was
becoming more complex ; the men of property felt that they
should have a say in the formation of economic policy ; and the
House of Commons did not want the King to become financially
independent of the taxes they voted. If James established a
right to levy impositions at will, he might soon gain a revenue
far in excess of the £70,000 a year which the 1608 Book
of Rates gave him. Sir John Eliot later pointed out that in the
Netherlands customs *revenue* was far greater because customs
rates were far lower, since there the government encouraged
trade and benefited from its extension.

In 1605 a Mr Bate had refused to pay an increased duty on
currants, and in 1610 the House of Commons took up his case.
The judges had decided against him, rightly in law ; but this
verdict, the House told James in 1610, might be extended ' to
the utter ruin of . . . your subjects' right of property of their
lands and goods '. The King ultimately agreed to remit some
of the impositions, and the Commons to grant him the

---

[1] *Thurloe State Papers*, i, 747

remainder on condition that levying impositions without consent of Parliament was henceforth declared illegal. But Parliament was dissolved before the bargain was completed. Attempts to settle the question in later Parliaments were unsuccessful. The new impositions laid a heavy burden on trade and the taxpayer, and played their part in allowing Dutch merchants to grab our carrying trade. As a result of this failure to agree about impositions, the House in 1625 took the revolutionary step of refusing to grant tunnage and poundage—the traditional customs dues—to Charles I for life, and voted them for one year only. Charles dissolved Parliament before this Bill was passed, and continued to collect tunnage and poundage without Parliamentary authority. So were initiated the quarrels which led on to the Petition of Right.

In 1610 it was proposed to solve the King's financial problems, and reduce burdens on landowners, by abolishing feudal tenures and wardship. When military service had been the method by which tenants-in-chief (*in capite*) paid for their lands, it was natural that the King should take over the property when the tenant's heir was a minor. But feudal tenure had ceased to have any military significance by the seventeenth century. The right of wardship had become little more than an erratic system of death duties. If the heir chanced to be a minor—and men died earlier then than now—either the family had to buy the wardship from the King, or the property was likely to be handed over to a courtier, who would make what profit he could out of the estate during the minority, and no doubt marry the heir or heiress to some needy kinsman of his own. In those days of narrow margins, when continuous careful estate management was necessary to economic success, a minority might prove disastrous to a family's fortunes. 'Much money was not raised this way,' Bishop Burnet wrote of the Court of Wards (in fact an average of about £65,000 a year) ; 'but families were often at mercy, and were used according to their behaviour.' It 'became then a most exacting oppression, by which several families were ruined '. ' Reviving tenures *in capite*,' Wentworth thought, ' was the greatest means of drawing the subjects to depend upon his majesty.'

The proposed Great Contract of 1610 would also have abolished purveyance, the right of the King to purchase

supplies for his vast household below the market price. Purveyance arose in medieval times when the royal household
moved around the country ; it was an irritating anomaly now
that production for the market had become a normal activity.
It had become a fixed levy, equivalent to an annual tax of
£50,000, not voted by Parliament. Yet less than a quarter of
what was paid in wardship and purveyance came in to the
national treasury. Most of it went to courtiers.[1]

The proposal discussed in 1610 was that the King should
be granted a regular income of £200,000 a year in place of
wardship and purveyance. The Contract broke down because
on reflection neither party was satisfied with it. The Commons
thought the price too high, and asked in addition for cancella-
tion of all grants and pensions to courtiers, enforcement of
the recusancy laws and abandonment of the royal claim to
impositions. The King began to realise that he would be
giving up his power to influence and control his greater
subjects, a power whose value could not be expressed in money.
The abolition of feudal tenures, thought Sir Julius Caesar,
James's Chancellor of the Exchequer, would facilitate ' a ready
passage to a democracy, which is the deadliest enemy to a
monarchy '.[2] The failure of the Great Contract meant that
the exactions of the Court of Wards were increased. Charles I's
exploitation of wardship during the sixteen-thirties was one of
the main grievances of the landowning class. Feudal tenures
were eventually to be abolished in 1646. But meanwhile the
Great Contract had put into men's minds the idea that the
prerogative might be for sale.

Yet whilst the yield to the crown from traditional sources
of revenue was proving difficult to expand, the wealth of the
propertied classes in the country was increasing rapidly. The
government made various ineffective attempts to tap this
wealth, by increasing customs dues and by selling monopolies.
But it proved essential to supplement the regular revenue still
further by Parliamentary grants. What was needed was a
settled income, provided by regular taxation. But who was
going to control collection and expenditure of the money

[1] G. E. Aylmer, ' The Last Years of Purveyance, 1610–60 ', *Econ.
H.R.* (2nd Ser.), **10**, 1
[2] J. Hurstfield, *The Queen's Wards* (1958), p. 313

voted ? The government ? Or the House of Commons, representing the taxpayers ? If the government, then how could it
be ensured that its policy did not clash with the economic
interests of the country and of the propertied classes ? In
short, control of finance ultimately raised the question of
control of the executive : the question of confidence.

The problems of adjusting taxation to rising prices and
expenditure were common to the whole of western Europe.
But in England the crown was in an especially weak position.
In France the real value of royal revenue doubled in the
century before 1640 ; in England it just kept pace with prices.
The French *gabelle* in 1641 brought in about twice the total
English revenue ; in England no such tax could be established.
In France something like 8s to 10s per head of the population
was raised each year ; in England about 2s 6d. And since in
France the nobles were exempt from taxation, the disproportion
was even greater than these figures suggest. Lower taxation
of course contributed to England's prosperity as well as to the
government's poverty.

Under James two serious attempts were made to tackle the
financial problem. The first was by Robert Cecil, who made
peace in 1604, adopted an increased tariff, and farmed the
customs ; improved revenue further by the impositions of 1608 ;
started to raise rents from crown lands, to increase profits from
the Court of Wards, and then inaugurated the Great Contract.
This attempt at an overall settlement was frustrated by a
combination of courtiers with the House of Commons. Cecil's
rule really came to an end with the failure of the Contract,
though he remained Lord Treasurer until his death in 1612.
In the next few years, corruption and plunder were rampant.
Cecil's successor as Treasurer appropriated £60,000 of public
money, and though imprisoned apparently never repaid it.
The last attempt at a total solution came with Cranfield, Lord
Treasurer in 1621. He cut fees, pensions, and sinecures ; and
he stipulated that the King should make no grants without his
consent. But the courtiers, with Buckingham at their head,
allied with the Commons to overthrow him—the same combination as had defeated Cecil. After that there was no hope
of the government's ever solving its financial problem by
economies. In the sixteen-thirties Laud and Strafford fought

a continual losing battle against what they called Lady Mora—
the power of the privileged groups now protected by Henrietta
Maria.

Lack of an efficient bureaucracy was also a handicap. The
merchants who farmed the customs—i.e. paid a lump sum in
advance for the right to collect them—naturally made what
profits they could for themselves. Parliamentary taxes were
assessed by the gentry in their counties, with the result that
the richest families paid far less than they should have done.
A gentleman worth £1,000 a year was assessed as though his
income was only £20, said Cranfield in 1615. He himself
was taxed on £150 in 1622, two years after he had estimated
his total wealth at £90,000. The Duke of Buckingham was
rated at £400; his income in 1623 was £15,000. In consequence, the Parliamentary subsidy at 4s in the pound of men's
assessed incomes or salaries gradually shrank in value. At the
beginning of Elizabeth's reign one subsidy brought in about
£140,000; by 1628 this had fallen to some £55,000. In one
part of Suffolk, 66 persons had been assessed in 1557 on £67
land and £454 goods; by 1628, only 37 persons were assessed,
on £54 land and £23 goods. The average sum at which 78
Sussex families were assessed fell from £48 each in 1560 to
£14 in 1626.[1] So more subsidies had to be voted to raise the
same sum of money, even without allowing for its depreciation
in value. In an age innocent of economic theory, this contributed to the view of the average member of Parliament
that he was being ruinously overtaxed, that the government
was extravagant and must be brought to book. Ministers may
have argued, with more reason, that their financial expedients
were justified by this refusal of the landed class—the richest
in the country—to pay a fair share of taxation.

Meanwhile another source of conflict had arisen. When
the Parliaments of 1625 and 1626 had been dissolved without
voting supplies for wars into which the King felt they had
encouraged him to enter, he tried to raise a forced loan.
Those who refused to pay were imprisoned; men of humbler

[1] R. H. Tawney, *Business and Politics under James I*, p. 146; F. C. Dietz,
English Public Finance, 1558–1641 (1932), p. 393; J. E. Mousley, 'The Fortunes
of Some Gentry Families of Elizabethan Sussex', *Econ. H.R.* (2nd Ser.), **II**,
479

rank were impressed for military service under martial law, or had soldiers billeted on them. Five knights who in 1627 were imprisoned for refusing to contribute to the loan sued out a writ of *habeas corpus*, to which a return was made that they were imprisoned ' by the special command of the King '. The courts accepted this, and refused to bail the prisoners. The judgment was legally sound ; but it placed impossibly wide powers in the hands of an unscrupulous government. In 1628 martial law was proclaimed in many southern and western counties, overriding the authority of Justices of the Peace.

All these grievances were brought together in the Petition of Right in 1628. Its four clauses laid it down (i) ' that no man hereafter be compelled to make or yield any gift, loan, benevolence, tax, or such-like charge, without common consent by Act of Parliament ' ; (ii) that no free man be detained in prison without cause shown ; (iii) that soldiers and sailors should not be billeted upon men without their agreement ; (iv) that commissions for proceeding by martial law should be revoked and never issued in future. So the House of Commons hoped to safeguard property by preventing arbitrary taxation and arbitrary arrest : to re-establish the supremacy of the Justices of the Peace in local government ; and to make it impossible for the King to build up a standing army in order to dispense with Parliaments altogether. The Petition had not been presented in the form of a Parliamentary Bill, out of deference to Charles ; but it was a petition *of right*, asking for confirmation of old liberties, not the granting of new. The King and the Lords fought hard to obtain the insertion of a clause saying that the Petition intended ' to leave entire the sovereign power ' or ' the royal prerogative '. But this would have nullified the Commons' intention, which was, while ostensibly only stating the existing law, to redefine that law for the future. In words the House of Commons got its own way here, as it did also in forcing Charles to accept the Petition with the reply normally used for assent to a private Bill.

But more was required than verbal definitions. Charles continued to collect tunnage and poundage without Parliamentary authorisation, arguing that it was not covered by ' or such-like charge ' in the Petition—i.e. that the attempt to define the limits of the royal prerogative had not really defined anything. Merchants refused to pay, and when the Commons tried to come to their rescue in 1629, Charles decided to dissolve Parliament. In a revolutionary scene the Speaker was held down in his chair whilst the House passed three resolutions. Anyone who advised or abetted the levying of tunnage and poundage, unless granted by Parliament, should be regarded as ' a capital enemy to the kingdom and commonwealth ' ; so should any merchant who paid tunnage and poundage not granted by Parliament, or anyone who introduced ' innovation of religion '. With this breakdown the eleven years' personal government began. The ringleaders in this scene, Sir John Eliot, Denzil Holles, and Benjamin Valentine, were imprisoned.

Stuart governments always had to be fertile in financial expedients. James I created the rank of baronet in order to sell it : £100,000 was raised by this means. Peerages and offices were also sold. Forced loans were aimed especially against those newly-rich who were thought to be under-assessed to taxation. In 1625 Deputy Lieutenants in Cheshire were ' careful to inform themselves of moneyed men, who employ the same in usury ', and to tax them heavily. Sir Richard Robartes of Truro, whose father had made money by lending at interest, was told at his father's death that the King had the right to ' seize on all gotten by these usurious courses ' but was content of his clemency merely to borrow £20,000 without interest. Robartes finally compromised for £12,000. He was still rich enough to buy a peerage for £10,000 in 1625. His son, rather naturally, was later a leader of the Parliamentary opposition in Cornwall.

During Charles I's personal government all sorts of schemes were tried : fines for enclosure, for encroachments on royal forests, for all those with incomes above £40 a year who refused to incur the expense of being knighted. This last brought in over £150,000 in two years. Prodigious efforts by Lord Treasurer Weston raised the ordinary revenue by twenty-five per cent. In 1635 the budget was all but balanced, although crown debts amounted to £1 million. Between 1636 and 1641 Lord Treasurer Juxon further improved the position by raising the customs farms and reducing pensions and annuities. The City was mulcted for allegedly failing to carry out its obligations in colonising Londonderry. But the greatest of all expedients was Ship Money. This extended to the whole kingdom the King's traditional feudal claim to demand ships (or their equivalent in money) from certain ports—a claim which had been exercised in the reigns of Elizabeth and James I. It could reasonably be argued that the whole realm should pay for national defence and commerce protection, not merely the ports. In many technical ways Ship Money marked a great advance. It tried to tap the new commercial and professional wealth of the country by a re-assessment on the ' true yearly value of rents, annuities, offices '. Whereas hitherto the clergy had been taxed separately, Ship Money taxed them together with the laity. Assessment and collection were centrally controlled : the sheriff replaced local commissioners, too likely to be partial, though the crown's lack of a bureaucracy led to failure here, since sheriffs had to rely on constables and petty constables.

But the importance of Ship Money for contemporaries was political, not technical. If it could be established as a regular tax which the King was entitled to collect without Parliamentary consent, the fundamental constitutional issue of the century would be decided in favour of the monarchy. This was the question underlying the Ship Money Case of 1637, not the £1 which the very rich John Hampden refused to pay. Chief Justice Finch declared that any Act of Parliament was void which claimed ' to bind the King not to command his subjects, their persons and goods . . . and money too '. When the verdict went against Hampden, the Venetian Ambassador observed that this meant royal absolutism and the end of parliaments. It was ' an utter oppression of the subjects' liberty ', the antiquarian Sir Simonds D'Ewes wrote. ' What shall freemen differ from the ancient bondsmen and villeins of England if their estates be subject to arbitrary taxes ? '

Legally the judges had a case ; but politics proved stronger than law. The crown obtained its verdict by the narrowest possible margin (seven to five) from a bench already subject to governmental pressure. The moral and political victory was with Hampden. As Hyde, later Earl of Clarendon, put it, when men ' heard this demanded in a court of law as a right, and found it by sworn judges of the law adjudged so, upon

such grounds and reasons as every stander-by was able to swear
was not law . . . they no more looked upon it as the case of
one man, but the case of the kingdom '. The judges' logic
' left no man anything which he might call his own ', so men
' thought themselves bound in conscience to the public justice
not to submit '. Hyde was to be a Royalist in the Civil War.
Almost the whole propertied class united in opposition to Ship
Money. In 1636, of the £196,600 assessed, only £7,000 odd,
or three and a half per cent, failed to come into the Exchequer.
Next year the figure rose to eleven per cent ; but in 1638,
when the Scottish troubles gave men the opportunity to resist,
sixty-one per cent was unpaid.

When they could not balance their budgets, governments
got into debt. Bills were left unpaid, and state contractors,
instead of pressing for payment, trebled their prices. Loans
were not repaid for decades. That made to the King by the
Corporation of London in 1617, for instance, was paid off in
1628, and then only in the form of crown lands. In 1640
the City refused to lend to the government because of its
resentment of past treatment. Charles's credit became so
bad that he could only borrow from persons like the customs'
farmers, upon whom he could put pressure and who hoped to
obtain future favours.

Before the existence of banks (that is, before the establishment of confidence between government and business community) a merchant might invest in land, if he became wealthy
enough, or in plate ; but normally he lent his money to other
merchants, or tied it up in goods. He was thus very susceptible
to fluctuations in the market, and to the kind of uncertainties
which early Stuart governments were all too skilful at creating.
Hence he was often short of ready cash, especially at those
times when governments found themselves most inclined to
demand forced loans or to billet troops on him. Erratic
government policy created the crises, and then arbitrary government finance intensified them. The business community longed
for stability, regularity, confidence. It was a London merchant
who complained, ' The merchants are in no part of the world so
screwed and wrung as in England.' ' Our estates are squeezed
from us,' declared another. These laments were not strictly
true ; but they accurately represent men's feelings.

FOREIGN POLICY

Finance and trade were the most obvious sources of dis-
agreement between King and Parliament. But quarrels also
arose over foreign policy. In the Thirty Years' War the
Habsburgs were trying to reverse the effects of the Reformation. Many Englishmen feared that, if this policy succeeded
on the Continent, its consequences would be felt in England
too. Nearly a century of history and propaganda lay behind
the identification of Protestantism and English patriotism.
The heretics burnt in Mary's reign had been popularised as the
victims of Spain by Foxe's *Book of Martyrs*, of which there was a
copy in many churches. The tortures of the Spanish Inquisition,
the Netherlands Revolt, the Massacre of St Bartholomew in
France, the Spanish Armada, Gunpowder Plot, all had been
skilfully exploited to build up a picture of cruel Papists striving
to dominate the world, and of God's Englishmen bravely
thwarting them. (This last was the contribution of Richard
Hakluyt's *Principal Navigations . . . and Discoveries of the English
Nation*, published in the years after the defeat of the Armada.)
A papal victory, moreover, would threaten those who had
acquired monastic lands at the Dissolution of the Monasteries,
in England as in Germany. Protestantism, patriotism, and
property were closely linked. The association of ideas was
strong and popular. The danger from Catholicism was both
real and imaginary. Few English Catholics were Spanish fifth
columnists, and Cecil and Archbishop Bancroft had skilfully
played on their divisions. Yet the Jesuits certainly wanted a
forcible reconversion of England, and if the Catholic cause had
prevailed in the Thirty Years' War they might have got it.

James was pacifically inclined, by temperament and from
financial necessity. He disapproved of his son-in-law's acceptance of the Bohemian crown, since he regarded it as subversive
of European order and of the rights of the Habsburg family.
He, like Queen Elizabeth, had always thought of the Dutch
republicans as rebels against the crown of Spain rather than
as Protestant heroes. James and Charles both admired the
Counter-Reformation monarchies of Spain and France. The
Spanish Ambassador Gondomar told James how to rule
without Parliament. He was very influential at court, and for

long prevented English intervention in the Thirty Years' War. James hoped by an understanding with Spain to restore peace in Europe—and so avoid having to call a Parliament.

This policy was strongly opposed. A Puritan group conducted vigorous propaganda in favour of English assistance to the Elector Palatine. In the Parliament of 1621 voices were raised in favour of war with Spain, on economic and strategic as well as religious grounds. When James dissolved it Gondomar reported that this was ' the best thing that has happened in the interest of Spain since Luther began to preach heresy a hundred years ago '. The visit of Prince Charles and Buckingham to Madrid in 1623 to negotiate a marriage with the Infanta aroused the gravest apprehensions in England. These were justified, for this marriage implied concessions to English Catholics which would have been utterly unacceptable to Parliament. The return of Charles, unmarried, in October 1623, was the occasion of nation-wide rejoicing.

In the Parliament of 1621 James had, in the Elizabethan manner, refused to allow the Commons to discuss foreign policy. But in 1624 Buckingham and Charles, now set upon war with Spain, virtually put themselves at the head of the Parliamentary opposition. They forced a new foreign policy on the King and overthrew Cranfield, who opposed war because it would ruin his policy of financial retrenchment. With what would have seemed intolerable insolence a few years earlier, Parliament made its grant of three subsidies conditional upon James's reversing his foreign policy. ' Upon your Majesty's public declaration of the utter dissolution and discharge of the two treaties of the marriage and Palatinate, in pursuit of our advise therein, and towards the support of that war which is likely to ensue, . . . we will grant . . . the greatest aid which was ever granted in Parliament to be levied in so short time.' This grant—only a quarter of what had been asked—was to be paid into the hands of London citizens, nominated by Parliament, who were answerable to the House of Commons for its expenditure.

Buckingham and Charles had given Parliament the right to initiate foreign policy, to control expenditure, and to displace ministers. James warned them that they were preparing a rod for their own backs. Their alliance with Parliament was short-lived. Mansfeld's expedition to the Palatinate in 1624 was a dismal failure. Buckingham thought, correctly enough in terms of power politics, that war against Spain necessitated an alliance with France. So Charles married Henrietta Maria, no less popish than the Infanta, and by secret agreement promised to make extensive concessions to English Papists. Worse still, in 1625 England agreed to send ships to help Louis XIII to suppress the Protestants of La Rochelle. This was not the foreign policy for which Parliament had clamoured; and in this instance at least Parliament represented public opinion. The crews of the ships intended to be put at French disposal mutinied. Buckingham light-heartedly reversed his policy and declared war on France. Yet his failure to relieve La Rochelle in 1627 was ' the greatest dishonour that our nation ever underwent '. Buckingham had finally lost the confidence of the opposition. ' I see little hope of any good,' wrote Isaac Penington to his cousin, ' unless the King and Parliament shall agree, for without that no money will be forth-coming, and without money nothing can be done. I pray God incline the heart of the King to yield to that which may further God's glory . . . that so we may enjoy peace and prosperity under him. I mean peace with all the world but war with Spain.' [1] Penington thought that war with Spain meant prosperity ; the King must yield if God's glory and domestic harmony were to be won. Penington was an important merchant, later Lord Mayor of London and a close ally of Pym in the Long Parliament. His opinion was echoed by Sir Edward Coke, doyen of the common lawyers : England ' never throve so well as when at war with Spain '.

This view was not shared by the government. As Gustavus Adolphus of Sweden marched into Germany to fight Pro-testantism's battles there, Charles I secretly promised the Spanish envoy in London 12,000 English levies, though he never dared to send them. In return, when Charles proposed to subject Scotland by force in 1637 he conducted secret negotiations with Spain for veteran troops. It was a natural reflection of the two different foreign policies that the Stuart kings always treated Catholics leniently, whilst Parliament

[1] V. L. Pearl, *London and the Outbreak of the Puritan Revolution* (1961), p. 178

was as determined to tighten up the collection of fines for breach of the recusancy laws. Parliament's motive was in part to finance the Exchequer at the expense of its foes, partly to weaken an irreconcilably hostile group at home. Papists were solidly Royalist in the Civil War. The queens of both James and Charles were Catholic, and especially in the latter's reign there were numerous conversions of politically important figures—Buckingham's mother, Lord Treasurer Portland, Secretaries of State Calvert and Windebanke, Chancellor of the Exchequer Cottington, and many great court ladies. A papal agent was received at court in 1637 for the first time since the reign of Bloody Mary. We know now that Laud opposed the Papist trend at court, and refused a Cardinal's hat. But to contemporaries his policy seemed to be approaching Popery, and after all the Pope thought the offer worth making. The accusation of Popery was damaging just because of the close association between Protestantism and English patriotism. Parliament's Grand Remonstrance of 1641 saw behind royal policy ' a malignant and pernicious design of subverting the fundamental laws and principles ' of English government, of which ' the actors and promoters ' were ' (i) the Jesuited Papists . . . ; (ii) the Bishops and the corrupt part of the clergy . . . ; (iii) such councillors and courtiers as for private ends have engaged themselves to further the interest of some foreign princes or states '. Certainly there were courtiers who took Spanish bribes : but the Grand Remonstrance was also a propaganda statement. ' We charge the prelatical clergy with Popery to make them odious,' observed Selden, ' though we know they are guilty of no such thing.'

THE STRUGGLE FOR SOVEREIGNTY

Impeachment was a fifteenth-century process, whereby the House of Commons accused an individual of crimes and presented him for trial before the House of Lords. In 1621 Sir Giles Mompesson had been impeached as a monopolist, and Lord Chancellor Bacon for bribery. Buckingham had been prepared to sacrifice Bacon to win popularity ; in 1624 he organised the impeachment of Lord Treasurer Cranfield. Buckingham's turn came in 1626. He was accused of monop-

olising offices of state. This was not a crime, but the clumsy
process of impeachment was the only way in which the Commons
could register lack of confidence in a royal minister. It was the
first step on the way to establishing responsibility of ministers
to Parliament.

The years 1604 to 1629 have been described as those in
which the House of Commons ' won the initiative '.[1] By a
series of procedural devices control of debates was wrested
from the Privy Councillors who were the King's agents in the
House. Extended use of committees reduced the formality of
debates and enabled private members to make their influence
felt. The Speaker was invariably a royal nominee, whose
duty was to manage debates in the government's interest. The
invention of ' the committee of the whole House ' enabled the
Commons to replace the Speaker by a chairman of their own
choosing. Longer sessions gave experience and the habit of
working together : leaders began to emerge who were not
courtiers and whom the House would follow rather than Privy
Councillors. In 1604 the House successfully opposed James's
attempt to refer to the Court of Chancery a disputed election
in Buckinghamshire, and so won the right henceforth to
decide election disputes, though James's action had had good
Elizabethan precedent. In 1614 there was so great an outcry
in the Commons over allegations that the government had tried
to manage the House through ' undertakers ' that Parliament
had to be dissolved after nine weeks of contentious inactivity.
The experience of this 'Addled Parliament' made governments
much more cautious in future.

In 1621 James rebuked the Commons' claim to discuss
foreign policy, asking, ' What have you left unattempted in
the highest points of sovereignty in that petition of yours,
except the striking of coin ? ' He added that the privileges of
the House were ' derived from the grace and permission of our
ancestors '. The House replied in a protestation, which the
angry King tore from the Journal of the House : ' The liberties,
franchises, privileges and jurisdictions of Parliament are the
ancient and undoubted birthright and inheritance of the
subjects of England ; . . . the arduous and urgent affairs

[1] W. Notestein, *The Winning of the Initiative by the House of Commons*
(Ralegh Lecture, 1924)

concerning the king, state and defence of the realm and of the
Church of England, and the maintenance and making of laws,
redress of mischiefs and grievances . . . are proper subjects
and matter of comment and debate in Parliament ', in discussing which speech should be free. The resolutions of 1629
were a similar assertion of the Commons' rights. The Speaker
had to be held down in his chair whilst they were passed.
But in 1642, when Charles I came to arrest five members of
Parliament, Speaker Lenthall said to him, ' I have neither
eyes to see nor tongue to speak in this place, but as the House
is pleased to direct me, whose servant I am.' So the revolution
was completed by which the Speaker ceased to be the King's
servant and became the servant of the Commons.

It is important to be clear what ' winning the initiative '
meant. Constitutional historians sometimes write as though
members of Parliament valued their ' liberties and privileges '
as things in themselves, as though they revived extinct pro-
cedures like impeachment out of pure antiquarianism. There
were devoted antiquarians in the House ; but all these procedural devices, old and new, were means to an end : to
imposing the will of the Commons on the government. There
were plenty of sources of conflict, in finance, religion, and
foreign policy ; the constitution was the sphere in which
attempts were made to adjust the conflict, by compromise or
by the victory of one side over the other. The opposition
gradually organised itself to wrest the initiative from the
Privy Councillors, not for the fun of the thing, but because it
wished state power to be put to different uses. And in this
the Commons were acting on behalf of those whom they
represented. Although debates were supposed to be secret,
the text of all important speeches circulated in the country,
and already members were appealing to the bar of public
opinion in a way that was to be deliberately extended during
the Long Parliament. The remonstrance of 1629 declaring
tunnage and poundage illegal, for instance, was intended to
encourage merchants to refuse payment.

Looking back, we describe the early seventeenth-century
conflicts as a struggle for sovereignty. Who was to be the boss,
the King and his favourites, or the elected representatives of
the men of property ? Contemporaries did not see it in this

light. Only Royalist thinkers had a clear theory of sovereignty. Parliamentarians agreed with Coke that ' Magna Carta is such a fellow that he will have no sovereign '. Pym denied ' sovereign power ' to ' our sovereign Lord the King ', but did not claim it for Parliament. The most remarkable case is that of Sir John Eliot. After the dissolution of 1629 Eliot was imprisoned by the King, and deliberately allowed to die in the Tower of London. He could have obtained his release by grovelling. He did not do so. He was a man of principle and of courage. In the Tower he composed a treatise, *De Jure Majestatis* (' Of the Rights of Sovereignty '). In normal times, Eliot said, the sovereign may not touch property without the owners' consent ; in case of necessity he may tax arbitrarily. There is no contract between King and people ; bad kings must be obeyed, lest greater evils result. Any liberty granted to subjects is without prejudice to royal sovereignty ; Charles had vainly tried to get this stated in the Petition of Right. Subjects cannot share sovereignty ; and in England, since Parliaments can be summoned only by the King, he is sovereign. So Eliot, slowly being done to death in prison for acting on the principle that Parliament's authority must prevail over the King, was unable to express this idea in theoretical form. This remarkable stop in the mind was not peculiar to Eliot. It was shared by all the Parliamentarian leaders before 1640. It may help us to understand Wentworth's acceptance of royal office in 1628, although he had previously been a member of the opposition. Pym and his fellows regarded Wentworth as a time-server who had betrayed his principles. He did indeed profit greatly in the royal service. But was he not in fact acting on Eliot's principle in deciding that, now Buckingham's rashly bellicose foreign policy had been abandoned, His Majesty's government must be carried on ?

In this light James I appears not unreasonable. Historians are apt to castigate him as ' a tactless Scot ', who did not understand the English constitution, and who by putting forward extreme claims on behalf of the monarchy roused members to make counter-claims for Parliament. But in fact James was a shrewd, conceited, lazy intellectual, who before he succeeded to the English throne had been a great success at the difficult job of governing Scotland. His ideas on the

prerogative or Divine Right were no more extreme than
those of Elizabeth had been. James expressed them more
often, and more forcibly, but there were perhaps reasons for
this. Parliament was already challenging the royal authority
by the end of Elizabeth's reign ; but in theory and practice
the position of the crown was much the stronger. The King
had been the focus of law and order in Tudor England. The
emotional loyalties of Protestant Englishmen centred on the
head of their Church. Shakespeare's historical plays illustrate
the Elizabethan sense that a strong monarchy was essential to
defend national unity against foreign invasion and domestic
anarchy. The danger from the monarchy's point of view was
that the position might go by default. It was to James's
advantage to define his position and dare Parliament to
challenge it. The ' stop in the mind ' ensured that the furthest
that Parliamentarians could go was to speak of the sovereignty
of King in Parliament, or more often of a mixed monarchy,
a balanced constitution. In case of conflict it was difficult,
historically, legally, and emotionally, for anyone to deny the
ultimate authority of the King. And much that seems offensive
to us in James's way of expressing the theory of Divine Right
would not have shocked contemporaries. A Privy Councillor
said in Star Chamber on one occasion, apropos of a gentleman
who had sued a village constable, the lowest official in the
hierarchy, ' Let all men hereby take heed how they complain
in words against any magistrate, for they are gods.' To call
a right divine in the seventeenth century meant no more than
that you attached importance to it. James's theory of the
royal prerogative had much to commend it in law, logic, and
common sense.

Both sides agreed that the King had certain prerogative
rights, such as the right to mint coin or to create peers. (It is
of course an over-simplification to speak of ' sides ' at this
stage.) What James and Charles also claimed was an
absolute prerogative right to take any action outside the law
which they thought necessary for national defence or national
security as defined by themselves. This prerogative the House
of Commons and the common lawyers denied to the government, but it is a right which Parliament exercises today. It is
the ultimate right of sovereignty, which in any state some

authority must exercise. Parliament and lawyers denied such prerogative to the King, because they had no confidence that he would use it for what they regarded as the interests of the country ; and they were quite correct. But from the King's point of view they seemed to be acting in a merely negative and obstructive way, and to justify their position they were forced to resort to unconvincing legal fictions.

Hence the legal antiquarianism of Sir Edward Coke and so many of the Parliamentary opposition. The 'stop in the mind' prevented them saying, 'We wish to force such and such acts upon the government because we believe them to be in the interests of the country, and because we, the taxpayers' representatives, are strong enough to insist that our views prevail.' Instead they had to pretend they were exercising immemorial rights of the Commons, and that those who advised the King otherwise were the innovators. (Since both sides were trying to cope with new problems there was of course some truth in the latter accusation.) So the Long Parliament kept Sir Simonds D'Ewes as its tame antiquarian, sending him off to the archives in the Tower every now and then to ' search for precedents ' which would justify what the House wanted to do. The sad day came when Sir Simonds reported that he could find no precedent. This did not stop the House from acting as it wished, but it helped men to overcome the ' stop in the mind ' and evolve a theory of sovereignty which countered that of the Divine Right of Kings.

The balanced or mixed constitution was one theory put forward to evade the issue of sovereignty. King, Lords, and Commons were jointly sovereign ; and so the Upper House might be expected to hold the balance between the two rivals. But this theory was foundering when it could be said that the House of Commons could buy the House of Lords three times over. During the disputes over the Petition of Right, Eliot said he was confident that ' should the Lords desert us, we should yet continue flourishing and green '. Moreover the issues which drove a majority of the Commons into opposition also divided the upper House. ' In 1621,' writes Mr Manning, ' the Earl of Southampton was the real leader of the opposition in the lower house ; in 1626 the Earl of Pembroke was behind the parliamentary attack on the Duke of Buckingham.' The

eleven years' personal rule was an affront to the Lords no less
than to the Commons. The crown could rely on the Lords
only because of the solid block of episcopal votes there. It
was with reference to the theory of the balanced constitution
that Harrington made his famous remark, 'A monarchy
divested of its nobility has no refuge under heaven but an
army. Wherefore the dissolution of this government caused
the [Civil] war, not the war the dissolution of this government.'

Another anti-sovereignty theory was the concept of fundamental law. Somewhere—in the breasts of judges, in Magna
Carta, or in the liberties of Parliament—were laws so sacred,
and so essential to social stability, that no government could
override them. (For Jean Bodin, one of the most influential
sixteenth-century political thinkers, such laws were those
protecting property and the family.) The beauty of the concept
of fundamental law lay precisely in its vagueness and in the
assumption that it was self-evident. All could agree about the
importance of something that was never defined. In 1641
Strafford was impeached, among other charges, for subverting
the fundamental laws of the kingdom. The Commons were
just about to vote the charge when the witty and malicious
Edmund Waller rose and, with seeming innocence, asked what
the fundamental laws of the kingdom were. There was an
uneasy silence. No-one dared to attempt a definition which
would certainly have divided the heterogeneous majority, agreed
only in its view that for Strafford 'stone dead hath no fellow'.
The situation was saved by a lawyer who leapt to his feet to
say that if Mr Waller did not know what the fundamental
laws of the kingdom were, he had no business to be sitting in
the House. That was all right for the time being. The theory
of fundamental law was the Commons' only answer to royal
claims to absolute prerogative, so long as they could not
claim sovereignty for themselves ; and adherence to fundamental law increased the impossibility of thinking in terms of
sovereignty.

So far we have discussed the constitutional conflicts with
little reference to the common law. This would have seemed
incomprehensible to the men of the seventeenth century,
whose difficulty in grasping the issue of sovereignty sprang
largely from the fact that they thought in legal terms. A

statute declared what law was ; it did not create it.   Parliament
was a High Court.   The problems of the day were seen as
matters calling for adjudication between rights and privileges,
liberties and prerogatives.   Sir Edward Coke, a professional
lawyer who became a leader of opposition in the Commons,
liked to think it was the task of the common-law judges to
act as ultimate court of appeal in constitutional matters, as a
supreme court.   The law itself was sovereign ; and the judges
alone understood its mysteries.   Under Coke the common-law
judges tried to hem in the royal prerogative, to restrict the
jurisdiction of prerogative and ecclesiastical courts which
derived their authority direct from the crown.

Coke believed that the common law had survived from
the time of the ancient Britons, and that the Roman, Anglo-
Saxon, and Norman conquests had left it virtually unchanged.
Yet the law was changing, radically, in Coke's own time ;
and Coke himself was the main instrument of change.   He it
is, more than any other lawyer, to whom legal historians
attribute the adaptation of the medieval law to the needs of a
commercial society.   By 1621 a member of Parliament could
even make the historically absurd claim that ' the common
law did ever allow free trade '.   When in 1624 Parliament
declared monopolies illegal, it insisted that they should be
' tried and determined according to the common laws of this
realm and not otherwise '.   Similarly the Act abolishing the
Star Chamber in 1641 said that all cases involving property
should be tried at common law.   The common law was the
law of free men.   ' All free subjects are born inheritable as to
their land so also to the free exercise of their industry,' said
Sir Edwin Sandys in the Commons of 1604.   The cost of
litigation in the royal courts meant that only the well-to-do
could enjoy this birthright.

So there was not merely a ' conflict of courts ', in the
sense that the common lawyers grudged business and fees to
Church or prerogative courts, though that entered into it.
More important was the type of justice which the courts
administered.   The common-law courts—King's Bench and
Court of Common Pleas—increasingly defended absolute
property rights, the right of every man to do what he would
with his own.   The prerogative courts became more and more

organs of the government. During the personal rule of Charles I they enforced monopolies and rode roughshod over the private-property rights of enclosing landlords. So the alliance between the House of Commons and common lawyers was natural. The law, Parliament declared in August 1642, was that by which ' the nobility and chief gentry of this kingdom . . . enjoy their estates, are protected from any act of violence and power, and differenced from the meaner sort of people, with whom otherwise they would be but fellow servants '.

Because of the antiquarianism of the Parliamentary opposition, because of their appeal to the common law and their alliance with the common lawyers, early Stuart governments needed judges who accepted the general lines of royal policy. In 1616 Chief Justice Coke was dismissed for refusing to defer to James I in giving judgment. Ten years later Charles dismissed Chief Justice Crew for refusing to admit the legality of a forced loan. In 1628, apropos the verdict in the Five Knights' Case, Wentworth in his opposition phase complained that the judges were ' tearing up the roots of all property '. During the personal government of Charles I repeated dismissals reduced the judges to a state in which they enforced monopolies, abandoned Coke's attempt to restrict the jurisdiction of Church courts, and declared Ship Money legal. But the loss of reputation which the Bench suffered in consequence probably did the government more harm in the long run.

COURT AND COUNTRY

Throughout this period we are conscious of a growing divergence between the standards of the court and those of the mass of the propertied class. James I was a pedantic and undignified person with gross and unseemly personal habits. He distributed wealth and honours with a lavish hand, first to Scottish favourites, then to the upstart tribe of the handsome George Villiers. The drunkenness of the court, the sordid scandals of the Essex divorce and the Overbury murder, reflected on the King personally since the Countess of Essex was divorced to marry a royal favourite, the Earl of Somerset. Such goings-on outraged the sense of decency of the increasingly Puritan gentry and merchants. Under Charles I the court's outward behaviour improved, but the continued domination of Buckingham offended the old aristocracy ; the influence of his Catholic relations shocked Puritan opinion ; and after his assassination in 1628 the party of Henrietta Maria was more ostentatiously Catholic than Buckingham's had been. In 1640 nearly one in five of the peers was a Papist. The better moral tone of the court was accompanied by the ascendancy of Laud, whose henchmen were ' lordly prelates raised from the dunghill ', ' equal commonly in birth to the meanest peasants '. The Bishops, adds Hyde, no enemy to episcopacy, ' by want of temper or want of breeding did not behave themselves with that decency in their debates towards the greatest men of the kingdom as in discretion they ought to have done '. And so they incurred ' the universal envy of the whole nobility '. In 1640 the Root and Branch Petition denounced ' the encouragement of ministers to despise the temporal magistracy, the nobles and gentry of the land '. Many Londoners signed it.

So there were deep divisions between ' court ' and ' country '. This had constitutional consequences, since those who were asked to pay taxes felt that the money largely went to pay for court luxury and extravagance. In 1610 a member of Parliament said he would never ' consent to take money from a poor frieze jerkin to trap [i.e. adorn] a courtier's horse withal '. Catholic influences at court meant failure to fine recusants as the law demanded. The ' country ' saw this as a lost source of revenue, which they must make good ; and as lenience to a potential fifth column at a time of national danger.

For over a decade Buckingham personified those evils which ' the country ' saw at court. He was an upstart who pushed his own family, and excluded the aristocracy from the offices and the disposal of patronage to which they thought they had a right. He protected monopolists and Papists. As Lord Admiral he failed to protect trade. His foreign policy was unprincipled, vacillating, and disastrous. He became so megalomaniac that he actually thought of establishing himself as independent sovereign of a West Indian island reputed to contain a gold-mine.[1] Under him the sale of offices and honours was systematised. Selling peerages, baronetcies, and offices might be defended as a form of taxation, which tapped

[1] M. Roberts, *Gustavus Adolphus*, ii (1958), 376

the wealth of the richest and most under-assessed elements in the population. It was a significant if incalculable source of revenue, through which courtiers could be rewarded without expense to the government, by giving them ' the making of a knight '. But considered as a tax it was extremely clumsy and inadequate. It also had grave social disadvantages. The government's object was to maintain the stable hierarchical society of degree : yet sale of honours undermined it. The inflation of honours diminished respect for the peerage, infuriated the older peers—and progressively reduced the value of the commodity sold. In 1640 there were more than twice as many English lay peers as in 1603, four times as many Irish.

Nor was much gratitude felt by those who had to pay heavily for their honours. Sale of offices led to inefficiency and corruption. A man who purchased his post could hardly put service to the public first : he had to recoup himself by taking fees and bribes. His office was a freehold, and so governments had little or no control over him. In the sixteen-thirties office-holders may have received £300–400,000 a year —half the total royal revenue. When a commission was set up to inquire into the taking of excessive fees, two of its clerks and its messenger had to be dismissed or reprimanded for bribery, blackmail, or similar offences.[1] There were not enough jobs at court and in the government to meet the aspirations of all those newly ennobled or knighted ; and sale of offices diminished the supply as sale of honours increased the demand. So the gentry were alienated too. ' When great favourites came in,' said the Duke of Newcastle, they ' jostled out ' the gentry. In 1626 the House of Commons made Buckingham's ' trade and commerce of honour ' one of the chief grounds for his impeachment : which did not prevent him financing the expedition to La Rochelle the next year by the same methods.

What could the government do ? Two of the periods in which honours were most actively sold (1608–12 and 1618–24) were ' reforming ' periods, in which serious attempts were being made to balance the budget. Charles I saw the social

[1] For these paragraphs, see L. Stone, ' The Inflation of Honours,' *P. and P.*, **14** ; C. R. Mayes, ' The Sale of Peerages in Early Stuart England ', *Journal of Modern History*, **29** ; G. E. Aylmer, ' Charles I's Commission on Fees, 1627–40 ', *Bulletin of the Institute of Historical Research*, **31**, 65 ; ' Office-holding as a Factor in English History, 1625–42 ', *History*, **44** (New Ser.)

objections to sale of honours, and after Buckingham's assassination he abandoned it. But his revenues remained inadequate : the King simply had to get at the wealth of his subjects by other means, for example by reviving an antiquated claim to fine those who refused to buy the knighthoods debased by his father. Even the Commission on Fees was used to raise money, by fining those who extorted too much. There could be no permanent solution so long as confidence was lacking between 'court' and 'country', between crown and Parliament : until the court had ceased to be parasitic on the country.

It was ' as necessary for princes to have places of preferment to prefer servants of merit as money in their Exchequer,' said Richard Lloyd in 1641, defending the Council in Wales. The ability to distribute offices was an essential means of governing the country. Throughout the century a major reason for wanting to occupy high office was the money to be obtained from it. Even a man like Strafford, who was very critical of the corruption of others, increased his income by nearly £17,000 a year in eleven years of royal service.[1] Except possibly during the Interregnum, we must never forget this economic point underlying the political struggles. The conflicts of the century aimed, among other things, at controlling distribution of the spoils of office, and transferring this lucrative patronage from the King to those who regarded themselves as the natural rulers of the country. Just as excessive concentration of power in Wolsey's hands helped to bring about the Reformation, so the monopolisation of patronage by Buckingham did much to cause the division between court and country, the split in the ruling class, which made possible the Civil War.

When we speak of the ' country ', to whom do we refer ? We mean those of ' the free ' who did not occupy court or government office, the main body of the gentry. On them the ultimate stability of government depended. No domestic policy could succeed in the long run without the co-operation of unpaid Justices of the Peace, who controlled local government. The constitutional conflicts of the century were not only a struggle between crown and greater landlords for disposal of government patronage ; they were also a struggle

[1] P. Williams, *The Council in the Marches of Wales under Elizabeth I* (1958), p. 148 ; H. F. Kearney, *Strafford in Ireland* (1959), chap. 12

of lesser landlords to escape control from Whitehall. The
patent for licensing ale-houses held by Mitchell and Mompesson
threatened the local influence of Justices of the Peace : it was
overthrown by the House of Commons in 1621. Martial law
overrode the powers of Justices of the Peace. It was
forbidden by the Petition of Right. In the sixteen-thirties the
Privy Council tried to impose a stricter policy of economic
regulation and poor relief on Justices of the Peace. In 1640–1
they hit back. Similar challenges to the local authority of
the natural rulers of the countryside, made later by Levellers,
by Cromwell's Major-Generals, and by James II, were similarly
overthrown. Justices of the Peace enjoyed real power and
patronage in their localities, and had the opportunity to impose
and maintain the type of social discipline that seemed best to
them. British freedom as established by 1714 meant, among
other things, the unimpeded right of the Justice to regulate
in minutest detail the lives of his social subordinates.

The reigns of the first two Stuarts thus taught a number
of lessons to those Englishmen who counted in politics. The
first was that administration could be carried on, and the
royal budget (just) balanced, without Parliamentary taxation,
if the government abstained from foreign war. This had been
shown during the two eleven-year periods when no Parliamentary grant had been voted, 1610–21 and 1629–40. The
warfare which followed in the sixteen-twenties and after the
Scottish invasion necessitated the calling of Parliaments. A
corollary was that no expansionist foreign policy, such as many
of the propertied classes conceived to be in the best interests
of the country, could be embarked upon without regular
sessions of Parliament. Patriotic Englishmen in the sixteen-
thirties were filled with shame when they saw German Protestants rescued by Gustavus Adolphus, whilst their government continued to negotiate with Spain ; when in 1639
Spanish and Dutch fleets fought an engagement in English
waters whilst the English fleet looked helplessly on. In the
same year Lord Admiral Northumberland wrote to the English
Ambassador in Paris that Laud, Wentworth, and the Scottish
Marquis of Hamilton, ' the persons that do absolutely govern,
are as much Spanish as Olivares ', the Spanish first minister.

A second and more sinister lesson was that by control of

the judicial bench the King had secured, in Ship Money, a source of regular taxation, which in time might enable him to dispense with Parliaments ; and that in Privy Council and Star Chamber he possessed the means for enforcing the government's will. Only the exceptional circumstances of the Scottish invasion in 1639, in agreement with an important section of the English opposition, broke the power of the government.

A third lesson, or rather apprehension, was that in order to dispense with Parliaments altogether and establish a monarchy on the French pattern, an army would have to be built up. Englishmen in the seventeenth century were very conscious that representative institutions were coming to an end all over Europe. The French Estates-General met in 1614 for the last time before 1789. ' What once were voluntary contributions in Naples and Spain have become due and certain,' said a member of the Parliament of 1625, arguing that the same might happen to tunnage and poundage. ' England is the last monarchy that yet retains her liberties,' added Sir Robert Phelips. Charles rubbed the point home by telling his next Parliament that ' Parliaments are altogether in my power for the calling, sitting and dissolution. Therefore, as I find the fruits of them to be good or evil, they are to continue or not to be.' In the sixteen-thirties Wentworth, as Lord Lieutenant of Ireland, was believed to be building up an army which could be used in Britain, an army composed largely of Papists. Here again Scottish intervention was decisive, since it supplied the opposition with an organised military force before the Irish army had been used. The gravest charge against Strafford in his impeachment was probably the report of his words in the Privy Council : ' You have an army in Ireland which you may employ here to reduce this kingdom.' Strafford argued that ' this kingdom ' meant Scotland, not England. But that was little better. For if the Scottish revolt had been suppressed by military power, there would have been small prospect of a Parliament's meeting in England.

Among the causes of the Civil War we must include the character of Charles I. Much stupider than his father or his eldest son, Charles was governed first by the disastrously vain and incompetent Buckingham, and then by the disastrously popish and arbitrary Henrietta Maria. He never gave his full confidence to the men who served him best, Laud and Strafford. If one shares Charles's prejudices, it is possible to argue that he was actuated by devotion to principles so noble that they override ordinary moral considerations ; if one does not share these prejudices, it looks more like the petulant obstinacy of the weak man. In any case, the King's high idea of his own station, his rigid inability to compromise in time, and his transparent dishonesty, made it impossible for him ever to have functioned as a constitutional monarch. Time after time in the sixteen-forties he demonstrated that his word could not be relied on. His execution became, in words doubtfully attributed to Oliver Cromwell, a ' cruel necessity '.

5 Religion and Ideas, 1603-40

> Archbishops and Lord Bishops . . . have claimed their calling
> immediately from the Lord Jesus Christ, which is against the
> laws of this kingdom.
>
> The Root and Branch Petition (December 1640)

THE STATE CHURCH

THE Civil War used to be called the 'Puritan Revolution'.
The tendency of historians recently has been to emphasise its
social and political causes, sometimes almost to the exclusion
of religion. Yet questions of religion and Church government
loomed large for contemporaries, even in spheres which today
we should not regard as religious at all. Professor Tawney's
Religion and the Rise of Capitalism, which every student of the
period should read, suggests that Puritan ways of thought
contributed to the development of a capitalist outlook ; most
historians would agree that there is some connection between
the Puritan and the *bourgeois* virtues. The very idea of a
Puritan Revolution is more complex than we used to think.

'There is not any man of the Church of England,' wrote its
most subtle defender, Richard Hooker, ' but the same man
is a member of the commonwealth, nor a member of the
commonwealth which is not also a member of the Church of
England.' The Church played a much larger part in the
lives of all English men and women in the seventeenth century
than it does today. Everyone had to attend services in his
parish church every Sunday, and was liable to legal penalties
if he did not. He had to pay tithes, one-tenth of his produce or
his profits, to a clergyman whom he had no say in choosing,
and of whom he might heartily disapprove. He was liable
to the jurisdiction of Church courts, which punished him not
only for ' heresy ', non-attendance at church, or sexual

immorality, but also for working on Sundays or saints' days, for non-payment of tithes, sometimes even for lending money at interest. Church courts were no less an irritant because their censures were often ineffective. The rich could buy themselves off, but many people had to waste time and money attending them.

In the isolated villages the parish was a real social unit. For all except perhaps the very poorest the church was the centre of public life and amusement as well as of local administration and taxation. Faint survivals of this still remain in the notices which can be seen fluttering in church porches. Military training went on in the churchyard, military stores and evidences of title to property were kept in the church. Parish officials were local government officials, responsible for poor relief and the poor rate, and for flogging vagrants ' until his or her body be bloody '. The pulpit was used for making government announcements, and ministers were frequently instructed by the government to preach sermons slanted in a particular way. Thus in 1620 James I ordered the Bishop of London to instruct his clergy to preach against ' the insolency of our women and their wearing of broad-brimmed hats, pointed doublets, their hair cut short or shorn '. A fortnight later a news-letter records, ' Our pulpits ring continually of the insolency and impudency of women.' Under Charles I positive attempts to dictate the contents of sermons were more frequent. For instance, in 1626 the clergy were instructed to preach that refusal of financial support for the King was sinful.

In days before the existence of newspapers, with no radio or television, we can scarcely exaggerate the influence of the parson in forming the political, economic, and moral outlook of his parishioners. Books were strictly censored, and the censorship was in the hands of the Bishops. Education was an ecclesiastical monopoly. Fellowships at Oxford and Cambridge were with few exceptions restricted to clerics : and in the thirties Laud was tightening thought-control in the universities. No person might teach in a school or private family unless licensed by his Bishop. The parson was likely to be the best-educated man in his parish, with the possible exception of the more remote squire. Moreover Christianity was the real (if conventional) belief of almost everyone. The Bible was universally believed to be an inspired text, offering guidance on all life's problems. Therefore the unchallengeable opinions of the accredited expounders of Christianity carried infinitely greater weight with their illiterate hearers than, say, those of press lords with their readers today. Competition had not yet reduced man's opinion of the value of the commodity supplied. In the forties the radicals attacked, in the same breath, the Merchant Adventurers' export monopoly, the Stationers' printing monopoly, and the Church's monopoly of preaching.

Politicians fully appreciated the political significance of the Church. 'People are governed by the pulpit more than the sword in time of peace,' said Charles I. 'As the Church can never flourish without the protection of the crown, so the dependency of the Church upon the crown is the chiefest support of royal authority.' 'Religion it is that keeps the subject in obedience,' Sir John Eliot agreed. Such expressions of opinion must be borne in mind when we try to assess the religious element in the seventeenth-century conflicts.

The parson was a key figure in the struggles of the time. It is therefore important to know who appointed him. The answer is revealing of the nature of seventeenth-century society. Apart from a mere handful of parishes where the congregation, a town corporation, or a London Company had the patronage, presentation was invariably in the hands of the landed ruling class. More often than not this was a layman—the King, a local squire, or a great man like the Earl of Warwick. But the higher clergy—Bishops, Deans and Chapters, Oxford and Cambridge colleges—also enjoyed much patronage. The Bishop of Lincoln's 150 livings were mostly very poor ones, but they made him a power in the land. 'If the patron be precise,' wrote Robert Burton in *The Anatomy of Melancholy*, 'so must his chaplain be : if he be papistical, his clerk must be so, or else be turned out.' The Bishop was legally bound to accept a patron's nominee unless he was manifestly scandalous in morals or knowledge. John Earle, later a Bishop, could take it for granted that for the humble villager ' his religion is a part of his copyhold, which he takes from his landlord and refers it wholly to his discretion '.

Patronage thus produced a majority of ministers whose political outlook, if they had one of their own, was conservative. 'No Bishop, no King, no nobility'; this version of King James's famous epigram was recorded by a Bishop. The three stood or fell together. Puritan patrons might appoint Puritan ministers; but their Puritanism would be moderate. When real religious radicalism appeared in the sixteen-forties, it was among men who rejected the patronage system altogether, and refused to pay tithes to ministers who, they thought, should be elected by their congregations. A social revolution was involved in this apparently simple point of conscience.

So before 1640 the demand for democracy in the Church was as unable to make itself heard as the demand for democracy in the state. Only a tiny minority of sectaries who had sought refuge in the Netherlands or New England were able to attack the concept of a state Church as such. The conflicts before the Civil War raged between rival views of what the national Church should be. Bishops gave the crown twenty-six safe votes in the House of Lords. Convocation taxed the clergy separately from the laity, and was much more generous in its subsidies than the House of Commons. It legislated, independently of Parliament, for laity and clergy alike. In 1604 it published canons, enforced by the Church courts, whose authority rested only on a royal proclamation.

Bishops were also civil servants and administrators. Gerrard Winstanley in 1649 spoke of 'Kings, Bishops, and other state officers'. They depended on the crown for protection and promotion, so as a group they naturally tended to elevate the royal prerogative. Under Laud ecclesiastics were being drawn increasingly into civil government. Consider the following extract from the Archbishop's diary for 6th March 1636 : 'William Juxon, Lord Bishop of London, made Lord High Treasurer of England. No churchman had it since Henry VII time. . . . And now if the church will not hold up themselves under God, I can do no more.' (Juxon's appointment, among other things, was intended to help to put pressure on Londoners whose tithe payments Laud was then trying to increase.) John Robinson, pastor to the Pilgrim Fathers before they left for America, accurately described the Church as 'the state-ecclesiastical'.

The High Commission, the supreme power in the Church, was as much an organ of the royal bureaucracy as the Star Chamber. Its censorship of books was used for political as well as religious purposes. Excommunication was used both for political offences and for technical and procedural offences, against great and small alike, with an impartiality which seems to us one of its virtues, but which did not so strike most contemporaries. 'What was it,' the Presbyterian divine Thomas Edwards asked in 1646, 'that ruined the Bishops and that party, but their grasping and meddling with all at once, Church and commonwealth both, provoking also all sorts of persons against them, nobility, gentry, City, ministers, common people . . . ? ' This fusion of the secular and ecclesiastical civil services led to a union of oppositions, and gave a political significance to what seemed on the surface purely religious questions. Many good churchmen, like Pym and Sir Simonds D'Ewes, ' allowed ancient and godly bishops ', but ' disliked their baronies and temporal honours and employments '.

Parliament in 1610 asked for drastic curtailment of the powers of the High Commission, and restrictions on the activities of ecclesiastical courts. Church courts were nominally supervised by Bishops, but in fact run by their lay officials. These courts were an impersonal part of the state machine, bitterly resented for their delays and extortionate fees. Many Puritans wanted to replace them by a parochial discipline, administered in a more paternal and intimate way by the minister assisted by elders elected from the congregation. It was assumed that elders would normally be drawn from the propertied class ; the Puritan scheme of discipline had supporters among the well-to-do laity, who saw themselves playing a large part in the control of the Church, and replacing the nominated officials of the Bishops' courts who owed everything to hierarchy and crown. This is an essential element in the Puritan alliance—those laymen of the propertied class (including common lawyers) who objected to the political and administrative powers of Bishops and their courts, and who were beginning to reject the whole idea of punishing ' sin '. The Protestant emphasis on the individual conscience as opposed to external ceremonies, on penitence rather than penance, also worked against the Church courts. Such men disliked Church courts for the same sort of reasons that they disliked prerogative courts. They wished to subordinate them to Parliament at the centre, and in the parishes to elders from the class which Parliament represented. This lay element might express its views in either ' Puritan ' or ' Erastian ' form, that is, it might emphasise either reforming the Church or subordinating it to the state. It was always strongly represented in the House of Commons.

Again this is more than a mere ' conflict of courts '. The type of justice would vary according to the court in which a case was tried. A jury of tithe-paying neighbours in a common-law court would be more sympathetic to a man accused of evading tithe payments than the Bishop's commissary would be. It was thus a matter of some consequence when, under James, Chief Justice Coke began to try to draw all tithe cases into the common-law courts, by the issue of ' prohibitions ' to stop Church courts dealing with them. In the thirties Church courts tried to insist that men should pay in tithe a fair ten per cent of their produce ; the common-law courts held that if it could be proved that less had been accepted in the past, the full amount need not be paid. So Laud's determined attempt to bring the common-law courts under government control was crucial for the success of his policy.

PURITANISM

The full Puritan programme for the Church involved an administrative revolution with far-reaching consequences for the state. The abolition of Bishops, or their removal from the House of Lords, and the abolition of Deans and Chapters and Church courts, would have ended ' the dependency of the Church upon the crown ' which, Charles I told his son, ' is the chiefest support of regal authority '. At the Hampton Court Conference in 1604, although the demands put forward by the spokesmen of the Puritan ministers were very moderate, James smelt underneath them the Presbyterian system from which he had suffered in Scotland. This, he thought, ' as well agreeth with a monarchy as God and the devil. Then Jack and Tom and Will and Dick shall meet, and at their pleasures censure me and my council and all our proceedings.' James exaggerated the democratic element in Presbyterianism ; but there was sense in his remark to the Bishops : ' If once you were out, and they [the Presbyterians] in place, I know what would become of my supremacy.' They must conform, James told the Puritans, or he would ' harry them out of the land '. As in the sphere of political theory, James here was merely stating the principles upon which Elizabeth had acted. In the light of subsequent history, who shall say that he was wrong ? ' No Bishop, no King, no nobility' proved true : monarchy and House of Lords were abolished in 1649, three years after episcopacy.

Under Elizabeth an attempt to capture the Church for a Presbyterian form of organisation had been defeated, and savage repression in the fifteen-nineties had broken the Presbyterian party. But Presbyterianism, with its special emphasis on the equality of ministers, is a clerical theory. What survived its suppression was a broader, looser brand of Puritanism, which appealed to the laity no less than to the clergy. This was the school associated with the name of William Perkins (d. 1602), which supplied the main body of Puritan clergy in the early seventeenth century. It had great influence on an important section of laymen who had been to Cambridge or had received some legal education at one of the Inns of Court. Perkins's school has been studied in Professor Haller's *The Rise of Puritanism*. The essence of its teaching was the distinction between the sheep and the goats. The former co-operate with God's purposes and strive to bring about his kingdom ; the latter serve the world. The former are the serious, conscientious minority ; the attitude of the latter is irresponsible. The Puritans saw a cosmic drama being played out around them. On the Continent God's cause was being endangered by the advance of Catholicism, and England was failing to play its part in this great battle because the royal advisers were at best supine, at worst popish or ' Arminian ', the name given to the Laudians who rejected Calvinist theology. At home there was insufficient preaching, insufficient attempt to educate and discipline the mass of the population.

The Puritans had high ideals of integrity, of service to the community. Their preachers taught a doctrine of spiritual equality : one good man was as good as another, and better than a bad peer or bishop or king. If men honestly studied the Scriptures, honestly searched their consciences, they could not fail to agree about God's will (just as Parliamentarian lawyers thought men could not disagree about fundamental law). No effort, no sacrifice, would then be too great to bring about God's wishes. Nothing else mattered, literally nothing else in the world. This was, as Professor Haller says, a doctrine which gave men courage to fight tenaciously, if necessary alone. Puritanism supplied a superb fighting morale. It appealed to men with social consciences, to those who felt that the times were out of joint (as they were) and that they could and therefore must help to set them right. Thomas Taylor neatly summed up the distinction between justification by faith and justification by works, as the Puritans saw it, in words which illuminate the social context of the two doctrines. ' We teach that only Doers shall be saved, and by their doing though not for their doing. . . . The profession of religion is no such gentlemanlike life or trade, whose rents come in by their stewards, whether they sleep or wake, work or play.' Puritanism was for doers only : for those who often look into their account books and cast up their reckonings. ' But a bankrupt has no heart to this business.'

Of the many aspects of Puritanism three only can be touched on here, because they have a bearing on our main theme : preaching, discipline, and Sabbatarianism. The emphasis on preaching, on the intellectual element in religion as against the sacramental and liturgical, dates from the Reformation. It is revealed in architecture : Protestant churches were no longer primarily places in which processions were held ; they were auditoria for the pulpit. Nonconformist chapels are often indistinguishable from lecture halls. The sermon was directed to men's understanding, music and ritual to their emotions. Hence the dislike which many Puritans felt for anthems, polyphony, and organ music in church. Congregational singing of psalms, with music as merely an edifying accompaniment to the Word, was different. The object of worship was to rouse men to think and act about the problems of this world. Preaching of the Word, Stephen Marshall told the House of Commons in November 1640, was the chariot on which salvation came riding into the hearts of men.

Royalists disagreed. 'There should be more praying and less preaching,' wrote the Duke of Newcastle ; 'for much preaching breeds faction, but much praying causes devotion.' In 1622 instructions were issued that preachers should adhere strictly to their text, and that afternoon sermons should be limited to expositions of the Catechism, the Creed, the Ten Commandments, or the Lord's Prayer. In 1626 writing or preaching about controversial matters in religion was prohibited. This silenced the Puritans on the subjects they most wanted to discuss. Nevertheless, their devotion to preaching gave them the advantage over their opponents. For the demand for sermons and religious discussion was almost insatiable, so aware were men of a spiritual crisis in their society. In 1607 the Commons petitioned James for a restoration of silenced ministers, in view of the great shortage of preachers ; and this remained their consistent wish.

To men who felt as the Puritans did, Laud's emphasis on ritual and ceremony, on 'the beauty of holiness', seemed little better than Popery. Some of his innovations—railing off the altar, for instance, and insistence on kneeling at Communion, suggested to Puritans the doctrine of the Real Presence of Christ's body and blood in the sacrament, and so seemed to be deliberately reversing the Reformation where it most closely concerned laymen. For Luther's doctrine of 'the priesthood of all believers' had denied the need for a mediator between man and God, who alone could perform the miracle of the mass ; and so had reduced the priesthood to an equality with the laity. Restoration of priests to a position of privilege and power in society, which Laud certainly intended, *was* Popery for most lay Englishmen. Hence Milton's reference to the railed-off altar as 'a table of separation' ; hence the fact that in 1639, in the army scraped together to fight against the Scots, when the troops got drunk of a Saturday night they tended to let off steam by pulling down and burning Communion rails. The distinction which Laud saw between his own theology and that of Rome was not clear to such men. The Archbishop's ideals were little appreciated by contemporaries, who were more aware of his quick temper and his savage persecution of opponents.

Thanks to Protestantism and especially Puritanism, the

well-to-do were becoming more sensitive to the age-old problem of poverty. On the relation of Presbyterian discipline to the possibility of overcoming poverty altogether, I will limit myself to two quotations. One, dating from before our period, is from Sir Francis Walsingham : 'Because multitude of rogues and poverty was an eyesore and dislike to every man, therefore they [the Puritans] put it into the people's head that, if discipline were planted, there should be no beggars nor vagabonds : a thing very plausible.' The other is from a sermon which Hugh Peter, brought back from New England by the outbreak of the Civil War, preached before Parliament and the Assembly of Divines in 1645. 'I have lived in a country,' he told them, 'where in seven years I never saw beggar, nor heard an oath, nor looked upon a drunkard. Why should there be beggars in your Israel where there is so much work to do ? ' (Note the attitude to New England, common at the time, which saw it as a sort of laboratory in which experiments were tried out for subsequent use in England. That was how the Pilgrim Fathers regarded it.) Here undoubtedly was one element of the Puritan appeal—the view that a parochial discipline, supervised by lay elders and backed up by excommunication, would be effective in solving England's unemployment problem. It would provide relief for the impotent poor, work for the sturdy, and punishment for the idle. Discipline was something that concerned this world as well as the next. It is one of the many points at which Puritanism appears to serve the needs of early capitalism. Those to whom it especially appealed were the small employers : Puritanism was always strongest in the economically advanced areas of England—in London, the Home Counties, East Anglia, towns, and the clothing areas generally. Part, though only part, of the appeal of Puritanism to the urban propertied classes derived from its emphasis on the duty of working hard in one's calling. Men served God here on earth by productive labour for the welfare of the community.

Puritan Sabbatarianism is often regarded as mere irrational Bibliolatry. But it seemed very different to contemporaries. For it was combined with the demand that saints' days should no longer be holidays. In medieval England, and in Catholic countries in the seventeenth century, the year was marked out by over a hundred holy days, on which no work was done. Many besides Puritans thought a regular weekly rest more appropriate to the regular rhythms of industrial society. There should not be so many holy days, wrote Nicholas Bownde, the great Puritan Sabbatarian, 'lest thereby men should be hindered from the necessary works of their callings, which hath moved the reformed churches . . . to cut off many that were used in time of popery '. Yet throughout the reigns of James and Charles, Church courts were proceeding against men for working on saints' days.

For Puritans the importance of the Sabbath was its association with preaching, Bible reading, and household prayers. Hence their disapproval of the traditional Sunday sports, which kept men away from afternoon sermons. But the Justices of most of the clothing counties, and of many towns, were also taking action to enforce Sunday observance. James I in 1618, and his son in 1633, by authorising Sunday sports, were flying in the face of respectable middle-class opinion, appealing to all that was unregenerate, undisciplined, and popish in men. When James justified his Declaration of Sports, his reasons were : (i) men would associate the traditional sports with Popery, and become dissatisfied with the established Church if deprived of them ; (ii) 'the common and meaner sort' would become unfit for military service ; (iii) they would go in disgust to ale-houses, and there indulge in 'a number of idle and discontented speeches'. The Laudian Bishop Pierce, a few years later, added a fourth objection : if men had no sports to occupy them on Sundays, they might meet for illegal religious discussion. Pierce was notorious for putting down sermons because they hindered church ales—the riotous jollifications at which money was raised for parish funds.

William Kiffin tells us how he and his fellow apprentices 'had no opportunity of converse but on the Lord's Day'. They used to meet before six o'clock in the morning for religious discussion. The government feared that unoccupied men would talk sedition, whether it was in ale-houses or in conventicles. The traditional sports, the Duke of Newcastle assured Charles II later, 'will amuse the people's thoughts, and keep them in harmless action, which will free your Majesty from faction and rebellion'. So employers who wished for regular labour, prentices who wanted a chance to talk theology and politics, Justices and judges who disliked the brawls and bastards produced by church ales, could all unite with Puritans who took the Bible literally. When the clergy were ordered to read Charles's Declaration of Sports, one followed it by reading the Ten Commandments, and told his congregation, ' You have heard now the commandments of God and man. Obey which you please.' Encouragement of Sunday sports by Bishops and the court, the official historian of the Long Parliament tells us, made many not very godly men see unsuspected virtues in Puritanism, and increased the divergence between ' court ' and ' country '.

ECONOMIC PROBLEMS OF THE CHURCH

The Puritan demand for a preaching clergy brings us to another point of conflict—the poverty of the clergy. The rise in prices had increased economic divisions in the Church. Some rectors, obtaining their full tithe in kind, were relatively better off in 1640 than their predecessors three generations earlier. Many vicars, especially those in towns where the full ten per cent of merchants' and craftsmen's profits proved impossible to collect, were much worse off. But since the Reformation the parson was allowed to marry, and might have a family to sustain ; lay standards of living for the middle and professional class had risen. If educated men were to be attracted into the ministry, its rewards must be enhanced. A sense of the urgency of this problem was common to hierarchy and Puritan alike ; but their solutions were different. Archbishop Bancroft in 1610 put an ambitious programme before the House of Lords. All tithes were to be paid in kind (many had been commuted before the inflation, for what had now become merely nominal sums) ; the powers of ecclesiastical courts should be strengthened in tithe cases, and all exemptions from tithes abolished ; mortuaries (death duties to the Church) and other Church fees should be revived. 3,849 parishes (over forty per cent) were ' impropriated ', that is, the right to tithes and patronage was held by laymen. Bancroft wanted a fund to be raised, by Parliamentary taxation, to buy out these laymen, and the right of presentation to be given to Bishops. If this was not possible, Bishops should be authorised to compel impropriators to increase payments to vicars.

This vast programme would have solved the Church's economic problems. It would have given incumbents something like a fair tenth of the produce of the country, and so have made possible the payment of stipends adequate to attract a learned ministry, and the abolition of pluralism (the holding of several livings by one cleric). But it would have involved a frontal attack on the property rights not only of nearly 4,000 impropriators, strongly represented in Parliament, but also on the vested interests of almost every tithe-payer, that is, every man of any property in the country. The scheme was dropped. The hierarchy continued to authorise pluralism. By this means a privileged minority of the clergy, including most Bishops, enjoyed handsome revenues ; but at the cost of leaving some congregations totally unprovided for, or with only a miserably paid non-preaching curate. In 1603, on the Bishops' own figures, there were only 3,804 licensed preachers with degrees for the 9,244 parishes of England. Nearly sixty per cent of benefices were occupied by persons either too stupid or too politically unreliable to be allowed to preach. Pluralism intensified inequalities and jealousies between ' court ' and ' country ' inside the Church. The worst pluralists were the Bishops and the cathedral, university, and court clergy. It was over a case in which the King had licensed a Bishop's pluralism that Coke was dismissed from his judgeship in 1616.

It was often suggested that the lands with which the higher clergy were endowed should be confiscated and used, like monastic property under Henry VIII, to solve the government's financial problems, and to enrich courtiers. The Puritans wanted the revenues of Bishops and Deans and Chapters to finance a preaching ministry in every parish, and so to abolish pluralism, as well as to establish schools and endow poor relief. Alliance between the godly and the land-grabbers seemed possible when in 1624 the Puritan leader, John Preston, urged on Buckingham the confiscation of Dean and Chapter lands, and the favourite, who had other reasons for flirting with the Puritans at the time, considered the idea seriously before rejecting it. In every Parliament in this

period proposals were put forward for increasing the revenue
of ministers, usually at the hierarchy's expense. The Bishops
managed to defeat them ; but no alternative policy of theirs
had a chance of passing through Parliament. And meanwhile
the poverty of ministers continued. Careful study of the New
Testament by Puritans failed to reveal any justification for
the type of inequality which prevailed among the clergy of the
Church of England. None of the apostles was called ' My
lord '. The Presbyterian movement was in part an egalitarian
movement among the lower clergy.

Failing achievement of their full programme, the Puritans
tried piecemeal solutions. A group of twelve Feoffees (four
lawyers, four merchants and four ministers—a significant
combination) was established in London to collect money to
buy impropriations. In eight years they raised over £6,000,
as well as having impropriations bequeathed to them. By
1633 they had installed at least eighteen ministers in livings
of which they owned the patronage, and their activities were
expanding. They tended to appoint men of radical religious
views ; and—ominously—they specialised in supplying
preachers for boroughs represented in the Commons. Laud
was frightened. He thought the Feoffees intended ' to overthrow the Church government by getting to their power more
dependency of the clergy than the King and all the peers and
all the Bishops . . . had '. So the Feoffees were suppressed and
their assets confiscated. Laud, Prynne observed, ' would rather
keep people in ignorance than see them instructed with the
Gospel's light '. Laud thought the Feoffees were spreading
political opposition rather than the Gospel's light. Recon-
struction of the Church raised the whole issue of power in the
state. Both sides agreed that reform was necessary. Neither
side could allow the other to secure the vast accession of
political strength which would come from reform on its own
terms. Nevertheless, since Laud was more successful at frustrat-
ing others than at carrying out his own plans, Prynne's accusation struck home. Laud's suppression of this scheme forced
men who wanted a well-paid preaching clergy to look to
Parliament for it.

Meanwhile there were two other piecemeal solutions which
the Puritan laity could adopt. One was to augment stipends

by voluntary contributions. This inevitably tended to give congregations, or their richer members, power over their ministers. Donations could be withheld if the contributor did not like the minister's theological or political outlook. In 1625 Sir John Eliot wrote to his Bishop asking him to present a named individual to a living in the parish in which Sir John resided. ' The stipend belonging to it is small, and not worthy of a scholar, or able to maintain him without helps.' But these helps ' have heretofore been added by some particulars [i.e. individuals] and I believe will be still to a man of their affection and choice '. So in effect the parish chose its own minister ; for the Bishop had to agree. This was happening in very many parishes, especially in towns, where maintenance was particularly inadequate. It was a big step towards congregational independency. It was a practice which Laud did his best to discourage.

Congregations could also get the type of preaching they wanted, in spite of the hierarchy, by establishing lectureships. A lecturer was paid a salary for preaching an agreed number of sermons a year. He was not subject to the same supervisory control by the Bishop as a minister with cure of souls. When the rich few who ' rule the roost' could not get their nominee appointed to a living, Thomas Powell wrote in 1636, ' ten to one but they will strain themselves to bring him in as a lecturer, which is a thing they reverence beyond the parson of the parish '. The lecturer might preach quite a different theology in the afternoon from that which the incumbent preached in the morning. Lectureships gave those who financed them a great measure of control, since the stipend could be withdrawn, increased, or diminished at the will of the contributors. Lecturers were often endowed by London merchants or town corporations. Hull, the first town to oppose Charles I in the Civil War, had been ' corrupted ', Bishop Hacket thought, by its lecturers. Since the dominant group in most towns tended to be Puritan, there were continual quarrels with the hierarchy over the lecturers whom they appointed. Lecturers were especially important in London, where three-quarters of the parochial livings were in the gift of ecclesiastics, peers, and the crown. Looking back after 1660, Archbishop Sheldon thought that ' nothing had spoiled the late King's affairs so much as

the credit that the factious lecturers had in all corporations ',
because of their influence on Parliamentary elections. It was
necessary, he assured Charles II, ' in order to the having a good
Parliament that all the clergy should be hearty conformists '.

Lecturers, said Laud in 1629, ' by reason of their pay are
the people's creatures and blow the bellows of their sedition '.
Under his influence the government made desperate attempts to
put an end to lectureships altogether. By 1638 this policy
had very largely succeeded, especially in London. Many
lecturers had been forced to emigrate, some taking their
congregations with them. In parishes up and down England,
especially in towns, there must have been a rueful feeling that
men could never get the preaching they wanted, even by paying
for it, so long as the hierarchy retained its power. Lord
Falkland, no Puritan, a Royalist in the Civil War, said in the
Commons in February 1641 that the Bishops had ' cried down
lectures, . . . either because other men's industry in that duty
[preaching] appeared a reproof of their neglect of it, . . . or with
intention to have brought in darkness that they may the easier
sow their tares while it was night '.

Laud put down lecturers. He ordered ministers not to
preach on controversial subjects, to catechise rather than to
preach. He suppressed the Feoffees for Impropriations. He
stopped the use of prohibitions by the common-law courts,
publicly disgraced Chief Justice Richardson, and reversed a
number of earlier legal decisions, thus making, to quote
Falkland again, ' as it were a conquest upon the common law
of the land '. He harried foreign Protestant refugees out of the
country. But we must also recall the more positive aspects
of his policy. He devoted fines in the High Commission to
the rebuilding of St Paul's. He began to enforce Bancroft's
scheme for authorising Bishops to increase the sums which
impropriators were legally bound to pay their vicars. He
persuaded individuals to restore impropriations to the Church,
and told Sir Arthur Haslerig that he hoped ' ere long not to
leave so much as the name of a lay fee [i.e. impropriation] in
England '. He conducted a campaign to increase tithe payments in London and other towns, and here too was beginning
to enjoy success when the Scottish army came to the rescue
of impropriators and City merchants.

So we come back to the Scots again. In Scotland the policy which Laud pursued in England had been carried to greater lengths. In 1625 the Scottish Act of Revocation tried to resume all Church property which had been acquired by laymen since the Reformation. Compensation was offered, but not nearly so much as the owners thought reasonable. Simultaneously a commission was set up to buy out impropriators, again at what seemed inadequate rates. The united opposition of the nobility caused both schemes to be modified, but all contemporary observers agree that these measures were decisive in convincing the Scottish aristocracy of the virtues of Presbyterianism. When the new Prayer Book of 1637 roused popular hostility, the nobility put themselves at the head of the movement against it. Their behaviour on this occasion persuaded Charles and Laud that religious reform was merely a popular rallying cry used cynically by men with economic grievances. So the King failed to appreciate the genuinely religious and mass support for Presbyterianism and national independence in Scotland, and floundered on to defeat ; while, in England, observers of Charles's behaviour in Scotland saw that the defence of property and Protestantism went hand in hand. Events in Ireland were equally alarming. Under Wentworth's patronage Bishop Bramhall was said to have recovered impropriations worth £30-40,000. But he did it by an open attack on property rights.

The Laudian clergy went out of their way to drive the men of property and the Puritans into one another's arms. The High Churchmen were also the supporters of personal monarchy. A well-known jest related how James I had asked some Bishops whether he might tax without his subjects' consent. Neile said yes. Lancelot Andrewes said James might take Neile's property, since he consented. Neile was Laud's patron, and by him made Archbishop of York. Robert Sibthorpe taught that 'if a prince impose an immoderate, yea an unjust tax, yet the subject . . . is bound to submit'. Roger Mainwaring preached that 'no subject may, without hazard of his own damnation in rebelling against God, question or disobey the will and pleasure of his sovereign'. These were not irresponsible personal opinions. Sibthorpe was promoted by Charles I. Mainwaring, though condemned by the House of Commons, became a Bishop under Laud, and was an eager defender of his policy. Canons voted by Convocation in 1640 ordered that once a year every minister should explain to his congregation that ' the most high and sacred order of kings is of divine right. . . . A supreme power is given to this most excellent order by God himself.' The Commons resolved in November 1640 that these canons contained ' many matters contrary to . . . the fundamental laws and liberties of the realm, to the right of Parliaments, to the property and liberty of the subjects.' One of the few occasions in 1641 on which the House of Commons was unanimous was in formulating the charge against Laud.

PURITANISM AND SCIENCE

Puritan ways of thought had influence far outside the circle of religious ideas. Puritan divines insisted on the duty of actively serving God, mankind, the Commonwealth, by working faithfully in one's calling. The idea is wholly traditional. Degree is preserved, we are kept in our proper stations. But hard work in the sixteenth and seventeenth centuries led some men to prosper. This, surely, was a sign of divine favour, of God's reward for diligence. As men prospered, however, they tended to rise above the station into which it had originally pleased God to call them. So divine sanction was given to a certain amount of social mobility. The Puritan doctrine of the calling ceased to maintain ' degree ' and became its opposite, a doctrine of individualism.

Calvinism liberated those who believed themselves to be the elect from a sense of sin, of helplessness ; it encouraged effort, industry, study, a sense of purpose. It prepared the way for modern science. Historians have noted the Protestant origins of many of the early scientists. The Puritan preachers insisted that the universe was law-abiding. The Reverend George Hakewill published in 1627 *An Apologie or Declaration of the Power and Providence of God in the Government of the World*. This raised the standard of the Moderns against the Ancients, and argued that scientific observation was more important than traditional authority. It was man's duty to study the universe and find out its laws. This would help to restore the human mind to the primitive vigour which it had enjoyed before the Fall. Within a year of publication Hakewill's book was set as a subject for disputation in Cambridge, and provoked a Latin poem from the twenty-year-old John Milton, who of course was on the side of the Moderns.

Looking through the wrong end of the telescope, we may imagine that the new scientific ideas broke through without difficulty. But men escaped no more easily from the tyranny of the past ideas about the world than of past ideas about politics. We meet with many ' stops in the mind '. They can all be summed up as respect for authority and fear of independent reason. In every sphere there were authorities—in philosophy Aristotle, in medicine Galen, in geography and astronomy Ptolemy. The Reformation demolished one authority, that of the Pope ; but it did so by elevating other authorities—the Divine Right of Kings, the authority of Scripture. Always men had to have an authority to lean on. Against the King one could set up Parliamentary statutes, the common law, medieval precedent ; against Bishops men appealed to the New Testament, to the primitive Church. Men's lives were dominated by the past. Because of Adam's sin in Paradise all men and women risked suffering an eternity of torment ; for all inherited the taint of original sin. Men looked to the Bible for solutions to moral and economic problems, to the Anglo-Saxons for solutions to their political problems.

The initial challenge to authority came from the Protestant appeal to the individual conscience. ' Here I stand, so help me God, I can no other,' cried Luther, though he refused to allow Anabaptists, whom he regarded as anti-social heretics, to appeal to their consciences against Lutheranism. Economic individualism in society (the breakdown of village community and gild, the rise of capitalism) combined with individualism in religion to produce a quite new authority, that contained within each man's breast. It was long before even the most radical thinkers recognised this : men said they were appealing to the authority of Scripture, when in fact they were appealing to their own interpretation of Scripture. But they were against any authority that was merely traditional. After refuting papal infallibility John Preston explained in a sermon before Charles I, ' Hence we may learn to take nothing merely upon trust, nor to think things are so, only because the Church hath said.' If Laud heard the remark, he can hardly have been pleased. ' They believe only what they see,' it was later said of the Independents. Francis Bacon was the son of an intensely Puritan mother. His programme of industriously collecting facts with the object of ultimately building up a body of knowledge which would help to improve man's lot on earth was entirely in the Puritan tradition. It suggests also one of the many connecting links between Puritanism and the productive needs of an expanding industrial society.

Bacon called men to study the world about them, the activities of craftsmen rather than the speculations of philosophers. He referred specifically to the new industries—dyeing, glass-making, gunpowder, paper-making, agriculture—as the proper objects of scientific investigation. He pleaded for a restoration of ' the commerce of the mind with things '. ' The empire of man over things depends wholly on the arts and sciences. For we cannot command nature except by obeying her.' His belief that knowledge grows by increments, and so that the Moderns can advance beyond the Ancients, helped to make possible a theory of progress, an optimistic confidence in man for which Puritanism had already, paradoxically, prepared. He turned men's faces to the future. Like Hakewill, he envisaged getting back behind the Fall by pushing forward the frontiers of learning. Despair, he thought, was the greatest of all hindrances to the progress of science. Even Bacon's method had forward-looking implications. ' My way of discovering sciences goes far to level men's wits ' : it depended on the co-operative activity of many researchers. The end of knowledge was ' the relief of man's estate ', ' to subdue and overcome the necessities and miseries of humanity ', ' to endow the condition and life of man with new powers and works '. Learning and power were identical. Acceptance of this novel doctrine constituted the greatest intellectual revolution of the century. James I had little use for the philosophy of his Lord Chancellor. Bacon's ideas began to be widely influential only after 1640. Almost all the early Baconians were Parliamentarians.

Conservatives were frightened by the sceptical implications of the new scientific method, its refusal to accept traditional authority, its readiness to test everything by reason and experiment. If the earth was no longer the centre of the universe, this had implications which reached far beyond the science of astronomy. In Donne's famous words :

> [The] new philosophy calls all in doubt ;
> The element of fire is quite put out ;
> The sun is lost, and th' earth, and no man's wit
> Can well direct him where to look for it.
> And freely men confess, that this world's spent
> When in the planets and the firmament
> They seek so many new ; then see that this
> Is crumbled out again to his atomies.
> 'Tis all in pieces, all coherence gone ;
> All just supply and all relation.
> Prince, subject, father, son, are things forgot,
> For every man alone thinks he hath got
> To be a Phoenix, and that then can be
> None of that kind of which he is but he.

So Donne linked the new philosophy with atomic individualism and political subversion. Contrast the confidence of a man who accepted the new spirit, Sir John Eliot :

'All things are subject to the Mind. . . . It measures in one thought the whole circumference of heaven, and by the same line it takes the geography of the earth. The seas, the air, the fire, all things of either, are within the comprehension of the mind. It has an influence on them all, whence it takes all that may be useful, all that may be helpful in its government. No limitation is prescribed it, no restriction is upon it, but in a free scope it has a liberty upon all. And in this liberty is the excellence of the mind ; in this power and composition of the mind is the perfection of a man. . . . Man is an absolute master of himself ; his own safety and tranquillity by God . . . are made dependent on himself.'

It is perhaps no accident that Donne had a successful political career at court, and that Eliot was in prison when he wrote those words. We might equally well have quoted from that *History of the World* which Ralegh composed in jail, and which was almost a second Bible for the Puritans. For the new scientific optimism (like Puritanism) gave a confidence in the future and a courage which could not be daunted by misfortune ; and those who accepted this philosophy were unlikely to be successful at Stuart courts.

CONFLICT IN THE ARTS

The juxtaposition of the passages from Donne and Eliot recalls some of the great themes of late Elizabethan and Jacobean drama. The boundless individualism of Marlowe's heroes, or of Macbeth, their unlimited desires and ambitions for power beyond power, set them in conflict with the standards of existing society. Yet their world itself has lost stability. Authority has gone, nothing can be taken for granted. ' What is truth ? said jesting Pilate ; and would not stay for an answer.' All old conventions are being challenged. We could tell simply by reading the literature of the time that two sets of standards were in conflict. In *King Lear* traditional feudal, patriarchal loyalties are challenged by the blind individualism of Goneril, Regan, and Edmund : the themes of *The Merchant of Venice* and *Coriolanus* are similar. In *Hamlet* the conflict has entered the soul of the hero, who knows there is something rotten in the state, that the time is out of joint, yet can only bewail the cursed spite that called him to set them right. In later Jacobean and Caroline drama the poetic tension is lost. There had always been a sharp divergence of sympathies between court and City drama : Jonson and Middleton on the one hand, Shakespeare and Heywood on the other, wrote different types of play and had different social attitudes. But after the first decade of James I's reign, as the conflicts in society became more acute, as the censorship became tighter and Puritanism extended its influence, so the popular theatre suffered a decline. Shakespeare ceased to write for the stage whilst still in his forties. Most of the later Jacobean and Caroline dramatists remembered today wrote for the select coterie of courtiers and intellectuals with whom pessimism and melancholy became a fashionable pose. Their plays became more bawdy and more horrific (though still, in Webster and Tourneur, with a central theme of the lone wolf against his society). The golden age of the drama had ended long before Parliament closed the theatres in 1640. Only in the grounds of Ludlow Castle could a Milton show an individual at last triumphing over her worldly environment, because she had submitted to godly discipline. Harnessing the turbulent force of individualism was not the least important social function of Puritanism.

In 1611 the Authorised Version of the Bible was published, the most popular and influential book of this or any century. It drew on many previous translations into English, and did much to standardise popular speech and ways of thought. The need for a new translation had been pointed out by the Puritans at the Hampton Court Conference, and Puritan divines played a large part in the work alongside members of the hierarchy. So in many ways the Authorised Version, together with Shakespeare's retirement from play-writing at the same time, may be taken to symbolise the last moment of national unity. As the conflict came home to men's bosoms, as it became too intensely personal to be played out on the censored stage, it was more and more expressed in what we call metaphysical poetry. The essence of the metaphysical lyric is its paradox, its sharp antitheses, its clutch at connections between objects apparently the most incongruous, its agonising soul-questionings and search for salvation, its sense of the contrast between subjective and objective, desire and possibility. Donne called on God :

> Take me to you, imprison me, for I,
> Except you enthrall me, never shall be free,
> Nor ever chaste, except you ravish me.

George Wither, another man who suffered imprisonment under the Stuarts, but who survived to fight for Parliament, wrote :

> But, oh my God ! though grovelling I appear
> Upon the ground (and have a rooting here
> Which hales me downwards) yet in my desire
> To that which is above me I aspire.

Henry Vaughan, a native of one of the outlying areas, like so many of the cavalier poets, saw the same contrast :

> Here in dust and dirt, oh here
> The lilies of his love appear.

So did Marvell :

> O who shall, from this dungeon, raise
> A soul enslaved so many ways ? . . .
> A soul hung up, as 'twere, in chains
> Of nerves and arteries and veins ;
> Tortured, besides each other part,
> In a vain head and double heart.

The decades immediately before the Civil War were years of a literary as well as an economic divide. George Herbert and Nicholas Ferrar saw the coming storm, and sought shelter in retirement from public life. Burton anatomised the melancholy that was characteristic of intellectuals in his society. Milton, ' church-outed by the prelates ', touched on the conflicts obscurely in *Lycidas* and *Comus* : only in 1641 could he freely denounce ' this impertinent yoke of prelaty, under whose inquisitorious duncery no free and splendid wit can flourish '. The censorship, Wither agreed, brought ' authors, yea the whole commonwealth and all the liberal sciences into bondage '. Among those who suffered from the censorship we may mention Chapman, Drayton, Ben Jonson, Donne, Ralegh, Fletcher, Massinger, Middleton, Burton, Joseph Hall, Fulke Greville, Selden, Coke, as well as Wither himself, who told John Taylor he must write against the government and get himself imprisoned if he wanted his books to sell. The idea that court patronage benefited literature under Charles I is a ludicrous travesty. The censorship was tightened as the revolution approached. In 1633 the Master of the Revels even laid it down that old plays being revived should be re-censored, ' since they may be full of offensive things against Church and state, the rather that in former times the poets took a greater liberty than is allowed them by me '.[1] All plays had to be licensed twice, for performance and for the press.

Until 1641 (as again after 1660) the publication of home news of any sort was a legal offence. There were no printed newspapers, only privately circulated news-letters, which none but the well-to-do could afford. This added to the political importance of the pulpit. In 1637, by decree of Star Chamber, the number of authorised printers in London was reduced to

[1] Ed. J. Q. Adams, *The Dramatic Records of Sir Henry Herbert* (1917), p. 21

twenty, and savage corporal penalties were denounced against illegal printing. All foreign books imported were to be vetted by the Bishops before they were put on the market. John Lilburne, later the Leveller leader, was flogged through the streets of London for breaking this regulation. No book was to be reprinted, even if previously licensed, without a new licence. Laud was alleged to have refused licences to print Luther's *Table Talk*, Foxe's *Book of Martyrs*, Bishop Jewell's *Works*, and Bishop Bayley's *Practice of Piety*. The Geneva Bible, with its anti-authoritarian marginal notes, had to be smuggled over from Holland. Sir Robert Cotton's library was raided. Sir Simonds D'Ewes decided not to write for publication. Even the saintly and conservative Nicholas Ferrar found his translation of a devotional work suppressed by the censor ; and he had long political arguments before he could publish George Herbert's apparently innocuous *The Temple*. 'Were the press open to us,' said Bastwick in the pillory, 'we would scatter [Antichrist's] kingdom.' He proved right.

There were similar conflicts in other arts. In music the golden age of Byrd, Bull, Morley, and Orlando Gibbons was coming to an end by the sixteen-twenties. The Church was still the greatest patron of music, and a new enthusiasm for polyphony was the stylistic accompaniment of Laudianism. This reinforced trends towards intellectualism and complexity fashionable in court circles. Composers, like metaphysical poets, sought the new and startling for its own sake, the subjective and the introspective. So a cleavage developed between the music of the few and the many, of the professional and the amateur. Polyphony was associated with Catholicism, ornament, ceremonies, luxury : the Puritans reacted towards simple tune-playing, towards utilitarianism in the arts as in science. In the sixteen-forties they sang psalms and destroyed organs.[1] Patronage of painting was monopolised by the royal family and a few courtiers. Charles I was a discriminating patron ; he conferred knighthoods on Rubens and Van Dyck, but he neglected native artists. Van Dyck has been described as a conscious ' propagandist in the cause of absolutism ', who ' falsified the truth of appearances and hopelessly corrupted

---

[1] E. Meyer, *English Chamber Music* (1946), *passim*

an honest British tradition in portraiture which was beginning
to be formed '.   His flattering portraits of Charles I, his
Queen, and his courtiers have contributed to a romantic view
of the Stuarts that contemporaries did not share.   Charles's
niece was ' surprised to find that the Queen, who looked so
fine in Van Dyck's painting, was a small woman . . . with
long skinny arms and teeth like defence works projecting from
her mouth '.[1]

There was an even more marked divorce between court
and country taste in architecture.   Inigo Jones, the
greatest name, was Surveyor to the Crown, 1615–42.   All his best
work was done for the royal family (the Queen's House at
Greenwich, the Banqueting House at Whitehall).   He introduced Italian styles of building into England, and in the late
sixteen-thirties was employed to design a palace whose general
conception ' reflects clearly enough the absolutist ideals of
the King '.   The fine imposed on the City for its failure to
colonise Londonderry was intended for this project ; fines in
the prerogative courts helped to pay for Jones's repair of
St Paul's.   It is a reflection of the cultural as well as political
divisions in English society that his most ambitious projects
were financed by abuses which made their contribution to the
causes of the Civil War.   Court patronage meant that the first
architect of his day had to spend much of his time on routine
work as Surveyor, or in designing sets and machinery for
ephemeral court masques.   In consequence of this isolation,
Inigo Jones, like Van Dyck, was the greatest but not the most
influential artist in his field.   ' English building proceeded at
its own pace and, quite independently of Inigo Jones, drew
influences from abroad and incorporated them in a style
which not only outlasted Jones's surveyorship and enjoyed a
mild triumph during the Commonwealth, but persisted till the
last quarter of the century.' [2]

[1] E. K. Waterhouse, *Painting in Britain, 1530–1790* (1953), esp. pp. 46,
49 ; M. Whinney and O. Millar, *English Art, 1625–1714* (1957), esp. chap. 4
[2] J. Summerson, *Architecture in Britain, 1530–1840* (1955) ; Whinney and
Millar, *op. cit.* ;   G. Shankland, ' A Study of the History of Architecture in
Society ', *The Architectural Association Journal*, **63** ; E. Mercer, ' The Houses
of the Gentry ', *P. and P.*, **4**
My brief and one-sided remarks on the arts are intended only to suggest
a few ideas about the connections between art and society, which should
be followed up in the references given.

6 Conclusion, 1603-40

> Miesta   Religion
> And liberty (most specious names) they urge ;
> Which like the bills of subtle mountebanks,
> Filled with great promises of curing all, though by
> The wise passed by as common cousenage,
> Yet by th' unknowing multitude they're still
> Admired and flocked unto.
> King   Is there no way
> To disabuse them ?
> Miesta   All is now too late.
>
>   Sir John Suckling, *The Tragedy of Brennoralt* (1639), III, i

IN THE three preceding chapters our arbitrary division between economics, politics, and ideas continually broke down. Monopolies have constitutional and political implications. Foreign policy involves economic and religious considerations, as well as political. The Church is a political as well as a religious organisation and a great landowner ; disputes over tithes involve religious, legal, and economic questions. Baconian science is linked with the ideas of Puritanism, and with the needs of the expanding economy : its supporters were mainly Parliamentarians. This impossibility of shutting off 'religious', 'constitutional', and 'economic' causes of the Civil War corresponds to the complexity of life in seventeenth-century England, and to the confusion of mind of men who lived in it. Commercial concepts like 'contract' and 'balance' abound in political and even religious as well as economic thought (the social contract ; covenant theology ; balance of trade, of property, of power, of the constitution). The Root and Branch Petition, listing 'the manifold evils . . . occasioned by the prelates and their dependants', sandwiched monopolies and Ship Money between the growth of Popery and the use of popish agents to defend episcopacy. We must be very careful not to force our later categories of analysis on seventeenth-century events.

The seventeenth-century English Revolution is often, and fruitfully, compared with the French Revolution of 1789. But there is one important difference. In France economic and political divisions roughly corresponded with social : the unprivileged Third Estate opposed aristocracy and monarchy ; the aristocracy took no part in trade and industry. But in England wool, cloth, and agricultural production for the market split the ruling class itself : many gentlemen and even peers engaged in economic activities which would have been impossible for a French noble. ' The landowner living on the profits and rents of commercial farming,' concludes Professor Tawney, ' and the merchant or banker who was also a land-owner, represented not two classes but one. Patrician and parvenu both owed their ascent to causes of the same order. Judged by the source of their incomes, both were equally bourgeois.' The division in England is not Third Estate *versus* gentry and peerage, but country *versus* court. Court and government offered economic privilege to some merchants (monopolists, customs farmers, ruling oligarchies in London and other towns) ; and perquisites to many members of the landed class. On the other hand, those gentlemen and merchants excluded from economic privilege—and they included some of the richest and most go-ahead members of these social groups as well as the middling men—thought that greater freedom of economic development would be of advantage to themselves and the country. They looked to Parliament and common lawyers to help them to get it. They looked for leadership to a group of peers excluded from court favour. In seventeenth-century France sale of offices diverted capital away from productive investment, thus delaying the development of trade and industry and widening the gap between nobility and bourgeoisie. Similar social consequences might have resulted in England if the old régime had survived.

But the cleavage between court and country was more than merely a matter of access to economic privilege. Under the Tudors the landed class had won a position rare in Europe. As Justices of the Peace, through control of wages and poor relief, they enjoyed great power over the masses of the popula-

tion who ' existed only to be ruled ' ; and this power was
virtually independent of a government which had no standing
army or bureaucracy. The Stuarts never had sufficient power
to hold the capitalist sector of the economy in check, to reduce
it to central regulation and control. Attempts to manage
local government from Whitehall only exasperated the ' natural
rulers ' of the country, many of whom felt that government
interference, even if well intentioned, had a detrimental effect
on the economy. Merchants and gentry in ten counties
voluntarily contributed £500,000 between 1601 and 1630
to schemes, which they devised and controlled, for relieving
poverty ; they fought tooth and nail against any attempt to
lay a local rate on them for this purpose, so that ' in no year
prior to 1660 was more than seven per cent of all the vast sums
expended on the care of the poor derived from taxation '.
Similarly they would contribute generously to a lecturer whom
they appointed, and violently resist attempts to increase legally
enforceable tithe payments. The effort of Laud and Wentworth to impose a programme on such men was a hopeless
failure : ' the structure of sovereignty in England had crumbled
well before the convention of the Long Parliament '.

Merchants and Puritan gentry, by endowing schools,
scholarships, assistance for apprentices and the other charities
studied by Professor Jordan, were building up a society in
which careers were much more open to the talents than in the
traditional hierarchical society which crown and Laudian
clergy wished to preserve. (It is significant that the peerage
played a far smaller part than merchants in these endowments.) ' Power,' Professor Jordan concludes, ' as history has
so often demonstrated, flows inevitably to those unafraid to
assume the burdens of responsibility.' [1] The instrument of the
transmission of power in the Civil War was the New Model
Army, an army of the career open to the talents.

Even reformers like Laud and Wentworth were pursuing
a policy which outraged wide sections of the population. They
dispensed with Parliament, and clearly would by preference
have called one only when the King had made himself financially independent—perhaps after Wentworth's army in Ireland
and the remodelling of corporations in England had deprived

[1] Jordan, *Philanthropy in England*, pp. 131–40, 151. See Appendix D, p. 321

Parliament of any independent power. A moral gulf was widening between the court and the mass of respectable Protestant Englishmen. The government protected monopolists and prosecuted enclosers ; tried to increase the revenue of the Church and to enhance the powers of the clergy ; suppressed Protestant nonconformists whilst not discouraging Papists ; in its foreign policy alienated potential Protestant allies and neglected to push the interests of English trade.

So when Parliament finally met in 1640, the propertied class was almost totally alienated from the government. 'The weaker faction in court did strive always to pull down the stronger by a Parliament,' the Duke of Newcastle noted. As in the revolt of the Netherlands and the French Revolution, revolution in England was precipitated by a 'revolt of the nobles'. Revolution happens only when the government has lost the confidence of an important section of the ruling class. But in France in 1789 the aristocracy quickly rallied to the crown once the Third Estate put forward revolutionary demands ; in England the House of Commons was split, and even in the Lords there was a considerable minority which carried opposition to the point of civil war. The difference can partly be explained by the importance of questions of religion and Church government in the English Revolution.

There were thus three contestants in all the spheres we have been looking at. Court-favoured monopolists were attacked by free traders who looked to Parliament and common law ; but below them was the mass of consumers and craftsmen, who also opposed monopolies but had little else in common with London merchants and gentlemen clothiers. Again, there was rivalry between those who profited by and those who suffered from the Court of Wards, between enclosing landlords and the government which fined enclosers ; but below this was the mass of tenants who wanted stability of tenure for their holdings and the throwing-open of all enclosures. In yet another sphere, there was rivalry between prerogative and Church courts on the one hand, common-law courts looking to Parliament on the other ; but spokesmen for those who existed only to be ruled will soon appear, declaring that the law itself is the enemy. In religion there was rivalry between Laudians and moderate Puritans who wished

to subordinate the Church to Parliament and elders; but
below them were sectaries who rejected the idea of a state
Church altogether. There was rivalry between those who
wanted to preserve a static hierarchical society and those who
were busy shaping a more fluid society in which men of ability
and means would be able to make their way to the top;
below both groups were those whose poverty prevented them,
in normal times, even conceiving the possibility of altering
the world in which they lived. In short, there was a quarrel
between two groups of the ruling class; but looking on was
the many-headed monster, which might yet be *tertius gaudens*.
Once the unity of the Parliamentary class was broken, social
revolution would be possible. That is why responsible leaders
on both sides were so anxious to get what they wanted without
war.

When the men of the Long Parliament wanted a shorthand
phrase to sum up their cause they said they were defending
' religion, liberty, and property '. We can now see how widely
these words extend. Religion could cover the various emotions
linking Protestantism and patriotism, the strategic anxieties
roused by the Thirty Years' War, the desire for an expansionist
anti-Spanish foreign policy. It could cover the traditional fear
for the safety of monastic lands, and the newer anxieties
caused by Laud's economic activities. It could cover dislike
of Bishops in state office, of the High Commission's savage
sentences, of the multifarious inquisitorial activities of Church
courts. It could cover the intense study of the Scriptures, and
the appeal to the Bible to criticise existing institutions and
practice. It could cover the Puritan sense of spiritual equality
and human dignity, and the appeal to the individual conscience with all its anarchist possibilities. It could cover the
demand for greater freedom of speech, publication, assembly,
and discussion.

Mrs Hutchinson, wife of a colonel in the Parliamentary
Army, illustrated the possible meanings of the word ' Puritan ':

' If any were grieved at the dishonour of the kingdom, or
the griping of the poor, or the unjust oppressions of the subject
by a thousand ways invented to maintain the riots of the
courtiers and the swarms of needy Scots the King had brought
in to devour like locusts the plenty of the land, he was a

Puritan ; . . . if any gentleman in his county maintained the
good laws of the land, or stood up for any public interest, for
good order or government, he was a Puritan. In short, all that
crossed the views of the needy courtiers, the proud encroaching
priests, the thievish projectors, the lewd nobility and gentry
. . . all these were Puritans.' Newcastle coal exporters
referred to London merchants who opposed their monopoly
as ' Puritans '.

Above all, religion was a useful rallying cry. We must
not exaggerate its intrinsic importance. In the Parliament of
1621, of 105 Bills prepared, only 10 dealt with religious matters
(including ecclesiastical economics) : 40 dealt with trade.
' Religion was not the thing at first contested for,' said Cromwell, probably the Parliamentary leader for whom religious
questions meant most ; ' but God brought it to that issue at
last.' The cry of Protestantism in danger stirred deep patriotic feelings, and was pleasantly vague. Many could agree in
denouncing Laudianism as Popery who were to disagree violently when it came to putting something in its place. ' I can
tell you, Sirs,' said Cromwell to two fellow members, ' what I
would not have ; though I cannot, what I would.' Selden
was more cynical and more intellectual than most of the
Parliamentarians. But his words show that some at least were
quite conscious of the use to which religion might be put.
' The very *Arcanum* of pretending religion in all wars is that
something may be found out in which all men may have
interest. In this the groom has as much interest as the lord.
Were it for land, one has one thousand acres, and the other
but one ; he would not venture so far as he that has a thousand.
But religion is equal to both. Had all men land alike . . .
then all men would say they fought for land.'

' Liberty and property ' were also words with wide meanings.
They could imply the right of every man to do what he would
with his own, unimpeded by Church or prerogative courts :
they included the possibility of freer trade, of industrial and
agricultural expansion. They could imply the supremacy of a
liberalised common law and Parliamentary control of the
economy, in place of incompetent royal interference and the
corruption of favourites and monopolists. They could imply
the right of the propertied class to tax themselves, and to

supervise the way in which their money was spent, including control of foreign policy. They could imply freedom for Justices of the Peace and corporations to run local affairs as they thought best, undisturbed by Privy Council or Star Chamber.

The personal government of Charles I broke down after eleven years in which it had every chance of succeeding. It broke down because it lost the confidence of the propertied classes. There were no safe investments under the English *ancien régime*. The City's charter for colonising Londonderry was revoked after £50,000 had been lost in a project which the crown had bullied the citizens into undertaking, and they were fined an additional £12,000 (originally £70,000). In 1635 Charles I licensed a second East India Company, to the great damage of those shareholders of the existing Company who had paid heavily for their monopoly. In 1640 the government resorted to the desperate measures of a fraudulent bankrupt. It bought pepper on credit for £63,000 and sold it immediately for £50,000 cash. It contemplated debasing the coinage. In July it seized £130,000 bullion which private merchants had placed in the Tower for safety, causing numerous bankruptcies. Sir John Davies had said, in a work dedicated to James I, ' The first and principal cause of making kings was to maintain property and contracts, and traffic and commerce among men.' James's son hardly performed this function.

The government was brought down by a revolt of the taxpayers. In 1639, encouraged by the presence of the Scottish army, they went on strike ; and the government was shown to be unable to exist without their goodwill. The City refused a loan, even to get the bullion restored : the Londonderry plantation had ' consumed their stocks ', they drily explained. The loan was forthcoming only after peace had been signed with the Scots. Even then the peers had to underwrite it, so low had royal credit sunk ; and the government got only a quarter of what it had asked. Everything waited on Parliament, which by 1640 had become the symbol for the defence of religion, liberty, and property.

PART TWO

1640–60

7 Narrative of Events, 1640-60

> What means had he [Charles I] to pay, what provision had he to arm, nay, means to levy, an army able to resist the army of the Parliament, maintained by the great purse of the City of London, and contributions of almost all the towns corporate in England ? . . . Those that helped the King in that kind were only lords and gentlemen.
>
> Thomas Hobbes, *Behemoth*

WHEN the Long Parliament met, the House of Commons at once impeached Strafford and Laud. Other ministers fled from the country. Strafford was executed in May 1641, under an Act of Attainder which had been substituted for impeachment. A Triennial Act provided for regular meetings of Parliament, with an automatic procedure if the King failed to summon them. An Act was passed against dissolving this Parliament without its own consent. It thus for the first time became a permanent part of the constitution. This revolutionary innovation was necessary if loans were to be raised, since only Parliament could inspire confidence. Tunnage and poundage was forbidden without consent of Parliament ; the judgment against Hampden and the levying of Ship Money were declared illegal, together with the other non-Parliamentary taxes of the eleven years of personal government. Prerogative courts— Star Chamber, Council of the North and in Wales—and the High Commission were abolished. Prynne, Burton, Bastwick, Lilburne, and other victims of the personal government were released and compensated.

In November 1641 a rebellion took place in Ireland, at last liberated from Strafford's iron hand. Many hundreds, probably many thousands, of Englishmen were killed. The opposition group in Parliament refused to trust a royal nominee with command of an army to reconquer Ireland. So the question of ultimate power in the state was raised. In the panic caused by news of the Irish rebellion the Grand Remonstrance was adopted, a comprehensive indictment of royal policy. It passed the Commons by only eleven votes. For by now parties had formed. Charles replied by bringing a body of armed men to the House in an attempt to arrest Pym, Hampden, and three other leaders of the opposition group. They took refuge in the City and resolutions in their support poured in from all over the country. Charles quitted London, of which he had lost control ; the Five Members returned in triumph. Almost the last act of the King was to agree to the exclusion of Bishops from the House of Lords (February 1642) and to a Bill for raising troops for Ireland. The conflict had now extended from Westminster to the country at large, and civil war became inevitable. Desultory negotiations took place as Charles roamed over the north of England. In April Sir John Hotham refused to admit him into Hull ; and in August the King raised his standard at Nottingham. The Earl of Essex was appointed to command the Parliamentary armies.

The first engagement of the Civil War was a drawn battle at Edgehill (23rd October). Charles advanced on London, but was checked by the trained bands at Turnham Green in November. He withdrew to Oxford. Meanwhile the Marquis of Newcastle secured the north of England for the King, and Sir Ralph Hopton the south-west. In 1643 an attempt was made to advance on London from these two centres and from Oxford. This was checked by the resistance of Hull, Plymouth, and Gloucester, and by the march of the London trained bands to relieve Gloucester. They fought another drawn battle at Newbury on their way back.

In September, in the hope of breaking the military deadlock, Parliament signed the Solemn League and Covenant with the Scots, and in January 1644 a Scottish army crossed the Border again. In July the Battle of Marston Moor was won by the combined armies of Scotland, Yorkshire (Sir Thomas Fairfax) and the Eastern Association (the Earl of Manchester and Oliver Cromwell). Control of the north passed to Parliament. But Parliament, with no united command, did not follow up its victory. The Earl of Essex was cut off in the south-west, and his army surrendered at Lostwithiel in September. This and the indecisive second Battle of Newbury (27th October) strengthened the hands of those who had been calling for the elimination of half-hearted officers and for a unified command. The New Model Army was formed with Fairfax as general, and the Self-Denying Ordinance (April 1645) deprived all peers and members of Parliament of their commissions. The immediate result was the decisive rout of the Royalists at Naseby (14th June). The rest of the war was a series of mopping-up operations, culminating in the surrender of Oxford in June 1646 after Charles had given himself up to the Scots. The latter handed him over to the English Parliament on 30th January 1647. Meanwhile Archbishop Laud had been executed in January 1645 and episcopacy abolished in October 1646. The same ordinance offered Bishops' lands for sale.

The controversies over the New Model Army and the Self-Denying Ordinance had seen the formation of two parties among the Parliamentarians. These we usually call Presbyterians and Independents, the conservatives and the radicals. Once the fighting had ended, the 'Presbyterian' majority in Parliament, which had always disliked and feared the Army, proposed to disband it, with its wages unpaid, offering the rank and file the chance of volunteering for service in Ireland. This led to a mutiny, and to the election of Agitators by the regiments. After some hesitation, Cromwell and most of the officers threw in their lot with the men. Those who did not were deprived of their commissions. Cornet Joyce was sent to take the royal prisoner out of Parliament's control into that of the Army. A General Council of the Army was set up, composed of the Generals and representatives of other officers and of the rank and file. The newly united Army issued a manifesto declaring that it would not disband or separate until its grievances had been met. It called for a purge of Parliament, an early dissolution and new elections. Impeaching eleven Presbyterian leaders, the Army occupied London and forced their withdrawal from the Commons (August 1647). But now divisions arose among the Independents. Negotiations took place between Charles and the Generals for the establishment of limited monarchy (the Heads of Proposals). These roused the suspicions of radicals in London (the Levellers) and in the Army who produced a rival, more democratic constitution, the Agreement of the People. The two constitutions were discussed in the Army Council at Putney in October, between spokesmen of the Generals and of the Agitators. Deadlock resulted, and finally Cromwell forcibly terminated the discussions. The Agitators were ordered back to their regiments (15th November). One of the Agitators was shot and the recalcitrant regiments subdued.

Cromwell was able to do this because on 11th November the King had escaped from the Army's custody and fled to the Isle of Wight. The Army had to reunite in face of imminent renewal of civil war. In December Charles signed an agreement with the Scottish commissioners in London, as a result of which a Scottish army entered England in July 1648. But it was an army led by Hamilton and the nobility, not the disciplined army of the Covenant. It was easily defeated at Preston by Cromwell, who had previously disposed of a ' Presbyterian '-Royalist revolt in South Wales, whilst Fairfax reduced a Royalist force in Colchester.

The ' Presbyterians ' in Parliament had meanwhile entered into negotiations with the King (the Treaty of Newport). But by now the Generals felt that the King could not be trusted, and were determined to settle accounts with him. They revived their alliance with the Levellers. London was occupied once more, some hundred members were excluded by Colonel Pride, and a court was set up to try the King. On 30th January 1649 he was executed as a traitor to the Commonwealth of England. Monarchy and the House of Lords were abolished. But there were no democratic reforms, and the republican government soon forfeited Leveller support. There were demonstrations against it, and in March the Leveller leaders were imprisoned. There were also mutinies in the Army, the most serious of which was put down at Burford in May. Henceforth the government had to face opposition from left as well as right.

Nevertheless, its achievements were considerable. The Irish revolt, which had dragged miserably on since 1641, was crushed in a whirlwind campaign by Cromwell, which started with the storming of Drogheda and the massacre of its garrison. An Act for the Settlement of Ireland (12th August 1652) provided for the expropriation of the owners of some two-thirds of the land, and for the transplantation of the bulk of the Irish population to Connaught. This was never fully carried out, but a great deal of Irish land passed to London merchants who had lent money to Parliament, and to soldiers in lieu of wages. In 1650 Scotland, where Charles II had been recognised, was invaded. Cromwell, succeeding Fairfax as Commander-in-Chief, won the Battle of Dunbar on 3rd September. Exactly a year later Charles and an invading Scottish army were routed at Worcester. Scotland, like Ireland, was united to England, and occupied by a military garrison. Meanwhile the Commonwealth's authority had been asserted over the colonies. Navigation Acts of October 1650 and October 1651 aimed at wresting the carrying trade from the Dutch. They led to the First Dutch War (1652–4).

The Rump of the Long Parliament was expelled by Cromwell in April 1653. It had sold crown and Dean and Chapter lands, and the lands of some 700 Royalists, but produced few domestic reforms. In July an assembly was summoned by Cromwell, composed of 140 men selected by the Army leaders from nominees of the Independent congregations. It came to be known as the Barebones Parliament, a social sneer directed against Praise-God Barbon, one of its members, who was a leather-seller. Proposals for radical reform frightened the conservatives in this assembly, and in December they engineered its dissolution. Power was handed back to the Lord General —i.e. to the Army. The officers produced a new constitution, the Instrument of Government, probably drafted by Major-General Lambert, under which Cromwell was given the position of Lord Protector. The franchise was redistributed. But when Parliament met, in September 1654, it refused to accept the Army's ascendancy, and was preparing a new constitution when Cromwell dissolved it in January 1655. A minor Royalist rising followed in March, and the opportunity was seized to extend the machinery of military rule. England was divided into eleven areas, and a Major-General was set over each, with wide powers. A decimation tax on Royalists was introduced, which it was hoped would finance the new system ; but it came nowhere near doing so. In November 1654 a merchant called Cony had challenged the Protector's right to collect taxation under the Instrument of Government. Cromwell managed to obtain a favourable verdict only after dismissing a judge and prosecuting Cony's counsel, in a way reminiscent of Charles I. Money was badly needed, and another Parliament was summoned for September 1656.

One reason for calling a Parliament was the foreign situation. In 1654 Cromwell had made peace with the Netherlands on favourable terms. He had signed an agreement which opened the Portuguese empire to English trade, and had established friendly relations with Sweden. He had equipped an expedition to attack the Spanish West Indies. This failed to capture its main objective, Hispaniola, but occupied Jamaica. In 1655 a Spanish treasure fleet was intercepted and in 1657 another destroyed. In 1655 England came to an agreement with France, by which the exiled court of Charles Stuart was expelled from France. This broadened into a treaty in March 1657 ; the Protector agreed to help France to defeat Spain in Europe. Dunkirk was captured at the Battle of the Dunes (June 1658) and handed over to England.

The government had hoped to use war against the traditional Spanish enemy to rally support in the Parliament of 1656. Money was indeed voted for the war, but even after many members of Parliament had been excluded, the House rejected a bill to continue the militia under the Major-Generals. The members showed their hostility to the government's policy of toleration by savage persecution of the Quaker James Nayler. Cromwell failed to intervene to save Nayler ; but after Nayler had been flogged, branded, and bored through the tongue, the Protector at once asked the House on what authority they had acted. This, together with discussions which had no doubt been going on behind the scenes since the rejection of the Militia Bill in January 1657, led to a constitutional debate and to the framing of the Humble Petition and Advice. This was a revised version of the Parliamentary constitution of 1654–5. Cromwell was offered the crown, and control of the executive was transferred to Parliament, which was to consist of two Houses. The new franchise instituted under the Instrument of Government was dropped. The Petition was fiercely opposed by the Army leaders, and after long hesitations Cromwell finally refused the crown but accepted the rest of

Plate 1 A VIEW OF LONDON. East of London Bridge, about 1600, by C. J. Visscher.

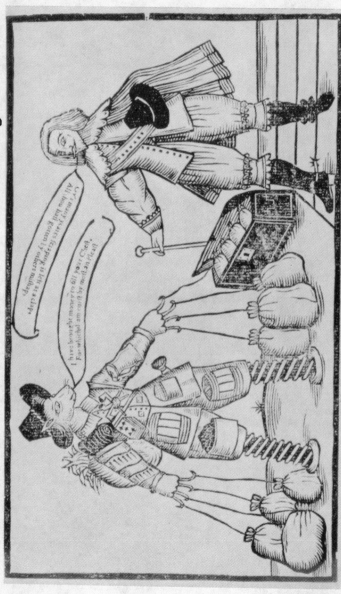

The complaint of M, Tenter-hooke the Projector, and Sir Thomas Dodger the Patentee/:

If any aske, what things these Monsters be,
'Tis a Projector, and a Patentee :

Such, as like Vermine o're this Land did crawle,
And grew so rich, they gain'd the Devill and all.

Plate 2   THE PROJECTOR AND THE PATENTEE.   One of the many caricatures of monopolists published after 1640.

Meefter Lilburn achter een kar gegeffelt.
Mr. Lilburne whipt after the Carts tail.

Plate 3 LILBURNE flogged through London at the cart's tail, 1637. From a Dutch print. (See p. 99.)

Plate 4 LAUD, BISHOPS, AND CITIZENS. From *The Bishops' Last Good-night*, a pamphlet of 1642.

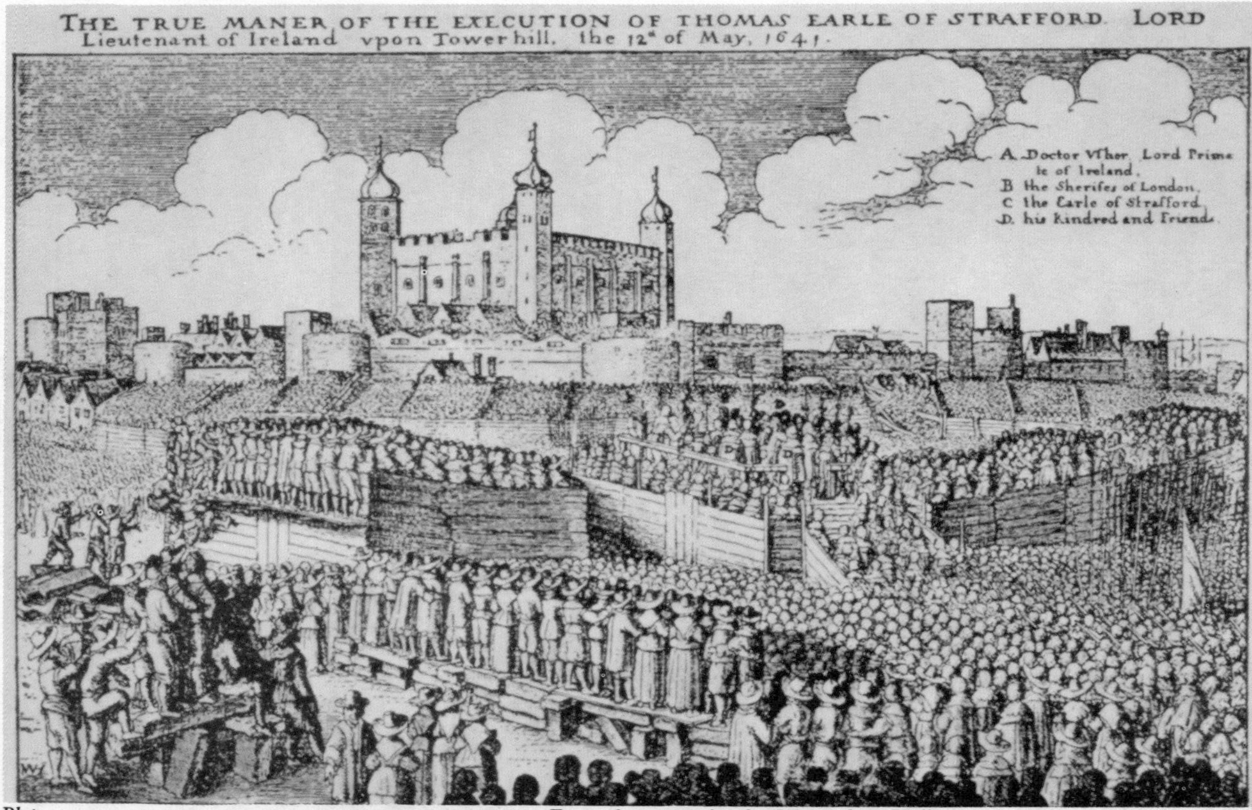

THE TRUE MANER OF THE EXECUTION OF THOMAS EARLE OF STRAFFORD. LORD
Lieutenant of Ireland vpon Tower hill. the 12° of May. 1641.

A. Doctor Vsher, Lord Prime
  te of Ireland.
B. the Sherifes of London.
C. the Earle of Strafford.
D. his kindred and friend.

Plate 5   THE EXECUTION OF THOMAS, EARL OF STRAFFORD. From the engraving by Wenceslaus Hollar.

Reade in this Image him, whofe deareft blood
Is thought noe price to buy his Countryes good,
Whofe name fhall flourifh, till the blaft of ffame
Shall want a Trumpet, or true Worth, a name.

Edw: Bower pinxit   G: Glouer fecit

Plate 6 PARLIAMENTARIAN LEADER—JOHN PYM. Print used in contemporary pamphlets, from the portrait by Edward Bower.

Dauentny

Brimidgham

The moſt Illuſtrious and High borne PRINCE RUPERT,
PRINCE ELECTOR, Second Son to FREDERICK
KING of BOHEMIA, GENERALL of the HORSE
of H's MAJESTIES ARMY, KNIGHT of the Noble
Order of the GARTER.

Plate 7 ROYALIST GENERAL—PRINCE RUPERT. Print from *The Bloody Prince,* 1643.

Plate 8 THE GREAT SEAL OF THE COMMONWEALTH, 1651, depicting
the House of Commons during a debate.

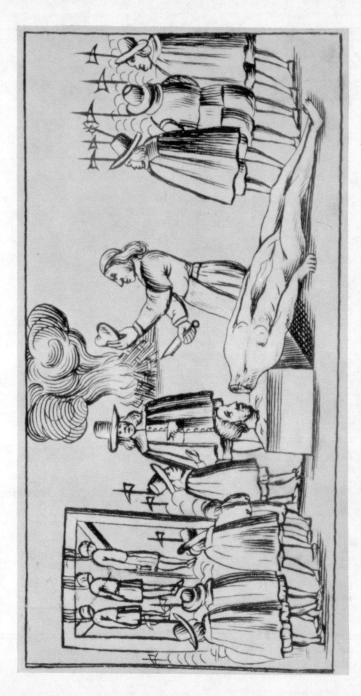

Plate 9 REGICIDES hanged, drawn and quartered. From a pamphlet of 1662.

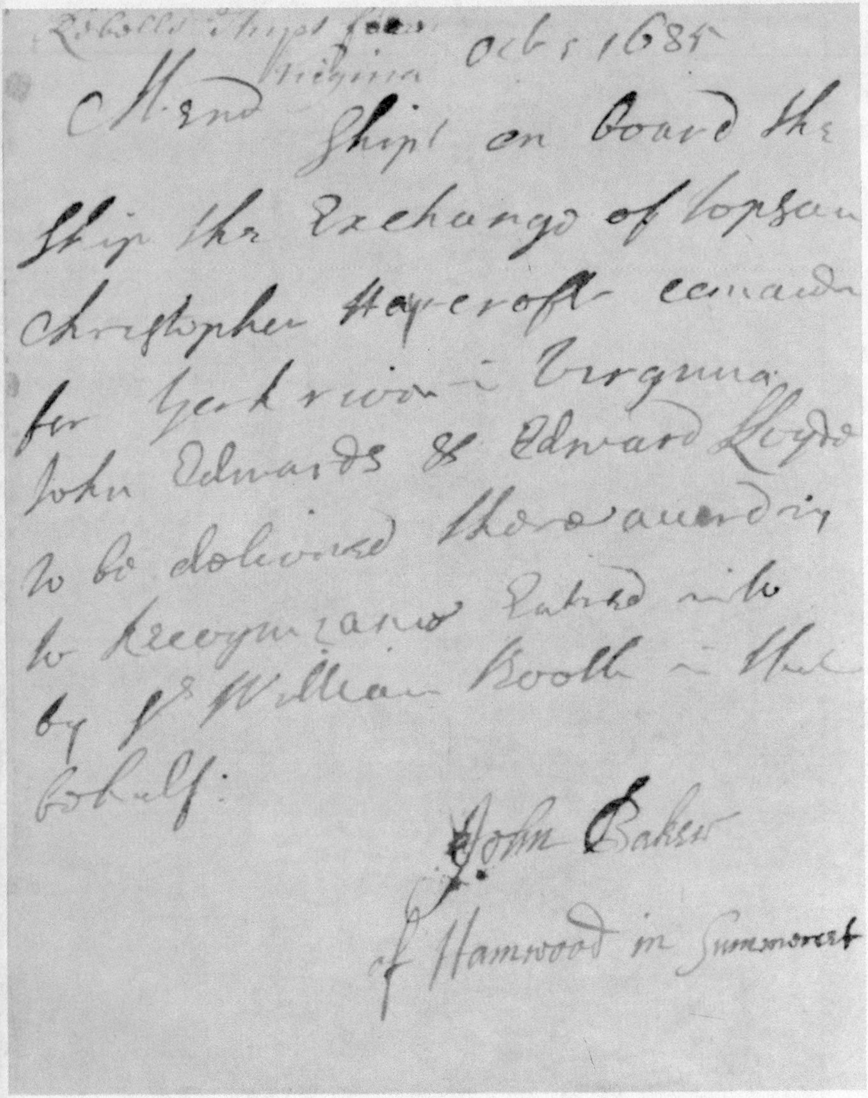

Rebells Shipt for ...

Virginia Octr 1685

Mem Shipt on board the
Ship the Exchange of Topsam
Christopher Haycroft comand[er]
for Yorkriver in Virginia
John Edwards & Edward Lloyd
to be delivered thereaccordin[g]
to Recognizance Entred into
by Sr William Booth in that
behalf:

John Baker
of Hamwood in Summersett

Plate 10   MONMOUTH'S REBELLION.
Invoice for transporting rebels to forced labour in Virginia.
(See p. 236)

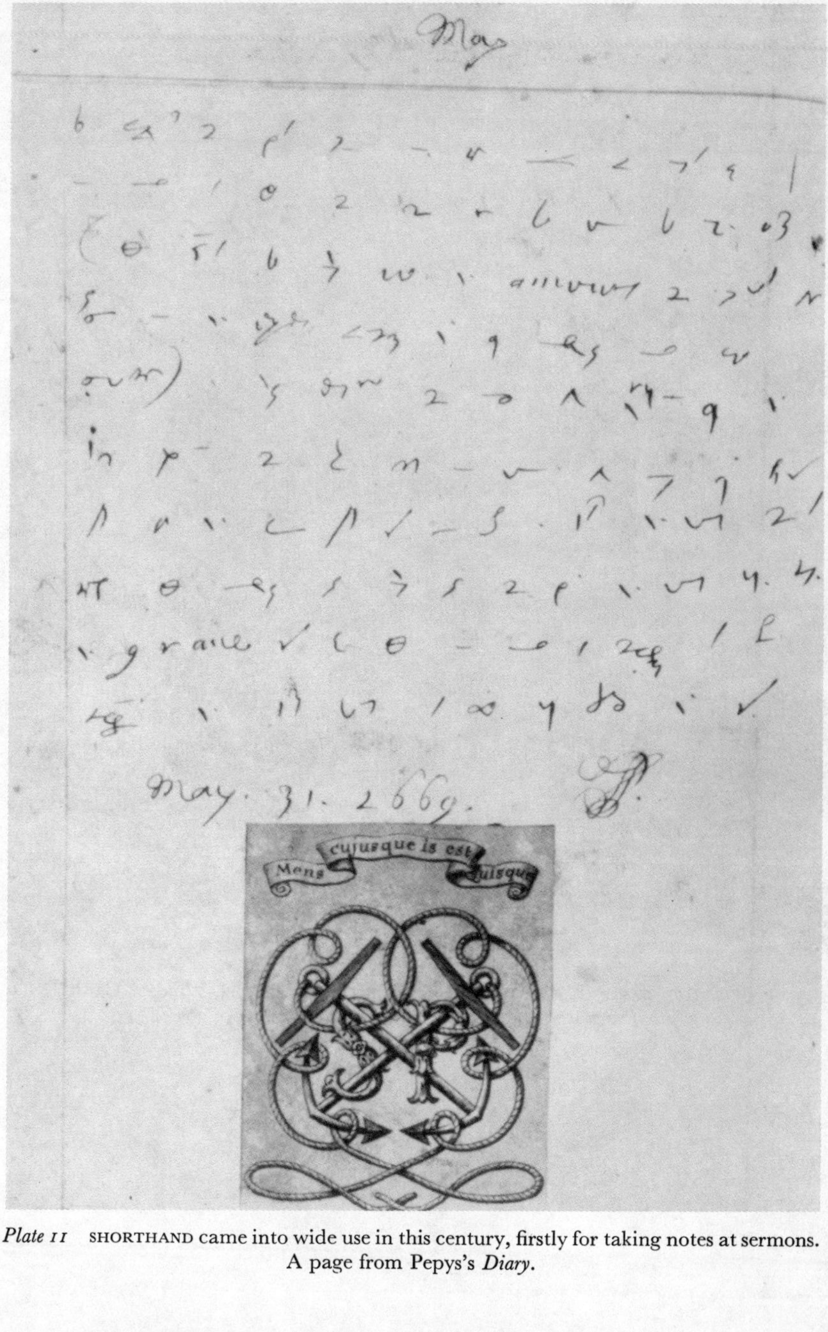

[shorthand text]

May. 31. 2 66g.

Mens *cujusque is est* quisque

Plate 11   SHORTHAND came into wide use in this century, firstly for taking notes at sermons.
A page from Pepys's *Diary*.

Plate 12 BAROQUE AND ABSOLUTISM. The Royal Chapel, Windsor Castle.
From the water-colour by C. Wild. (See pp. 303–4.)

A British Janus
Anglicè a Timeserver.

Since Moderation is so much in vogue,
And few can tell a Trimmer from a R——
I am perswaded such a Print as this,
Thus modell'd and contriv'd can't be amiss.
At such a juncture such a time as this,
When to be loyal is esteem'd a fault,
Obedience hist at, Scripture sett at nought,
And ỹ reverse for pure sound doctrine taught.
I mean by them this picture doth resemble,
Who preach not half so fine as they dissemble
Of Heterogeneous parts as opposite
Compos'd as darkness to Meridian light.
Made up of halves that can no more agree
Than Regal powr and Independency.
A British Janus with a double face.
A Monster of a strange Gigantick Race;
His head half Mitre, and half hat doth bear.
His looks are sainted; and refind his air.
Not more preposterous in his black, & white.

Than the true semblance of an Hypocrite.
Always Conformist to the strongest Party.
Always deceitful; Ever more unhearty.
The Moderate Man neer yet a Martyr dy'd.
But tack'd about, & chose the strongest side
Always recanted in the time of trial;
Is ever best extempore at denial.
Scorne to be moderate then in any thing.
But where to be immoderate is a sin.
In eating, drinking, and such things as these
Be moderate as moderate as you please.
But in Religion there's no Medium, No
Who is not truly zealous, is not so.
Glory to be esteem'd an High - c - h Man
Let them prove Low-c -h true c -h if they can
Zeal for the c -h's Cause a Crown will gain:
And Martyrdom for Heven's an easy pain.
Dare to be true, tho in a suffring time
A Base Denial then's a Double Crime

Plate 13 THE TIME-SERVER. A High Church caricature of about 1700.

London's Gazette here

Nouvelle Gazette

Chi compra gl'avisi di Londra

Plate 14 NEWSPAPERS originated in the revolutionary decades. Here is a newsvendor
of the late seventeenth century.

Plate 15 BLENHEIM PALACE, built at public expense for the Duke of Marlborough by Sir John Vanbrugh and Nicholas Hawksmoor.

Plate 16 THE MICROSCOPE opened up new worlds to scientists.
'Louse holding to a human hair', from Robert Hooke's epoch-
making *Micrographia* (1665).

the constitution with modifications. Lambert, who had been losing influence for some time, was dismissed from all his offices. But when Parliament met again in January 1658 the hitherto excluded members were admitted on taking an oath to be faithful to the Protector. In consequence opponents of the constitution captured control of the Commons, and in February Cromwell dissolved Parliament. Seven months later he died. The Petition and Advice had authorised him to nominate his successor, and his eldest son Richard succeeded him.

Richard had none of his father's prestige with the Army. A Parliament (elected on the old franchise) met in January 1659 and recognised the new Protector. The Commons also accepted the Other House, though reserving the right of peers who had been faithful to Parliament to sit in it. But the republican malcontents revived their alliance with Army malcontents, and the latter now included many higher officers. In April 1659 Parliament tried to assert control over the Army ; the Generals retorted by forcing the Protector to dissolve it. Power reverted to the Army. On 5th May the Generals restored the remnant of the Rump, and Richard retired into oblivion. A national 'Presbyterian'-Royalist revolt, planned for August 1659, took place only in Cheshire, where it was defeated by Lambert. But relations between Rump and Army deteriorated as the former tried to subordinate the latter to its control, and in October the Parliament was expelled once more. But it proved impossible to levy taxes except by military violence. The City of London refused to co-operate with the military government ; and General Monck, commanding the army in Scotland, was authorised by some of the deposed Council of State to take military action on their behalf. He advanced towards the Border. An army under Lambert was sent to oppose him. As long as this was paid, there were more rank-and-file desertions from Monck to Lambert than from Lambert to Monck. But Monck had more money and Lambert's army gradually melted away. The Generals in London capitulated and recalled the Rump in December ; but Monck crossed into England.

He was greeted on the way south with organised petitions for 'a free Parliament', but kept his own counsel until he

arrived in the capital (3rd February 1660). The first task
Parliament gave him was to arrest leading members of London's
government and to destroy its defensive gates and chains.
Monck complied, but immediately thereafter retreated into the
City and sent Parliament an ultimatum calling for a dissolution. Monck's surrender to the City ensured the downfall
of the Rump. He opened the doors of Parliament to the
members excluded in 1648, and they carried out a pledge to
Monck by dissolving themselves on 16th March, after providing
for elections to a new Parliament. This met on 25th April. It
was 'Presbyterian'-Royalist in composition. The House of
Lords was restored (though Royalist peers were still excluded),
and Parliament accepted the Declaration which Charles II
had issued from Breda on 4th April. By this he offered an
indemnity, settlement of disputes about land sales, payment
of arrears to the Army and liberty of conscience—all subject
to confirmation by Parliament. On 25th May Charles II
returned to England.

8 Politics and the Constitution 1640-60

> None more fond of a King than the English, yet they departed from him to ease their purses and consciences.
>
> Peter Chamberlen, *The Poor Man's Advocate* (1649)

> The war was begun in our streets before the King or Parliament had any armies.
>
> Richard Baxter, *The Holy Commonwealth* (1659)

TAKING SIDES

IN THE period before 1640 we looked at economics before politics. But in the revolutionary decades we must give first place to politics.

The House of Commons of the Long Parliament represented, as usual, a cross-section of the ruling class. It was composed of gentry, merchants, and lawyers. But the circumstances in which it was elected gave rise to some novel features. For almost the first time in English history, elections were contested on political issues. Many members were elected not merely because of their social standing but because they were known to adopt a definite political attitude. At Great Marlow all the contestants were gentlemen ; but one of them was a great local landowner who stood for the court interest, his father-in-law being Attorney-General. The two opposition candidates ' stood for the liberty of the commons in the election ', with the support of shopkeepers and labourers. Their victory was not only a defeat for the court but also a demonstration that ' the ordinary sort of townsmen ' felt free for once to vote against their powerful landlord, despite his threats of economic reprisals. At Leicester the contest looks like just one more example of that rivalry of two great local families, the Greys and the Hastings, which had characterised its politics since the fifteenth century. But we know that the townsmen were becoming restive under the dominance of the great families, whose privileges the Privy Council maintained. In the election of 1640 support for Lord Grey of Groby came from rank-and-file citizens. In 1649 he was one of those who signed the King's death-warrant : later he became a Fifth Monarchist. So we can see that this traditional family rivalry, like many others, had been transformed by political alignments.

Wherever we have evidence of disputed borough elections (and this is true of elections before 1640, too) it appears that the Royalists normally favoured confining the vote to the ruling oligarchy ; the opposition wished to extend it to all freemen or all propertied inhabitants. Only occasionally, in a borough with a wide franchise, Royalists wanted the vote to be extended to all inhabitants. Parliament's strength lay with the middling men. By several resolutions the Commons tried to stop peers interfering in elections.

Historians have analysed the personnel of the Commons of 1640,[1] though as yet there has been no full investigation of the political and economic affiliations of members which might, as with the Greys and Hastings, be more important than their social position. But some points are clear. Among 507 members 22 London merchants were elected. 12 monopolists were expelled from the House ; they were naturally Royalists. Of the 10 remaining London merchants, 9 were Parliamentarians. The few Royalist merchants from provincial towns seem to have represented ruling merchant oligarchies. Among the gentry with business connections there were more Parliamentarian than Royalist members. But we should not think of the House of Commons as in any sense creating the Civil War. There were Royalists of principle and Parliamentarians of principle in the House, but the evidence suggests that most members would have preferred neutrality, and were more concerned to preserve their own property than to be martyrs for a cause. About 100 members who opposed the court in 1641 but ultimately fought for the King had estates in areas controlled by the royal armies.

[1] e.g. D. Brunton and D. H. Pennington, *Members of the Long Parliament* (1954) ; M. Keeler, *The Long Parliament* (1954)

One problem is to decide how the King got a party at all. In May 1641 only 59 members voted against the attainder of Strafford ; six months later 148 voted against the Grand Remonstrance ; and some 236 were involved to a greater or less extent with the King's side in the Civil War. There was a group in the Commons, led with great skill and finesse by Pym and Hampden, determined to force the King to surrender to the domination of Parliament ; and there was a smaller group, round Henry Marten, of republicans. But the real strength even of Pym's party came from outside the House. It came primarily from London, which elected four radicals to Parliament in 1640, and where in December 1641 the Royalist clique was ejected from its governing positions just in time to make the City a safe refuge for the Five Members in January 1642. Pym, with his commercial connections and his sly burgher's face, was the ideal mediator between Commons and City. Pressure from London citizens was often exercised on Parliament—to get Strafford condemned, against Bishops. ' Whensoever there was anything proposed in the House of Commons,' wrote Laud, ' which it was thought the Lords would stick at, or the King not grant, by and by the rabble came about the Houses, and called for this or that justice, as they were prompted.' But pressure and support also came from outside—from the Buckinghamshire freeholders who rode up to London to protect Hampden when the Five Members were arrested ; from the 2,000 seamen who rallied among 140,000 Londoners to defend Parliamentary privilege and Protestantism on the same occasion ; from members of sectarian congregations in London, the Home Counties, and East Anglia, who would have no compromise with episcopacy. Similarly the formation of a royal party owed more to shifts of opinion among the propertied class all over the country than to the events in the House of Commons on which historians normally rivet their attention.

If we want to understand the Civil War, a glance at the maps on p. 122 is far more important than the most elaborate analysis of members of Parliament. Support for Parliament came from the economically advanced south and east of England, the King's support from the economically backward areas of the north and west. In Yorkshire, Lancashire, and

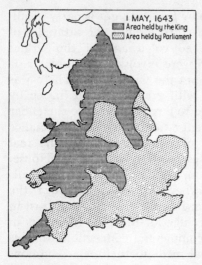

Sussex there was a clear division between Parliamentarian
industrial areas and Royalist agricultural areas.   In Yorkshire
the clothing town of Bradford, with no backing from the gentry,
summoned the countryside and forced Fairfax to lead them
into action against the King.[1]   In Staffordshire a group of
' Moorlanders ' led by ' a person of low quality ' bore the
brunt of the early fighting. ' A factious humour . . . possessed
most corporations,' said Clarendon, and led them to oppose
the King ; though often, as in London, town oligarchies were
Royalist, and had to be overthrown before the Parliamentarian
sentiments of the majority of citizens could express themselves.
Many towns in the area controlled by the King long held out
for Parliament : the defence of Gloucester, Hull, and Plymouth
frustrated the royal advance on London in 1643.   But only
cathedral cities like Oxford and Chester were Royalist.
Royalist strongholds were aristocratic houses like the Marquis
of Winchester's Basing House, the Earl of Derby's Lathom
House. The Earl of Worcester's Raglan Castle was the last
royal fortress to surrender.   The ports were mostly for Parliament. So was the navy. A few gentleman captains opted for
the King when war broke out, but they were easily replaced
by professional ' tarpaulins '. The defection of the fleet and

[1] B. Manning, *P. and P.*, **13**, 70

of the ports meant that the King could neither end the war by blockading London nor obtain the foreign help he tried so hard for.

The very names 'Cavalier' (swashbuckling officer) and 'Roundhead' (crop-haired citizen) imply a social sneer : the upper classes (including most of the Parliamentarian leaders) wore their hair long. The London trained bands or militia were the most reliable Parliamentary troops in the early stages of the war. They checked the Royalist advance at Turnham Green in 1642. In 1643 they marched across England to relieve Gloucester. At the Battle of Newbury, on their way back, the trained bands 'were . . . the preservation of that army . . . for they stood as a bulwark and rampart to defend the rest ', and frustrated even the dashing Prince Rupert after he had scattered their cavalry. Later the voluntary yeoman cavalry trooper came to be as typical on the Parliamentary side as were the Marquis of Newcastle's 'Whitecoats', his tenants and retainers, on the other, or the Catholic dependants of the Royalist Earl of Worcester, who even before the war started was said to possess arms for 2,000 men.

These social distinctions were very clear to contemporaries. The Duchess of Newcastle, writing of the West Riding, referred to ' those parts of the kingdom which were populous, rich and rebellious '.[1]   Clarendon said that 'Leeds, Halifax and Bradford, three very populous and rich towns, . . . depending wholly upon clothiers naturally maligned the gentry ', and were wholly at Parliament's disposal. In Wiltshire ' gentlemen of ancient families and estates ' were ' for the most part well-affected to the King ', whilst ' a people of inferior degree who, by good husbandry, clothing and other thriving arts, had gotten very great fortunes . . . were fast friends to the Parliament '. It is what such passages assume, as well as what they actually say, that is revealing. Chamberlayne, writing after the Restoration, named as Parliamentarians ' some of the . . . gentry, divers of the inferior clergy, most of the tradesmen and very many of the peasantry '. ' The wealth, insolence and pride ' of ' the lower sort of common people ' made them lose ' that humble respect and awful reverence which,

---

[1] Sources for most of the quotations in this and the next three paragraphs will be found in my *Puritanism and Revolution*, pp. 199–214.

in other kingdoms, is usually given to nobility, gentry and clergy'.

Baxter's careful analysis was similar. ' A very great part of the knights and gentlemen . . . adhered to the King. . . . Most of the tenants of these gentlemen, and also most of the poorest of the people, whom the other call the rabble, did follow the gentry and were for the King. On the Parliament's side were . . . the smaller part (as some thought) of the gentry in most of the counties, and the greatest part of the tradesmen and freeholders and the middle sort of men, especially in those corporations and counties which depend on clothing and such manufactures. If you ask the reason of this difference, ask also why in France it is not commonly the nobility nor the beggars, but the merchants and middle sort of men, that were Protestants. The two reasons which the party themselves gave was because (say they) the tradesmen have a correspondency with London, and so are grown to be a far more intelligent sort of men than the ignorant peasants. . . . And the freeholders, say they, were not enslaved to their landlords as the tenants are. The gentry (say they) are wholly by their estates and ambition more dependent on the King than their tenants on them.' ' Freeholders and tradesmen are the strength of religion and civility in the land ; and gentlemen and beggars and servile tenants are the strength of iniquity.' ' Many of the nobility and gentry,' Edmund Ludlow agreed, ' were contented to serve his [the King's] arbitrary designs, if they might have leave to insult over such as were of a lower order.' In Gloucestershire the Parliamentarians were ' a generation of men truly laborious, jealous of their properties, whose principal aim is liberty and plenty'. The gentry, ' who, detesting a close, hardy and industrious way of living, do eat their bread in the sweat of other men ', were mostly Royalist.

These accounts help to explain why numbers of gentlemen fought for the King, when even as late as 1642 many, like the republican Ludlow, expected he would find little support. By that time many of the propertied classes were beginning to draw back in alarm. The break had come not over religious questions, but over the crucial issue of political power, control of the armed forces. An army had to be raised to suppress the Irish revolt. The opposition in Parliament believed, or professed to believe, that the King was behind this revolt. They saw here confirmation of the international Popish Plot against the liberties of Protestant Englishmen which they had all along suspected. They refused to trust command of the army to Charles. He would not surrender it to Parliament. So they appealed to public opinion in the Grand Remonstrance, a carefully prepared propagandist statement of the opposition's case against Charles. ' I thought to represent unto the King the wicked counsels of pernicious counsellors,' said the conservative Sir Edward Dering of this document ; ' I did not dream that we should remonstrate downward, tell stories to the people, and talk of the King as of a third person.' It was over the question of printing the Grand Remonstrance that swords were first drawn in the House.

This appeal to opinion outside the ' political nation ' came at an ominous time. In 1641–2 there were many riots against enclosure ; there were refusals to pay tithes and rents. ' Men of mean or a middle quality ' were becoming politically active in London, so much so that few ' gentlemen, especially courtiers . . . durst come into the City : or if they did they were sure to receive affronts.' ' The gentry,' the vulgar were saying, ' have been our masters a long time, and now we may chance to master them.' ' Now they know their strength,' added the letter writer who reported this in the autumn of 1642, ' it shall go hard but they will use it.' In November the High Sheriff of Lancashire urged gentlemen to appear in arms with their tenants and servants, ' for the securing of our own lives and estates, which are now ready to be surprised by a heady multitude '.[1] The Royalist Sir John Oglander believed that ' such times were never before seen in England, when the gentry were made slaves to the commonalty and in their power, not only to abuse but plunder any gentleman '.

The abolition of the Star Chamber and High Commission, the breakdown of the censorship, the impotence of the government, allowed religious sects to emerge from underground. Preachings were made ' by tradesmen and illiterate people of the lowest rank '. Their discussions, not confined to purely

[1] W. Lilly, *The True History of King James I and Charles I* (1715), pp. 55–6 ; *Verney Memoirs* (1892), ii, 69 ; *Farrington Papers* (Chetham Soc., 1856), p. 88

religious subjects, attracted large audiences. To conservatives, it seemed that nothing was to remain sacred. 'Turbulent spirits, backed by rude and tumultuous mechanic persons, . . . would have the total subversion of the government of the state.' [1] Hyde defended episcopacy because he 'could not conceive how the government of the state could well subsist if the government of the church were altered ' ; the abolition of episcopacy was ' the removing of a landmark and the shaking the very foundations of government '. Another member of Parliament said in 1641 that 'if we make a parity in the church, we must at last come to a parity in the commonwealth '. No Bishop, no gentry : social conservatives rallied to the crown. Against this background the determination of the majority in the Commons to carry the quarrel outside the House, to break the traditional secrecy of debates in a deliberate appeal to the people, seemed black treachery and wild irresponsibility.

So there was strong pressure for a compromise peace. John Hotham, who with his father held Hull against the King in 1642, but changed sides the following year, explained in social terms why he did so : ' No man that hath any reasonable share in the commonwealth can desire that either side should be conqueror. . . . It is too great a temptation to counsels of violence.' He feared lest 'the necessitous people of the whole kingdom will presently rise in mighty numbers and . . . set up for themselves to the utter ruin of all the nobility and gentry '.

'PRESBYTERIANS' AND 'INDEPENDENTS'

This explains not only why many gentlemen rallied to the King when it came to civil war, but also why most men of high social rank on the Parliamentary side feared too decisive a victory. At the beginning of the war Parliament established county committees in all areas under its control, on which it naturally put the leading gentry of the shires. Command of the county militias likewise went by social rank in the traditional way. But gradually, in the course of the fighting, two parties appeared in the committees of all counties so far investigated. A conservative group, of higher rank,

[1] Quoted by B. S. Manning, ' The Nobles, the People and the Constitution ', *P. and P.*, **9**, 61

favoured a defensive war and a negotiated peace, whereas the win-the-war party found that its main support came from lower social groups. 'It had been well that men of honour and birth had entered into these military employments,' wrote Oliver Cromwell in September 1643. 'But seeing it was necessary the work must go on, better plain men than none.' 'I had rather have a plain russet-coated captain that knows what he fights for and loves what he knows than that which you call a " gentleman " and is nothing else.' (The turncoat John Hotham was one of those who objected to yeomen officers.) Sir William Brereton found he had to replace the governor of Stafford, even though he came from one of the best county families, by a rich merchant who happened to be more efficient and enthusiastic. The low-born 'Tinker' Fox of Walsall, who raised a troop among the small craftsmen of the Birmingham district, rose by efficiency to the rank of colonel. He was highly critical of his superior officers, and conducted a campaign to get rid of the Earl of Denbigh. In Kent, as in Staffordshire, members of old ruling families gradually dropped off the committee, or were squeezed out of controlling positions. The win-the-war party everywhere looked to London for a lead and for organisation, to the middling sort within the county for support.

This is the local basis for what we see at Westminster as a conflict between 'Presbyterians' and 'Independents'. The 'Independents' were those who wanted an all-out war fought to a decisive conclusion. They saw that this meant abandoning the county unit for recruiting and paying the armed forces; and getting rid of officers who were unwilling to lead their troops out of areas in which their property was situated. They wanted appointment by merit, irrespective of social rank, and the full mobilisation of Parliament's vastly superior resources in men and money. The two positions were stated in an exchange between Cromwell and his general, the Earl of Manchester, in November 1644. 'If we beat the King 99 times,' the Earl said, 'yet he is King still ; . . . but if the King beat us once we shall all be hanged, and our posterity be made slaves. . . .' ' My lord,' Cromwell replied, ' if this be so, why did we take up arms at first ? This is against fighting ever hereafter.' So the Self-Denying Ordinance and the

New Model Army were inextricably connected. The main point of the former was to relieve peers of their commissions, so that an army of the career open to the talents could be created. It was no accident that Manchester accused Cromwell of saying that 'he hoped to live to see never a nobleman in England'. (Cromwell and Sir William Brereton were among the members of Parliament who were re-appointed to commands after the Self-Denying Ordinance.)

Promotion by merit went together with religious toleration. If an appeal was to be made to people who hitherto had 'existed only to be ruled', they must be allowed freedom of discussion and organisation, and must be appointed for efficiency irrespective of their views. 'The state in choosing men to serve them takes no notice of their opinions,' Cromwell wrote to a Major-General in March 1644. 'If they be willing faithfully to serve them, that satisfies.' He was discussing the promotion of a man alleged to be an Anabaptist, someone who held religious and social views which respectable men of property had been taught to regard with horror. Cromwell selected his own officers and men from those who 'made some conscience of what they did', regardless of labels ; it was one reason for his early military success, and for his reputation as a dangerous man.

On the other hand, the ruling men in the City of London were 'Presbyterians'. They despised the 'thrift, sordidness and affected ill-breeding of the Independents', Clarendon tells us, and had no wish to see social revolution go too far. The Earl of Essex asked in 1644, 'Is this the liberty which we claim to vindicate by shedding our blood ? . . . Posterity will say that to deliver them from the yoke of the King we have subjugated them to that of the common people.' The Commander-in-Chief of the Parliamentary armies was making the same point as John Hotham, soon to be executed for deserting to the other side.

The Major-General to whom Cromwell wrote was a Scot ; and here was another distinction between 'Presbyterians' and 'Independents'. Both had agreed in asking for the assistance of a Scottish army. The Scots demanded as the price of their alliance the introduction into England of a religious system like their own, together with persecution of sectaries. Conservative Parliamentarians were happy to accept a Presbyterian national Church, though of a more Erastian type than the Scottish model ; the Independents, for religious, political, and military reasons, supported religious toleration.   In 1640 a Scottish army had enabled the opposition to impose terms on the King.   The 'Presbyterians' hoped in 1644 to use the Scottish army to impose their views on King, Parliament, and Army 'Independents'.   The correspondence of Robert Baillie, Scots commissioner in London, shows that 'we had no hope of any progress here' in imposing a Presbyterian establishment, 'till God gave [the Scottish army] victories'. The triumph of the Independent national Army meant that the Presbyterian national Church was still-born.

THE LEVELLERS

But just as the 'Presbyterian' opposition to the Royalists had been a coalition, so was the 'Independent' opposition to the 'Presbyterians' ; and it too disintegrated after victory.   Already in 1646 a group of democrats in London were saying that Parliament's resistance to the King, and the sovereignty of Parliament, could only be justified theoretically if that sovereignty derived from the people.   But if the people were sovereign, then Parliament must be made representative of the people.   'The poorest that lives hath as true a right to give a vote as well as the richest and greatest '—so a Leveller spokesman thought.   This democratic theory was combined with demands for a whole series of reforms : redistribution of the franchise, abolition of monarchy and House of Lords, election of sheriffs and Justices of the Peace, law reform, security of tenure for copyholders, throwing open of enclosures, abolition of tithes and therewith of a state Church, abolition of conscription, excise, and of the privileges of peers, corporations, and trading companies.   Their design, said a hostile pamphleteer, was ' to raise the servant against the master, the tenant against the landlord, the buyer against the seller, the borrower against the lender, the poor against the rich '.

The Levellers enjoyed a good deal of support among apprentices and small masters in London.   In 1647 they associated themselves with the demands of the Army rank and

file for arrears of pay and indemnity. They rapidly won much
influence among the Agitators. 'The thing contrived' by the
Agitators, Baxter wrote, 'was an heretical democracy.' The
words accurately portray the confusion between religion and
politics at the time. The seizure of the King by Cornet Joyce
in June 1647 forced the Generals to co-operate with the rank
and file. The Agitators told Cromwell that 'if he did not
forthwith come and head them, they would go their own way
without him'. Cromwell came. The day after the seizure
of the King the Generals agreed to the setting up of an Army
Council in which all ranks were represented. The Declaration
of 14th June 1647 was an acceptance by the Generals of Leveller
attitudes. 'We were not a mere mercenary Army, hired to
serve any arbitrary power of a state, but called forth and
conjured by the several declarations of Parliament, to the
defence of our own and the people's just rights and liberties.
And so we took up arms in judgment and conscience . . .
and are resolved . . . to assert and vindicate the just power and
rights of this kingdom in Parliament, for those common ends
premised, against all arbitrary power and violence and oppression.' So the Army justified its intervention in politics against
the 'Presbyterian' majority in the Commons. The soldiers
were citizens in uniform, who had regained the rights of freeborn
Englishmen.

At Putney in October 1647 the Leveller draft constitution,
the Agreement of the People, was debated in the Army Council.
Civil war, the Levellers held, meant that the constitution had
broken down. They offered the Agreement as a social contract
refounding the state. The franchise was to be granted to
every free man who accepted the Agreement. It demanded
the dissolution of the existing Parliament, redistribution of the
franchise, biennial Parliaments, and the absolute sovereignty
of the House of Commons, limited only by the reservation of
religious toleration and freedom from conscription as absolute
rights. There was to be complete equality before the law,
law reform, and an indemnity for all who had taken part in the
Civil War.

The Putney Debates turned very largely on the extent of
the franchise. Some Levellers spoke as though they were in
favour of manhood suffrage. Colonel Rainborough said, in

words that have become famous, 'The poorest he that is in England has a life to live as the greatest he, and therefore . . . every man that is to live under a government ought first by his own consent to put himself under that government.' But, rhetorical flourishes apart, the Levellers wanted the vote to be given only to ' freeborn Englishmen '. Unless they had fought for Parliament, servants and those in receipt of alms—that is, wage labourers and paupers—were excluded from the franchise, because these two groups were not economically independent. Thinking in terms of small household industrial and agricultural units, the Levellers held that servants—apprentices and labourers as well as domestic servants—were represented by the head of the household no less than were his womenfolk and children. ' Free ' Englishmen were those who could freely dispose of their labour, of their property in their own persons. (The Levellers' analysis is confirmed by the fact that the rank and file of the cavalry regiments—who provided their own horses, and so were men of some standing—were more politically radical than the infantry rank and file, many of whom were pressed men and so by definition not free.) [1]

The Leveller conception of ' free Englishmen ' was thus still restricted even if much wider than that embodied in the existing franchise. Their proposals would perhaps have doubled the number of men entitled to vote. But manhood suffrage would have quadrupled it. The Generals, genuinely horrified, pretended at Putney that the Levellers were more democratic than they were. Defending the existing franchise, Cromwell's son-in-law Ireton rejected the doctrine ' that by a man's being born here he shall have a share in that power that shall dispose of the lands here, and of all things here '. The vote was rightly restricted to those who have ' a permanent fixed interest in this kingdom ', namely ' the persons in whom all land lies, and those in corporations in whom all trading lies '. The present House of Commons represented them. Ireton further asked by what right the vote was demanded for

---

[1] This and the following paragraph are based on Professor C. B. Macpherson's *The Political Theory of Possessive Individualism* (1962), which the author kindly permitted me to read in advance of publication.

all free Englishmen. If by natural right—taking up the Levellers' point that all should be free who could freely dispose of their own labour—then Ireton could see no reason why men had not as much natural right to property as to the vote (for the vote had hitherto gone with particular forms of property, and the extension of the franchise would in effect expropriate existing voters). 'The liberty of all those that have the permanent interest . . . *that* is provided for. And liberty cannot be provided for in a general sense if property be preserved.' A doctrine of natural rights would lead to communism.

This argument confused the Levellers at Putney, for they were far from being communists. On the contrary, they expressed the outlook of men of small property, the artisan, yeoman, and husbandman majority of the population. They sharply differentiated themselves from the Diggers who advocated a communist programme and began communal cultivation of land at St George's Hill near London in 1649. Gerrard Winstanley, the Digger leader, extended the Leveller conception of liberty by saying, 'True freedom lies where a man receives his nourishment and preservation, and that is in the use of the earth.' The Diggers agreed with the Levellers that wage labourers were unfree ; but they drew the conclusion that wage labour should be abolished. The Generals may have believed that logically there was nothing to prevent so wide an extension of the franchise as the Levellers advocated, leading on to manhood suffrage and even to communism. As Colonel Rich put it, ' You have five to one in this kingdom that have no permanent interest. . . . If the master and servant shall be equal electors, then clearly those that have no interest in the kingdom will make it their interest to choose those that have no interest. . . . There may be a law enacted, that there shall be an equality of goods and estate.' The Generals feared that the Levellers might capture the Army ; then the many-headed monster would acquire a single head. Hence their forcible dissolution of the Army Council.

In November 1648 Cromwell warned a correspondent against the danger of stampeding towards the King and the ' Presbyterians ' through the empty fear that the Levellers would overthrow nobility and gentry ; yet four months later he told the Council of State, ' You have no other way to deal with these men but to break them in pieces. . . . If you do not break them they will break you.' Fear of popular revolt in 1642 had disintegrated the united Parliamentarian party; fear of the social consequences of religious toleration had set 'Presbyterians' against 'Independents' and the Army in 1645; and now the Levellers were beginning to extend their propaganda activities outside London and the Army. There was much in their programme to appeal to the men of small property. Unless 'normal' military discipline could be introduced, the Army which had been called into existence to establish the supremacy of the men of property might threaten that supremacy even more fundamentally than Star Chamber and Ship Money had done. So Cromwell proceeded to break the London Levellers and Leveller-led mutinies in the Army.

After defeating the most dangerous of these revolts at Burford in May 1649, Fairfax and Cromwell received honorary degrees from the traditionally Royalist university of Oxford. On their return to London they were fêted by the ' Presbyterian ' City Fathers. It was indeed the parting of the ways. Henceforth the Revolution has turned conservative. A restoration of Charles II was certainly not intended by those men who executed Charles I in 1649. But the Rump made overtures to the ' Presbyterians ' two days after the execution of the King. Once the propertied ' Independents ' had decided that tenants must not be equal with their landlords, it was only a matter of time before the ranks of the gentry would be re-united. Social conservatism led to conservative politics.

THE COMMONWEALTH AND THE PROTECTORATE

Nevertheless, there are some interesting halting-places on the road from Burford to Breda. The immediate effect of Pride's Purge and the execution of the King was that many ' persons of condition ' withdrew from local government, and were succeeded by ' a more inferior sort of the common people '. Clarendon exaggerated when he wrote that ' they who were not above the condition of ordinary inferior constables six or seven years before were now the Justices of Peace, sequestrators and commissioners '. The Royalist physician, George Bate, exaggerated when he said that in London ' the most sordid men and of the vilest condition ' replaced ' the most wealthy and grave citizens '. But that was the way it struck Royalists.

From 1649 to 1653 the republican government enjoyed an apparent affluence unique in seventeenth-century England. Sales of confiscated lands and fines on Royalists produced over £7 million. Much of this went to civil war creditors, but it also helped to finance the conquest of Ireland and Scotland, the building of Blake's fleet, and the fighting of the Anglo-Dutch war. Furthermore, by paying men more regularly, by shipping disaffected regiments off to Ireland and Scotland, later to Jamaica, and by judicious purges and promotions of radical leaders, the citizens in arms were reduced to something more like a professional army. The Leveller movement had perhaps always seemed stronger in the Army than it really was : the astonishing political sophistication of the leaders cannot have been widely reflected among the rank and file, for whom no doubt the demand for arrears of wages was the most popular plank in the Leveller platform.

Living on capital is a short-term solution. As the land fund was exhausted, so divergences began to appear between Parliamentary ' Independents ' and military leaders. Those members who sat in the Rump after Pride's Purge were a curious mixture. Some were men of high principle—either devotees of religious toleration, or convinced republicans, or advocates of the constitutional supremacy of the Commons. Others had leapt on to the bandwagon in order to share the spoils of office. They were united only in opposing a dissolution of Parliament, the second group for obvious reasons, the first because they knew that the electorate would never return a majority in favour of either religious toleration or a republic. So they wished either to prolong the rule of the Rump indefinitely, or, if there had to be a dissolution, to rig elections to ensure their own return in the next Parliament. The position of the Army leaders was different. Less theoretically attached to a republic, they wanted a more representative assembly which would vote regular taxes so as to give the Army a stable place in the constitution. Unlike the civilian members of the Rump, they did not fear a dissolution, for so long as the Army existed, its Generals could not be ignored. Yet they too were divided. The more conservative, headed by Lambert, wanted to come to terms with the 'natural rulers of the country', to have a Parliamentary settlement even if there had to be 'something of monarchical in it'; another group, led by Major-General Harrison, was prepared to use military dictatorship to put through a more radical policy, including law reform and the dis-establishment of the state Church.

After the dissolution of the Rump, the Barebones assembly was a stop-gap compromise between these two points of view. It was apparently originally intended as an advisory body, a party congress nominated by the local party cells—the Independent churches. But it took to itself the title of Parliament, and the radicals pushed forward with their programme. This was not, as is often said, an irresponsible programme. Much of it was taken over from Bills which the Rump had been preparing. But it was too radical for the men of property. Votes were passed for law reform, for the abolition of Chancery and of lay patronage; to establish civil marriage without the need of a religious ceremony, and for further sales of delinquents' and recusants' lands; and tithes were called in question. Vested interests, what Ludlow called the corrupt interests of the lawyers and the clergy, as well as the gentry, felt themselves threatened. They were directly challenged by the Leveller leader, Lilburne, who was brought up for trial while the Barebones Parliament sat. He had been exiled by the Rump, on pain of death if he returned to England, but he argued from its dissolution that this sentence was invalid, and returned. He was put on trial, but no London jury could be found to convict him. He was declared 'not guilty of any crime worthy of death', to the accompaniment of demonstrations of joy in London, in which the troops guarding Lilburne participated. The radicals in Parliament made no gesture towards Lilburne, and so sealed their fate. Their programme had no hope of realisation without popular support. The Barebones Parliament was dissolved without incident.

The Instrument of Government was the attempt of the more conservative Generals to find a *modus vivendi* between Army and electorate. The franchise was modified in two respects. First, it was redistributed, so as to increase the number of county seats and disfranchise a large number of smaller boroughs, whose representation was monopolised by a single

family. The House of Commons was made more representative
of new centres of wealth and population: Leeds and Manchester
were enfranchised for the first time. Secondly, following a
scheme drafted in the Rump, the forty-shilling freehold franchise was replaced as a qualification by ownership of real or
personal estate valued at £200. The effect was to disfranchise
many smaller freeholders (those most dependent on landlords)
and to give the vote to solid men of property among copyholders, leaseholders, clothiers, merchants, etc. It was not the
democratic reform the Levellers had wished to see, for it
restricted rather than enlarged the number of voters ; but it
was an attempt to create an independent middle-class electorate,
rather like that of 1832. In this it was relatively successful.
The Major-Generals succeeded in influencing some boroughs
in the elections of 1656. But boroughs were not enough to
create a Parliamentary majority, as they would have been
under the old franchise.

Yet the constitution looked after the interests of the Generals
too. First, a great deal of power was concentrated in the
hands of the executive, and to this (the Council) the Instrument
nominated a decisive majority of the Generals and their friends.
There was no procedure for removal except by death ; so,
though Parliament was to meet every three years, it was
effectively deprived of control over the executive. Cromwell
was appointed Protector for life. Secondly, the Commons'
financial control was greatly limited by writing an Army of
30,000 men into the constitution, as a first charge which must
be met. Thirdly, a considerable degree of religious toleration
was expressly guaranteed. None of these provisions proved to
the liking of Parliament when it met in September 1654, even
after many members had been excluded for refusing to sign an
engagement accepting government by a single person and
Parliament ; and others had withdrawn in disgust.

One horn of the dilemma of the Protectorate was now
obvious. No Parliament elected on any propertied franchise
that could be devised would abandon the claim to exercise
financial control over the executive, or to limit free expression
by persecuting sectaries thought to be socially subversive.
Nor would any Parliament representing the propertied classes
tolerate the expense of the vast Army, which now existed only

as a police force to hold down its enemies to right and left, and to collect the money for its own pay. Parliament showed its teeth on the issue of thought-control by imprisoning John Biddle, a Unitarian; and it proceeded to draft a new constitution in which its own supremacy over executive, Army, taxation, and Church should be clearly established.

The dissolution of January 1655 merely impaled the government on the other horn of the dilemma. The rule of the Major-Generals was honest and efficient. They filled a gap left after the abolition of prerogative and Church courts, the breakdown of the Presbyterian system, and the refusal of the leading gentry to act as Justices of the Peace. They began to drive the administrative machine, which had been running down for a long time. But they won only limited co-operation from the ' natural rulers ' in town and country. They had great difficulty in finding sheriffs, Justices, and juries. Major-Generals were put in command of the militia, traditionally controlled by the gentry. They purged town corporations. They restored to poor relief funds which town oligarchies had appropriated. They enforced religious toleration, and some of them even tried to check enclosure. They exhorted, bullied, and directed Justices of the Peace. For the last time in English history before the nineteenth century, local government was run from Whitehall. It was worse than the days of Laud, for now the representatives of the central authority were low-born intruders into the charmed circle of county politics ; and they had troops of horse at their command to give effect to their orders. The opponents of ' Thorough ' had not fought the Civil War to *strengthen* the central government. ' I love old England very well,' sighed Ralph Verney in 1655 ; ' but as things are carried here the gentry cannot joy much to be in it.'

The ' natural rulers ' hated these radical policies ; yet the Generals had broken irretrievably with those on the radical left who might have supported them. Military dictatorship was viewed with abhorrence by Rumpers like Sir Henry Vane and Ludlow no less than by Levellers like Sexby and Wildman, or religious radicals like Harrison and Vavasor Powell. The Protectorate was sitting on bayonets, and not much else. The Army itself was no longer a united revolutionary force. It had been purged of radicals. Representative assemblies of the rank and file had long been forgotten. Many officers speculated in ' debentures ' (the IOUs in which the troops had too often been paid), buying them up cheap and using them to invest in land. If local government was to be run *against* the ' natural rulers ', the expensive Army had to be kept up. The attempt to finance the Major-Generals by a decimation tax on the Royalists was a failure. A levy on property not voted by Parliament was disliked by all the taxpaying classes; and its failure made men fear that more land confiscations might follow. Slowly the logic of events was driving the men of property to reunite. All the efforts of the Major-Generals to influence elections, and their decision to exclude nearly a hundred members after the election, failed to produce a Parliament which would tolerate a continuance of their rule. The most determined opponents of the Protectorate came from the south-east and east of England, the main strongholds of Parliament in the Civil War. Only in the conquered Royalist areas (and in newly enfranchised Scotland and Ireland), where Royalists were disfranchised, were docile members returned.

When Parliament met, the decisive moment came when a proposal to continue the decimation tax was defeated. It was a vote of no confidence in the Major-Generals, supported, a member of Parliament noted, by those who ' were for hereditary rank '. The Humble Petition and Advice was an attempt to establish a limited Parliamentary monarchy in the house of Cromwell, and to restore cheap local government by the ' natural rulers '. The restoration of an upper house was proposed, its members to be approved by the House of Commons. The executive and the armed forces were to be made responsible to a Parliament elected on the old gentry-controlled franchise. An upper rather than a lower limit was set to taxation, and its control was restored to Parliament. Under pressure from the Generals, Oliver rejected the crown but accepted a revised Petition and Advice, which left the nomination of the upper chamber to him. When Parliament reassembled, the Other House contained only two of the old peers, and was packed with the Generals and their friends and relations. They had been winkled out of the Council, but they would still be able to veto any legislation they disliked.

Real Parliamentary control of the executive seemed as far off as ever.

A Cromwellian limited monarchy was impossible because Oliver was the creation of the Army and dared not disband it. No-one else could succeed where he failed, not Richard Cromwell, not Lambert or Fleetwood, not Monck. England plunged into anarchy. Two themes can be heard across the chaos. First, on the left, desperate pleas for reunion of republicans, democrats, and sectaries with the Army to defend the Good Old Cause. But the history of the past twelve years had split the radicals irretrievably. None of them trusted the others. The Generals still wanted a 'select senate', composed of themselves, which could veto legislation; they were terrified of any revival of Army democracy. The Levellers were a spent force. Too much idealism had been spilt, too many had already decided that political victory was impossible.

The other insistent theme is the gradual polarisation at the opposite extreme, the reunion of the 'free' against those who existed only to be ruled. Without the Army, Royalists and Episcopalians could not be held in forcible subjection. But as long as the Army existed, endless vistas of free quarter, of requisitions, of reviving radicalism, of further land confiscations, rose to terrify the men of property. In the winter of 1659–60 the taxpayers, led by the City of London, again went on strike. Once Monck had clearly identified himself with the City, the purse-strings were untied. The slogan of the men of property, with which they had greeted Monck everywhere on his march down from Scotland, was 'a free Parliament', by which they meant a Parliament of the free.

ADMINISTRATIVE CHANGES

One point must be emphasised before we leave the Army to disintegrate—how thoroughly it had done its job. The military and economic power of Irish Catholicism, so frightening in the thirties and forties, had been broken. One great bastion of the monarchy had thus gone, and even James II proved unable to restore it. Secondly, in England itself the Parliamentarian artillery had destroyed strongholds such as Basing House and Lathom House; after the war castles were in

turn 'slighted'. It was a symbolical destruction of military
feudalism ; and it made it so much the more difficult for the
crown ever again to impose its will on the country by military
force. Thirdly, the union of England and Scotland, unpopular
though it was in Scotland, established free trade between
the two countries, and the Lowlands at least remained within
the sphere of English civilisation. The conquest of Royalist
Wales, Cornwall, and the north, the activities of the Committees for the Propagation of the Gospel in Wales and the
North Parts, followed by the Quaker movement which
evangelised England and Wales from the north, and the
establishment of links between other churches—all this helped
to make Britain more conscious of its unity. This unity focused
on London ; the Highlands of Scotland and the Catholic areas
of Ireland were excluded from it. Those, the only areas in
which the later Stuart cause enjoyed any mass support, had
been isolated and defeated in advance.

Before 1640 the heart of government had been the court,
the royal household. Officers of state stood in a personal
relation to the King ; their subordinates were their personal
dependents. In 1642 the court left London. Most of the
great lords followed. Customs farmers and monopolists lost
their privileges. Parliament, now the permanent focus of
government, had to build up a new administrative apparatus
side by side with what remained of the old. Government was
perforce depersonalised. New financial departments were
formed, located significantly in the halls of City companies.
Committees were set up for trade, for sale of confiscated lands,
to administer customs and excise. The Committee for Plundered
Ministers ran the Church. The Committee of Both Kingdoms
became the supreme executive, dependent on Parliament,
foreshadowing the Cabinet. A habit of rule through Parliament was established. Semi-professional civil servants, who did
not owe their position to clientage or purchase, began to
establish a new tradition of public service. Ludlow says that
Sir Henry Vane, as Treasurer of the navy, brought men ' to
understand that they were not placed in employment to serve
themselves, but to serve the public '. This new ethic had
difficulty in surviving the Restoration, but an ex-Cromwellian
civil servant like Pepys took some of it into the world of

Charles II. Levellers boasted of 'the New Model, wherein there is not one lord'. The rise of new groups to rule the counties also helped to destroy the assumption that command must inevitably devolve upon social rank. The astonishing efficiency of the Army and navy in these years owed much to the new attitudes of those who ran them with a sense of public duty. Sailors were more regularly paid, sick and wounded better looked after, than under Charles I or Charles II.

Judges obtained legal security of tenure, which made them less subject to government pressure. In 1652 they were given a salary of £1,000, and forbidden to take fees or rewards. Similar attempts were made to substitute salaries for fees in the excise, customs, and navy. In other departments fees were limited and controlled. Nevertheless, in the long run the vested interests of lawyers and office-holders proved too strong for Parliamentary reformers no less than for Wentworth. With growing conservatism under the Protectorate the Exchequer was restored, and with it the traditional fees. But sale of offices was forbidden, and does not seem to have been reinstated until 1660. The abolition of the Councils of the North and in Wales, together with the Privy Council, led to changes in local government and to greater independence for Justices of the Peace. Close co-operation in the forties between members of Parliament and county committees gave the former a new importance. Parliament was no longer a court: it was recognised as the central representative of the interests of 'the county'. This status was not lost after 1660. 'Member of Parliament' henceforth means member of the House of Commons.

THE RESTORATION

We are now better placed to understand how the Restoration came about. Charles I, whose life had nearly ruined the monarchy, did much to save it by his death. During the Civil War he had not fully accepted, except for propagandist purposes, the position of Edward Hyde and the constitutional Royalists, that the monarchy's function was to protect law, order, and property against Parliament's arbitrary claims backed up by popular violence. But at his trial he not only stood

forward as a martyr for the Church of England but also argued
that there could be no security for anyone's life or property
if even he, the King, was subjected to unlawful violence.
Anyone who remembered Charles's earlier career must have
found this difficult to accept at the time ; but in the fifties a
nostalgic desire for ' normality ' and a hearty dislike for
military rule spread among the gentry, who began to see a
national Church as the bulwark of law, order, and stability.
The fraudulent but skilful *Eikon Basilike*, purporting to be
Charles's own reflections in captivity, helped to popularise the
legend of the martyred King. With great acumen the exiled
Charles II had chosen as his chief minister Hyde, who personified the constitutionalist opposition of 1640–1, and had
stuck to him against all the intrigues of his rivals. Hyde's
insistence that the King could not be restored by force, but
only by a revulsion in his favour inside England, now began
to pay dividends.

In August 1659 Sir George Booth published a manifesto
justifying his taking up arms on behalf of Charles II. As in
1642, Sir George drew his sword in defence of liberty and
property ; though this time, he thought, the threat came from
' a mean and schismatical party '. In 1659 Booth was defeated ;
but he lived to get a peerage at the Restoration, together with
many other ' Presbyterians '. His adherents had claimed to
be taking up arms against the Quakers. Now the early
Quakers were not pacifists. The Army leaders were said to
intend to arm them in 1659–60. But the word Quaker was
used as a generic term of abuse to describe religious and
political radicals : the propertied classes feared a return to
the 1647–9 policy of alliance between the Army leaders and
these radicals. Alternatively, an unpaid Army might get
totally out of hand and a condition of anarchy ensue of which
the many-headed monster might take advantage. By the end
of 1659 shops could no longer be opened with safety. The
law courts ceased to function. The Army had to live by free
quarter, and it was but a small step from this to unrestricted
plunder. In 1659–60, the censorship being once again unenforceable, pamphlets were published calling for law reform,
stable copyholds, and other Leveller objectives.

The Reverend Henry Newcombe supported the Restoration,

but was ejected from his living as a Presbyterian in 1662. Later he looked back and asked himself whether it had been worth it. He decided it had. ' Though soon after the settlement of the nation we saw ourselves the despised and cheated party, . . . yet, in all this I have suffered since, I look upon it as less than my trouble was from my fears then. They [the ruling powers before the Restoration] did me no hurt ; took nothing from me. These [the post-Restoration government] have taken all ; and yet I feel it not, comparatively, to what I felt from my fears then ; and I would not change conditions . . . to have it as it was then, as bad as it is. (i) Their malice and rage was so desperate and giddy and lawless. Affliction by law is known, and one may know how to frame to it, and more than is law cannot be inflicted. Then we lay at the mercy and impulse of a giddy, hot-headed, bloody multitude. (ii) A Münsterian anarchy [1] we escaped, far sadder than particular persecution. . . . If it then should have been said to us, well, you shall be eased of this power, and rid of the bloody Anabaptists, but you must have Bishops and ceremonies again, we should have then said, with all our hearts.' So the Presbyterians sacrificed religion to social order. In April 1660 Milton had warned of the danger that religion and liberty would be prostituted to ' the vain and groundless apprehension that nothing but kingship can restore trade '.

' Can you at once suppress the sectaries and keep out the King ? ' a Royalist pamphleteer asked ; his answer was no. The county election in Buckinghamshire in 1659 was described as being between ' the gentlemen ' and ' the Anabaptist party '. The gentlemen won. The decisive moment was the day in February 1660 when the militia was taken from the command of ' persons of no degree or quality ' and restored to ' the government of the nobility and principal gentry '.[2] Pepys stated the alternatives precisely in his *Diary* for 18th April 1660 : ' Either the fanatics must now be undone or the gentry and citizens throughout England, and clergy, must fall, in spite of their militia and army.' The gentry and citizens, the free, were

[1] The Anabaptist régime in Münster in 1535 had been short-lived, because repressed with terrible ferocity ; but it was long used as a horror story to suggest that all sectaries were bloodthirsty revolutionaries.
[2] *A Coffin for the Good Old Cause* ; *Verney Memoirs*, iii, 444 ; Clarendon, *History of the Rebellion* (1888), vi, 176

opposed by the fanatics, the republicans, the many-headed monster. Fear of the latter led the free to look to Charles Stuart, ' out of love to themselves, not to him ', Ralph Joscelyn noted in his Diary. ' Nor do we desire more to enjoy what is ours, than that all our subjects may enjoy what by law is theirs ', said Charles II in his Declaration of Breda, which referred all disputed questions to ' a free Parliament, by which, upon the word of a King, we will be advised '.

Popular rejoicing at the Restoration should not deceive us. Men of property were pleased to feel that law, order, and social stability, liberty and property, were being restored with the King, discipline with the Bishops. They bought rumps for the populace to roast, just as in 1623 they had paid for rejoicings at the return of Prince Charles from Spain. But as Cromwell had said to Lambert in 1650, ' These very persons would shout as much if you and I were going to be hanged.' Those who were not pleased with the Restoration, Sir John Reresby shrewdly observed, ' durst not oppose the current by seeming otherwise '. We do not know what the unfree thought, for in 1660 the shutters close. Henceforth they again exist only to be ruled, and we hear their inarticulate protests only through the distorting medium of trials and reports of Justices of the Peace.

9 Economics, 1640-60

Some cry, ' The land is poor and cannot give '.
'Tis poor indeed : and yet I do believe
Few kingdoms are so rich. . . .
'Tis poor if we on those reflect our eyes
On whom the labour of this kingdom lies :
Those people whom our great and wealthy ones
Have racked, oppressed and eaten to the bones
To fatten and adorn their carcasses. . . .
Yet we do nothing want that may conduce,
In war or peace, to serve a needful use. . . .
If we . . . could agree
This kingdom which so needy seems to be
Might with her superfluities maintain
Far greater armies than the King of Spain.

George Wither, *Brittans Remembrancer* (1628)

Whosoever commands the sea commands the trade ; whosoever commands the trade of the world commands the riches
of the world, and consequently the world itself.

Sir Walter Ralegh, *A Discourse of the Invention of Ships*

THE LAND

HISTORIANS are coming more and more to recognise the
decisive significance of these decades in the economic history
of England. ' The fall of the absolute monarchy,' writes Mr
Lipson, ' was the turning-point in the evolution of capitalism.'
' The issue between the monarchy as the champion of the
established economic order, and the rising middle class as its
assailant ' became involved with religious and constitutional
conflicts ; the struggle ' resulted in consolidating the ascendancy
of Parliament and in freeing the capitalist class from control
by the crown '. ' In the relaxation of that control lies the
economic significance of the Civil War. . . . It eliminated the
one barrier which obstructed the path of the *entrepreneur*, who
was allowed henceforth a freer hand in industry.' ' The first
condition of healthy industrial growth,' wrote Professor Hughes

apropos the salt industry, 'was the exclusion of the parasitic
entourage of the court.'

Employers and *entrepreneurs* were freed from government
regulation and control in various ways. Attempts to supervise
quality of manufactures and to fix prices were abandoned ;
industrial monopolies were abolished. Greater freedom was
established in relations between employers and workmen. The
government stopped trying to regulate wage rates, to compel
employers to keep their employees at work in time of slump.
Taxation became regular, if heavy, and (except under Army
rule) it was controlled by representatives of the taxpayers.
Henceforth employers were limited in expanding or contract-
ing their business solely by economic considerations. 'The
relation between masters and servants,' wrote Clarendon nos-
talgically, was 'dissolved by the Parliament, that their army
might be increased by the prentices against their masters'
consent.' The Act of 1563, insisting on a seven-year period of
apprenticeship, and excluding all but freeholders' sons from
apprenticeship, was not enforced. The common law, so
favourable to absolute property rights, triumphed over the
prerogative courts.

During these decades crown lands and rents were sold to
the value of over £2¼ million. The capital value of Church
lands sold is estimated at nearly £2 million. The estates of all
substantial Royalists were sequestrated, that is, taken over by
county committees, which collected rents and fines and
assigned leases. The lands of more than 700 Royalists were
confiscated and sold, for over £1¼ million ; and far more land
was almost certainly disposed of privately by Royalists. It
was an upheaval comparable with the dissolution of the
monasteries. Royalists who were willing to do so might
'compound' for their estates—i.e. buy them back for a fine,
assessed in relation to the degree of their delinquency, at anything from a half to a tenth of the capitalised value. Tenants
who had refused to pay rent to 'delinquent' landlords, or who
had co-operated too eagerly with the Parliamentary sequestra-
tion committees, were at the mercy of landlords who had
compounded. John Cook, the lawyer who presented Parliament's case against the King in 1649, dramatically represented
the attitude of such Royalists. 'Says the old miser, " I must pay

many thousand pounds to the Parliament, and must get it up again ! " . . . " Oh," says he, " I'll be sure to be revenged on that Roundhead ! " '

Purchasers of confiscated lands were anxious to secure quick returns. Those of their tenants who could not produce written evidence of their titles were liable to eviction. Tenants of former Church and crown lands, a Royalist wrote in 1653, ' do perfectly hate those who bought them, as possibly men can do ; for these men are the greatest tyrants everywhere as men can be ; for they wrest the poor tenants of all former immunities and freedoms they formerly enjoyed '. The land transfers must have had the effect of disrupting traditional relationships between landlord and tenant, of replacing them by purely monetary relations.

It is difficult to assess the effects of these transactions on Royalist landlords. Great men like the Earl of Newcastle and the Earl of Worcester each claimed to have lost little short of £1 million in the royal cause. These were inflated estimates, including expenses in raising troops for the King and loss of rents for nearly twenty years ; yet neither of these noblemen was in poverty after the Restoration. Other Royalists, who did not go into exile but compounded and got their estates back, could devote themselves to estate management during their fifteen years of exclusion from politics, with no court to force extravagant expenditure on them. Many Royalists, through agents or relations, bought their estates back before 1660, though some of them ran into debt in doing so. But many lesser Royalists must have got into grave financial difficulties. Nearly £1½ million was raised from over 3,000 Royalists by the Committee for Compounding, as well as £350,000 in rents and profits from their estates. Delinquents submitting to Parliament also had to pay a levy of one-twentieth of their real and one-fifth of their personal estates. On top of this came heavy taxation, culminating in the decimation tax of 1655.

In order to pay composition fines after a long period in which no rents had been received, Royalists were authorised to sell part of their lands. We have no idea how much was sold, but the amount must have been considerable ; these lands were not restored in 1660. Declining gentlemen whose financial position was desperate seem to have formed the backbone of the Royalist action party in the sixteen-fifties, fomenting military conspiracy which the greater landlords of their party frowned upon.[1] Unless such men were very fortunate in securing court favour after the Restoration, their families had a stiff fight to keep their heads above water. Still, the bulk of Royalist landlords retained their position. There was no social revolution in the countryside comparable with that which occurred during the French Revolution, though changes that had long been taking place may have been accelerated. It was estimated that half the land of Staffordshire came into the hands of new owners between 1609 and 1669. In 1609 there had been only three ' citizen owners ' in the county ; in 1669 there were three peers, four baronets, and twenty esquires who had purchased land with wealth made in trade.

Wardship and the Court of Wards were abolished by order of the two Houses in 1646, and by Act of Parliament in 1656. All lands formerly held from the King by feudal tenure were converted into freehold. Confirmation of this legislation was the first business the House of Commons turned to in 1660 after hearing the Declaration of Breda, so great was the significance attached to it. The effect of what Mr Ogg calls ' possibly the most important single event in the history of English land-holding ' was to deprive the crown of a vital means of maintaining its leading subjects in a proper subordination ; to relieve the landed class of the irritating and erratic death duties which wardship had imposed ; and to give landowners, whose rights in their estates had hitherto been limited, an absolute power to do what they would with their own, including the right to settle the inheritance of all their lands by will. Unconditional ownership and transmission of landed property was one essential for planned long-term capital investment in agricultural improvements. The other was that copy-holders—mostly smaller tenants with no security of tenure—should *not* win absolute rights in their holdings, particularly not an absolute right of inheritance, but could be evicted by landlords who wished to enclose or consolidate.

So there are three stages in the victory of improving land-lordism. First, the abolition of the Laudian régime and the prerogative courts, which had tried to check enclosure and to

[1] D. E. Underdown, *Royalist Conspiracy in England, 1649-60* (1960), *passim*

protect small men. Secondly, the abolition of wardship and
feudal tenures. Thirdly, the defeat of the movement to win
economic (and thus political) independence for copyholders,
to protect common rights against enclosure and to reform the
law on behalf of small proprietors. Winstanley was appealing
to deaf ears when in 1649 he asked the House of Commons
to ' let the gentry have their enclosures free from all Norman
enslaving entanglements whatsoever, and let the common
people have their commons and waste lands set free to them,
from all Norman enslaving lords of manors. . . . If you found
out the Court of Wards to be a burden and freed lords of
manors and gentry from paying fines to the King . . . let the
common people be set free too from paying homage to lords of
manors.' The Parliament of 1656 which abolished military
tenures rejected a Bill to set an upper limit to the entry fines
which could be imposed on copyholders (thus leaving landlords
free to evict those unable to pay). The same Parliament
rejected another Bill—introduced, significantly, by a Major-
General—which for the last time attempted to check enclosures.
These Bills would ' destroy property', it was said ; only the
property of the free seemed to count. The Act of 1660 con-
firming the abolition of military tenures specifically provided
that it should not benefit copyholders. Blackstone in the
eighteenth century thought this Act a greater boon to property
owners than Magna Carta itself. In no sphere was the defeat
of the radical movement more decisive than this. The century
of agricultural prosperity which followed the Civil War
victories of Cromwell's yeoman cavalry was also the century of
' the disappearance of the small landowner '.

It is thus from the Interregnum that new possibilities of
extending the cultivated area opened up. Woods belonging to
Royalist landlords were often turned over to cultivation, either
by sequestrators or by purchasers, or by necessitous Royalists
themselves. During the Civil War, popular protests checked
enclosures of common and waste lands. But the restoration of
central authority, and the defeat of the radical movements,
together with the fact that confiscated lands were sold by
Parliament in large groups, ensured that the great new areas
now available for cultivation came into the hands of men with
sufficient capital to be able to improve them. When lands

were surveyed for sale by Parliament, squatters on commons were always marked for eviction. Henceforth the encouragement of agricultural improvements was a major object of government policy; attempts to prevent enclosure were abandoned. Agricultural prosperity came in a way which favoured richer landlords and depressed their tenants. In 1649 Peter Chamberlen, protesting against this, advocated the nationalisation of confiscated lands, commons, and marshes; and Gerrard Winstanley and the Diggers started to take over waste land for communal cultivation. Such schemes were inevitably defeated. Parliament passed an Act for draining the Fens in the same month as the Levellers were put down at Burford. Lower rates of interest (making it easier to borrow money) also helped land reclamation and cultivation of the commons to go ahead; but not for the benefit of the poor, who had hitherto used fens and commons for fishing, hunting, grazing, and for their fuel supply.

Clover seed was on sale in London by 1650. Its use, recommended by agricultural writers, revolutionised the cultivation of barren land. Charles Davenant thought clover was introduced especially on crown lands during the Interregnum. Improved rotation of crops enabled animals to be kept alive through the winter. This in its turn increased the supply of fertilisers. Meanwhile purchasing power was increasing, thanks to government expenditure and rising wage rates. Greater purchasing power meant that men could eat more, which in turn was a great stimulus to agriculture. Agricultural production leapt forward; England ceased to import corn and soon began to export it. Cheaper corn and meat meant relatively lower labour costs, especially in the hitherto less-developed frontier areas of the north and west, in which both agricultural and industrial production expanded most rapidly. The victory of south and east in the Civil War, paradoxically, brought prosperity to Liverpool, and economic revival to Bristol and Exeter.

Public opinion altered too. Levellers protested against enclosure, but agricultural writers invariably favoured it, and after the restoration of the censorship in the fifties the note of moral disapprobation is more rarely met. The traditional rhyme might circulate verbally:

The law locks up the man or woman
That steals the goose from off the common ;
But leaves the greater villain loose
Who steals the common from the goose.

But the Reverend Joseph Lee argued that the free play of the market would succeed where government regulation had failed. If corn was ever again in short supply, ' men will plough up their enclosed land for their own profit ; it's an undeniable maxim that everyone . . . will do that which makes for his greatest advantage '. Agricultural improvement was increasingly becoming a matter of capital investment, which only rich landowners or lessees could afford. ' Any land,' wrote Blyth in 1652, ' by cost and charge may be made rich, and as rich as land can be.' By cost and charge—that was the point. In Parliament in 1657 Colonel Sydenham said of rank-and-file soldiers, ' They are poor, and if you assign lands to them they must sell again.' The rich inherited the earth.

INDUSTRY AND THE POOR

The Interregnum saw an advance in communications which made it easier for agricultural and industrial production to be specialised in different regions. Before 1640 opposition of vested interests to improvements in river navigation could be met only by an overriding power obtained by letters patent : this was subject to all the costs and hazards of negotiation at court. After 1640 the initiative passed to Parliament, more liberal in such matters. Coastal shipping trebled between 1628 and 1683. In 1654 surveyors were empowered by Act of Parliament to assess the inhabitants of a parish and to hire labour and carts for amending the highways. It was the beginning of a recognition of the state's duty in this sphere, anticipating the first Turnpike Act of 1663. Military and administrative necessity led to a great acceleration of postal communications. In 1656 letters from London were delivered in Winchester next day. Under Secretary Thurloe the Post Office developed as a national institution serving private as well as public customers. The first regular coach services date from the Interregnum.

In trade and industry the revolutionary decades were no less decisive. Purveyance was abolished ; the authority of the clerk of the market, whose supervisory control over weights and measures had often been used for the purpose of extortion, was transferred to the local magistracy. Local monopoly privileges and the system of apprenticeship were severely shaken. Down to 1640 England and France had moved along parallel lines of industrial regulation ; after that date they are poles apart. The rise in prices, which had created boom conditions for so long, had come to an end : the havoc of the Thirty Years' War led to drastic reductions in European demand. Political crises in 1648-9 and 1659-60 caused industrial and trading depressions, and the burden of taxation and free quarter was heavy throughout the period. But internal free trade was the essential prerequisite for industrial advance. Wages, left to supply and demand, rose steadily : Army rates of pay helped to force them up. The trend continued to the end of the period covered by this book.

In the Cornish tin mines complete *laissez-faire* created conditions of abounding prosperity. Miners who had left the industry in the depression caused by Stuart monopoly flocked back ; new mines were opened, production expanded, and wages rose. They fell again when monopoly was re-established in 1660.[1] In the clothing industry, John Aubrey wrote under Charles II, ' The art of spinning is so much improved within these last forty years, that one pound of wool makes twice as much cloth as to extent as it did before the civil wars.' Government expenditure, financed by confiscation, taxation, and customs dues on this increased trade, mounted enormously. It is difficult to estimate the effect of bulk purchases, novel on such a scale, in stimulating the armaments, shipbuilding, clothing, and leather industries, to mention only a few. Most important of all was a change in the intellectual and moral climate. As late as 1641, when the Commons discussed interest, it had to be called ' damages '. Medieval ideas about money-lending still prevailed, and ' interest ' was a rude word. By 1660 such prejudices were extinct. The rate of interest was lowered to six per cent in 1651, giving an additional fillip to industry.

[1] G. R. Lewis, *The Stannaries* (1924), pp. 220-1

Before 1640 many wage labourers could not legally depart from their place of work without a testimonial. But between the breakdown of conciliar government and the establishment of new and more drastic restrictions by the Act of Settlement in 1662, there was a period of greater mobility. Impressment for the forces snatched men away from their crafts and husbandry ; at the Army's insistence, apprentice regulations were waived on behalf of disbanded soldiers. Military operations and the billeting of troops in private houses (which continued long after the fighting was over) helped to mix up the population, to bring the ideas of the south and east into isolated areas of the north and west. Scots and Irishmen fought in England ; Englishmen in Scotland, Ireland, the West Indies, and Flanders. The period was in general one of great mobility. The marches of armies were succeeded by those of demobilised soldiers seeking work and of itinerant Quakers seeking the salvation of souls. The self-contained units of English society broke down at all levels. The Statute of Apprentices, which excluded three-quarters of the rural population from the clothing industry, was no longer enforced. After 1660 unemployment declined. Men ceased to think England was overpopulated.

Administration of poor relief continued without breakdown during the revolutionary decades, and there was no cessation of private charitable grants. A special Corporation for the Poor was set up in London in 1647. In fact the poor seem to have been better off in the sixteen-fifties than in any preceding decade.[1] The crisis years 1649 and 1659 produced a number of pamphlets making generous and imaginative proposals for abolishing poverty ; but the defeat of the radicals meant that such schemes were not put into practice. The Puritan emphasis on the duty of serving God by hard work in one's calling had provided theoretical justification for the law's distinction between the able-bodied poor, who were wicked and should be forced to work, and the aged or impotent poor, who should be relieved by the parish. So long as there were large numbers of unemployed unable to find work, this doctrine had proved unconvincing ; nor were early Stuart attempts to browbeat parishes into setting the poor on work successful. But the period of fuller employment which followed

[1] Jordan, *Philanthropy in England*, pp. 137, 198-9, 206-9, 369

the establishment of internal free trade made the doctrine
that beggars were idle and sinful more acceptable. 1640 ends
the period in which the central government had tried to
enforce a national system of dealing with the poor. Henceforth,
until the nineteenth century, each parish looked after its own
unemployed. Unsuccessful state paternalism ends ; trade
unionism slowly and painfully begins.

COMPANIES AND THE CITY

The Long Parliament abolished industrial monopolies. It
did not abolish the right of merchants to form privileged
trading companies to which access was restricted. The great
London companies lent money to Parliament, and there was,
in Mr Scott's words, ' a tendency to strengthen the position
of the companies far beyond what can be accounted for
exclusively by pure political motives '. But after 1647 the
companies' privileges came increasingly under attack. For
three years the East India trade was open to interlopers. The
Levant Company also suffered badly from unauthorised trading
rivals. The Levellers made themselves the spearhead of this
attack, demanding freedom from all restrictions on competitive production and sale, and the right of the small
producer to dispense with the middleman, who took much
of the profit. This was in effect a call for state intervention on behalf of small master craftsmen against the great
merchant capitalists as well as against local and monopoly
privileges.

In London there was a movement, parallel to that of
political revolt, against the oligarchical system of government
in companies and in the City. The small masters tried to
regain an active share in control of the companies, in order
to protect themselves against being depressed into the position
of wage labourers. Thus ' poor freemen and journeymen
printers ' complained that they were made ' perpetual bondsmen to serve some few of the rich all their lives upon such
conditions and for such hire, and at such times, as the masters
think fit '.[1] In at least twelve London companies the industrial
rank and file took part in a movement of this sort on quite

[1] Margaret James, *Social Policy during the Puritan Revolution*, pp. 207, 211

a new scale. Fierce battles resulted. Their simultaneity suggests the influence of general democratic theories as well as of particular discontents. The Levellers were influential in this movement too. The small masters frequently asked Parliament for support, alleging that the oligarchies who ruled the companies were Royalists. Successes were gained. The commonalty of the weavers were empowered to elect a representative body of 140. The right to print Bibles and Testaments, hitherto a monopoly, was extended to the whole body of printers.

But the democratic movement in the gilds achieved no substantial or lasting success. It was all over by 1656. In that year the government ratified the privileges of the Merchant Adventurers, and so restored one of the more powerful companies to their semi-monopoly of cloth export. In 1657 it was a Merchant Adventurer, Packe, who offered the crown to Cromwell. In that year too the East India Company recovered its charter. The Protector's government was abandoning its former radical allies and linking up again with the men of big property for whom formerly the ' Presbyterians ' had spoken. So in this field too the way was prepared for the Restoration.

In 1649-50 there was an attempt, again with Leveller backing, to democratise the government of the City of London itself. In February the Parliament which had just abolished the monarchy authorised the calling of a Common Council without the Lord Mayor ; his veto and that of the aldermen were abolished. But this was only a means of circumventing ' Presbyterian ' control of the City. It led to no lasting democratisation of City government. There were similar democratic movements in other towns, though few have as yet been properly studied.

TRADE AND FOREIGN POLICY

The end of the price-revolution boom saw Europe entering into a protectionist phase and an epoch of trade wars. It was fortunate for English merchants that power passed, just in time, to men more responsive to the interests of trade. There were two possible lines of foreign expansion. Some—for example those merchants engaged in trade with the West

Indies—saw the main enemy as the Habsburg power monopolising the American market and trying to establish political
and economic control over the Baltic. Against Habsburg
Spain and Austria the Protestant Dutch Republic was a
potential ally. The Merchant Adventurers favoured friendly
relations with the Netherlands, the recipients of their cloth
exports. Others, more interested in the East India trade, the
export of the New Draperies, fishing, or the European carrying
trade (particularly interlopers), saw the Netherlands as
England's greatest rivals. The Dutch were out-trading English
merchants in the European and colonial trades. They were
establishing a monopoly of shipbuilding materials and of the
supply of negro slaves. The years before 1646 and after 1656,
when 'Presbyterians' and City companies had the greatest
influence, were the periods of pro-French, pro-Dutch, and anti-
Spanish foreign policy; the policy of the Rump was pro-
Spanish and anti-Dutch. The Yorkshire clothing interest,
whether represented in the government by Wentworth or
Lambert, was consistently pro-Spanish. The antithesis between
the two policies was permanent, varying as the emphasis was
placed on Europe, where Dutch help might be needed, or the
colonies, where Dutch and English were trade rivals. It was
not resolved until, after three wars, the Dutch accepted the
position of subordination to and dependence on England which
was offered and rejected in 1651.

1651 saw a turning-point in colonial policy. During the
Civil War Parliament's main concern in this field had been to
win over the colonies by trading privileges and favourable
tariffs, and so to deprive the Royalist fleet of bases. Many of
the peers prominent in colonisation, like Warwick and Saye
and Sele, were supporters of Parliament, and so could not be
offended. But after Pride's Purge, Warwick was removed from
control of colonial affairs, which passed to 'citizens and
inferior persons' (Clarendon's words); Blake drove Prince
Rupert's fleet from the seas, and a new policy was adopted.
This involved a much more positive attitude than that of the
Stuarts. An attempt was made to build up a close-knit
imperial unit. Parliamentary legislation, enforced by the
navy, aimed at increasing colonial production so as to supply
England with all she needed. Bounties were introduced on

the production of naval stores, in order to free us from dependence on Dutch-carried Baltic supplies. Trade with foreigners—and that meant principally the Dutch—was forbidden to the colonists. So was inaugurated the ' old colonial system ', which was to last for well over a century.

By 1640 colonial products re-exported from London equalled in value all English exports other than textiles. Hence London's interest in colonial expansion, in the re-orientation of colonial trade, in making London an *entrepôt* for re-export of colonial produce. It was the way to shift the commercial centre of the world from Amsterdam to London. It involved a commercial revolution. Crucial were the Navigation Acts of 1650 and 1651, which challenged the Dutch to fight for the trade of the world. A Navigation Act had been introduced into the Parliament of 1621, and frequent suggestions were made in the ensuing decades that goods should be imported and exported only in English bottoms. But under the monarchy merchants had never been sufficiently influential to force this policy on the government. Its adoption by the Rump was not the triumph of any particular pressure group : it was a victory for a new governmental sense of responsibility for trade.[1] In 1648 the Dutch had secured the right of free passage into the Baltic for their ships, whilst English ships had to pay : only the intervention of state power could reverse this defeat. Between 1651 and 1660 over 200 ships were added to the British navy, thanks both to captures and to the building of more new vessels than in four decades of Stuart rule. This vast fleet was deliberately used to win commercial advantages. 1,700 prizes taken during the Dutch war of 1652-4 greatly strengthened the English mercantile marine. The Dutch agreed to pay compensation for the Amboyna massacre, a concession which no previous English government had been able to secure.

From the late sixteen-thirties, as the Dutch drove Portuguese ships from the eastern seas, English merchants had aspired to take over the role of carriers for the Portuguese. England's protection of the Portuguese empire was a contributory cause of the Anglo-Dutch war of 1652. Its successful conclusion enabled the signature of an Anglo-Portuguese treaty in 1654, which transferred the monopoly of trade with the

[1] Hinton, *The Eastland Company and the Common Weal* (1959), chap. vii

Portuguese empire from Dutch to English merchants, and permitted the latter to trade with Brazil, Bengal, and West Africa on terms more favourable than those of Portuguese merchants themselves. There was a marked revival of Anglo-Portuguese trade, which in 1656 was expected to be ' welcome news to our clothing towns, now their trade with Spain is shut up '.[1] In 1660 there were said to be sixty houses of English merchants at Lisbon, two in Spain. The long Portuguese connection had been established.

From the mid-sixteen-fifties, with the return to influence of Warwick and the ' Presbyterians ', there was a shift in the direction of foreign policy, but no change in the conscious use of state power for commercial ends. The Anglo-Spanish war indeed accentuated Anglo-Dutch rivalry, owing to Dutch merchants attempting to monopolise the trade with Spain. In the Western Design of 1655 Cromwell put into effect the policy of which a section of English opinion had dreamed since the days of Hakluyt, the policy of Ralegh and the Providence Island Company. It was not immediately successful : the attempt to seize Hispaniola failed, and the Spanish empire proved still too strong. But the Western Design for the first time made the Caribbean the theatre of European power politics which it was to remain for 150 years. The capture of Jamaica had far-reaching consequences. It was the first of the Greater Antilles to be lost to Spain, and its seizure inaugurated a new epoch in English commercial policy. Between 1640, when sugar cultivation was introduced, and 1651, the slave population of Barbados rose from 1,000 to 20,000, mostly supplied by the Dutch. It had doubled again by 1673, but now slaves came from Jamaica. Since political and religious emigration to the English North American plantations slowed down after 1640, slave labour was in demand there too. Jamaica also replaced the Dutch base at Curaçao as *entrepôt* for the Spanish American mainland. The prosperity of Liverpool and Bristol during the next century and a half was based on the slave trade.

The national importance of commerce was recognised when the navy began to provide regular convoys from 1649. After Royalist privateers had been crushed, Barbary pirates subdued,

[1] *Thurloe State Papers*, v, 165

and the old privateering base of Dunkirk annexed, the English navy began effectively to police the seas. Merchantmen no longer needed to be armed to the teeth. So freights began to be reduced to the Dutch level. Blake's fleet was used as a decisive instrument of policy. English power appeared in the Mediterranean, with immediate and lasting effects. Treaties with Tetuan and Tangier gave naval bases there. Already the government was casting eyes on Gibraltar (or Minorca) as a permanent base. English power was also exercised in the Baltic, still an essential source of naval stores and corn. Treaties of 1654 and 1656 gave English traders entry to Swedish ports on terms of equality with the Dutch, who hitherto had monopolised Baltic exports. Goodson's fleet at the Sound in 1658 looks forward to the eighteenth century.

So English foreign policy was transformed. In place of the feeble and pro-Spanish policy of James and Charles there was a deliberate concentration of England's strength on the use of sea power for an aggressive foreign policy. The Interregnum saw the acquisition of Jamaica, St Helena, Pulo Run, Surinam, Dunkirk, Nova Scotia and New Brunswick; trade with China began. Cromwell's greatness at home was but a shadow of his glory abroad, said Clarendon. Though Oliver talked of a Protestant Crusade, and did in fact extend protection to the Vaudois and other victims of persecution, his foreign policy was dominated by economic considerations. Even Sweden was opposed when she seemed to threaten English commercial interests in the Baltic. By the end of the sixteen-fifties the traditional anti-Spanish policy—part economic, part religious—had achieved its purpose. Spain's defeat in the Thirty Years' War, the dominance of commercial over religious motives in foreign policy, meant that henceforth the Dutch were our immediate rivals. Thurloe regarded Dunkirk, captured from Spain, as ' a bridle to the Dutch '. It would also have been a bridle to the French had Charles II not subsequently sold it and disbanded Cromwell's army. In consequence France succeeded Spain as the most dangerous European power, against which the struggle for the New World and India had ultimately to be waged. From the Interregnum, commercial interests acquired a primacy in the formation of foreign policy, which they were to retain.

FINANCE

This grandiose foreign policy cost money. It has been calculated that during the Interregnum over £80 million was raised in England—an average of over £4 million a year. To pay for the Civil War Parliament imposed new taxes, notably the assessment and excise. The former was a land and property tax modelled on Ship Money, and levied on the ' true yearly value of rents, annuities and offices '. It was introduced on the initiative of the City radicals in 1643. Hitherto the main burden of taxation had fallen on merchants and the smaller men of property. Now for the first time the gentry were made to pay a substantial proportion. One landed family was paying a quarter of its income in taxation between 1643 and 1646, one-eighth in the sixteen-fifties.[1] At the same time the excise taxed the poor. It could be regarded as a rationalised and more efficient substitute for monopolies (in their fiscal aspect) since it fell mainly on articles of popular consumption— beer, meat, salt, starch, soap, paper.

The revolutionary decades thus marked a turning-point in taxation. The changes worked to the advantage of the middling men, merchants and industrialists, and to the dis- advantage of the landed and landless classes. This heavy taxation came on top of requisitioning and free quarter, which hit the rich, and of conscription, which hit the very poor. Combined with state contracts, loans, and grants for the more fortunate among the well-to-do Parliamentarians, and with the profits made from money-lending and land speculation, the system of taxation helped to widen the gap between rich and poor, and to exacerbate relations between landed and moneyed men. In addition to the land sales, which only accelerated a process continuous throughout the century, plate was melted down, lead stripped from houses, timber from estates. The Puritans, Cowley wrote in 1643, ' turn the kingdom's gold to iron and steel '. Assets hitherto frozen were made available for productive investment. Davenant thought the years from 1630 to 1660 were those in which English stock increased most rapidly in the seventeenth century. This transfer and concen-

[1] H. J. Habakkuk, ' English Landownership, 1680–1740 ', *Econ. H.R.*, **10**, 8–9

tration of wealth by the use of state power has never been properly studied ; it may prove to have been a leap forward parallel to that in agriculture resulting from the availability of new land for cultivation. Again the beneficiaries were the moneyed men.

Land sales helped to pay for the Dutch war. But after confiscated lands had been sold, governments continued to spend each year some four times as much as had been thought intolerable under Charles I. Far better value for money was given to the taxpayer than under the monarchy. Nevertheless, no Parliament could be found which would vote the sums required. For much of the expenditure went to maintain the unpopular Army. So each Parliament under the Protectorate tried to reduce military expenditure, and to establish the principle that all taxation must be voted by representatives of those who paid it. Perhaps the most significant words in the Petition and Advice were those in Clause 7 concerning the revenue : ' No part thereof to be raised by a land tax.' For the land tax, the assessment, paid for the Army ; excise and customs between them brought in less than £1 million, which did not cover other government expenditure.

In view of the grudging attitude of the taxpaying classes, the government could raise only short-term loans. The Protectorate could never establish a funded National Debt, that is, one which the lenders would regard as a permanent interest-bearing investment. Charles I's government had been brought down when simultaneous invasion from Scotland and tax strike in England forced the summons of a Parliament. In a similar manner the Commonwealth collapsed in face of Monck's army, the only disciplined and paid force in the country, combined with a refusal to pay taxes. In each case the invading force from the north allowed the overwhelming combined strength of the City of London and the gentry to establish their natural supremacy. (Monck's army was paid because a Scottish assembly had voted him £50,000 in November 1659, which saw him through till February, the date at which he came to terms with the City.) After that, he could no more have dictated a settlement than the Scots could have done in 1640. He was too sensible to try ; he took a dukedom instead.

10   Religion and Ideas, 1640-60

Mansoul, it was the very seat of war.

Bunyan, *The Holy War*

Till about the year 1649 'twas held a strange presumption for a man to attempt an innovation in learning.

Aubrey, *Natural History of Wiltshire*

If in time as in place there were degrees of high and low, I verily believe the highest of time would be that which passed betwixt 1640 and 1660.

Thomas Hobbes

THE STATE CHURCH

IN SEPTEMBER 1641 the House of Commons voted, ' It shall be lawful for the parishioners of any parish . . . to set up a lecture, and to maintain an orthodox minister at their own charge to preach every Lord's Day where there is no preaching, and to preach one day in every week where there is no weekly lecture.' This was a double-edged weapon, intended partly to allow parishioners to force lecturers of their own choosing on Laudian or ' dumb dog ' incumbents ; partly to steal the thunder of the unauthorised ' mechanick preachers ' who were collecting congregations outside the parish churches. Numbers of parishes took advantage of the order, often after keen struggles, in which the House of Commons intervened to insist that ministers must allow free use of their pulpits to lecturers. ' Furious promoters of the most dangerous innovations ', Charles I called lecturers ; their prayers and sermons ' stir up and continue the rebellion raised against me '. Lecturers and ministers frequently acted as recruiting agents and propagandists. In August 1643 the House of Commons ordered ' divers godly ministers ' to go ' into divers counties . . . to possess the people with the truth and justice of the Parliament's cause in taking up of defensive arms '. Meanwhile the Commons ejected numbers of ' scandalous ministers ', many for reasons which made them scandalous in the modern sense, but others because of their political attitude. Ejected clergy were allowed one-fifth of the parochial revenue, at the expense of their successors. As the Parliamentary armies advanced, so the purge advanced with them ; until finally, under the Committees for the Propagation of the Gospel in Wales and the North Parts, groups of itinerant ministers were set up to carry the Puritan gospel into the hitherto ' dark corners ' of the land. So the state took over the task which the Feoffees for Impropriations had begun twenty-five years earlier. Church building, neglected for a century and a half, was resumed in the fifties—especially in the north and west—at government expense.

The other aspect of the Feoffees' work, augmentation of livings, was also resumed on a vastly expanded scale. Bishops' lands were sold under an ordinance of 1646, Dean and Chapter lands in 1649. The original Puritan hope of devoting the whole of the proceeds to the promotion of religion and learning was not realised : the demands of the Army were too great. Nevertheless, over £30,000 a year from Dean and Chapter lands went to augment stipends of ministers and schoolmasters. More important, Royalists were allowed to redeem part of their fine by settling impropriated tithes (if they owned any) on the vicar of the parish. From these two sources, and much greater sums from municipal and private generosity, a large number of the English clergy must have enjoyed far more substantial incomes than before 1640 or after 1660.

Before 1640 there had been considerable resentment at the Laudian attempt to increase tithe payments. Now the whole principle of tithes was challenged. The minister should depend on the voluntary contributions of his parishioners, it was claimed : otherwise he was a ' hireling '. If voluntary contributions were not sufficient, why should the minister not work like anyone else ? The Reformation doctrine of the priesthood of all believers would be carried to its logical conclusion by the abolition of a privileged caste of clergy.

These arguments carried vast political and economic consequences. If tithes were not paid to ministers, then they would not be paid to lay impropriators either. Would these

lay owners receive compensation, and if so at whose expense?
Or would they merely be expropriated? Few of the propertied
class regarded either proposal with anything but alarm. An
established church stood or fell with tithes. Election and
payment of ministers by congregations would mean the end of
any nationally controlled and disciplined church. It would
make anything but complete religious toleration virtually
impossible. The reasons for preserving a national church
were social as well as religious. Thus in 1650 Alderman
Violet, in a report to a Parliamentary committee on the decay
of trade, proposed as remedies, ' First, to settle able and godly
ministers in all churches throughout the nation, that will teach
the people to fear God, to obey their superiors, and to live
peaceably with each other, with a competent subsistence for
all such ministers.' The social function of religion was not
often so frankly expressed, but many men undoubtedly agreed
with Alderman Violet. Abolition of a state Church would be
an act of expropriation. Many thousands of gentlemen enjoyed
rights of patronage to livings, for which they or their ancestors
had paid hard cash. They did not wish to lose the right to
appoint to these livings their younger sons, brothers, tutors,
chaplains, or other dependants; nor to be deprived at the same
stroke of the squire's faithful ally, the parson. Sir William
Strickland spoke for many impropriators when he said in
Parliament in June 1657, ' The same levelling principle will
lay waste properties and deny rents, upon the same account
that they do tithes.' Tithes, a pamphlet said in 1641, were
paid especially by ' the meanest and poorest people '; ' the
richest citizen in London hardly paying so much as a country-
man that hath but £20 or £10 a year in his occupation '.
Opponents of tithes came from the middling and poorer sort;
the rich suffered comparatively little, and might even be
recipients of tithes. These are some of the reasons why the
question of tithes aroused the deepest passions and proved the
most bitter of all the issues which divided radical from conservative Parliamentarians.

The threat to tithes must have seemed very real. They
were opposed not only by Levellers, the Barebones Parliament,
and the more radical sects, but also, and insistently, by a
respectable civil servant like Milton, by the Lieutenant-General

in Ireland, Edmund Ludlow, and by very many in the Army.
Cromwell himself was alleged to have promised at Dunbar
that if God gave him the victory he would abolish tithes.
Tithes survived ; but ministers abandoned the claim to
collect them by divine right. The law of the land was a safer
plea. One reason for the survival of tithes was the view,
accepted by all parties, that very few ministers would be
maintained by voluntary contributions if legal compulsion was
removed. 'The minister,' wrote Blyth in 1652, 'might go
barefoot, and his family a-begging, for what the common
people would contribute to his subsistence.' We must remember
remarks like this (and many could be quoted) whenever we
are tempted to think that the seventeenth century was ' a more
religious age ' than the present.

PRESBYTERIANS, INDEPENDENTS, AND SECTARIES

Historians these days are cautious about the labels ' Presbyterian ' and ' Independent '. In November 1641, after
sitting a year in the House of Commons, Sir Edward Dering
said, ' I have not yet heard any one gentleman within these
walls stand up and assert his thought here for either of these
ways [Presbyterian or Independent].' Many ' Independent '
members became elders when Presbyterianism was the established Church ; many who voted for a Presbyterian establishment in 1646 were moderate Episcopalians or conservative
Erastians, choosing the lesser evil. Haslerig, one of the
' Independent ' leaders, was, in Clarendon's words, ' as to
religion perfectly Presbyterian '. In political usage, ' Presbyterian ' meant conservative Parliamentarian, ' Independent '
one who favoured religious toleration. Or, as an anonymous
Royalist pamphleteer put it, ' He that would rightly understand them must read for Presbytery, aristocracy ; and
democracy, for Independency.'

The Presbyterian establishment was virtually still-born.
By the time it reached the statute book (1646) power was
passing to the ' Independent ' Army. Only in London and
Lancashire was there much support from below for the Presbyterian system. Parliament had been careful to insist on its
own absolute control of the Church centrally, and had nominated

the ruling elders who were to function locally. When the Assembly of Divines proclaimed that ministers and elders held their power from Jesus Christ, the House of Commons was quick to point out that, on the contrary, they held it from Parliament. *Jure divino* doctrines were as unwelcome in new presbyter as they had been in Archbishop Laud. There was little danger here of ' a Pope in every parish '. The ' Independents ' also favoured a state Church, but with very loosely defined doctrine, with tithes maintained or replaced by some certain form of maintenance for ministers, and with toleration of law-abiding sects. Religious toleration, which has come to be thought of as the hall-mark of ' Independency ', was forced upon the ' Independent ' members of Parliament by political necessity. The Independent churches in New England were very far from tolerant. But the sects included the most radical and determined opponents of King and Bishops. Cromwell found that toleration (for those with ' the root of the matter ' in them) created the best possible fighting morale ; the members of Parliament who forced through the Self-Denying Ordinance and the New Model Army needed the political support of the sectaries.

For conservatives, religious toleration was anathema. It meant that the lower orders could collect together and discuss whatever they liked, with no control from above at all. Professor Notestein has suggested that the sectaries brought Christianity to some of the poorer classes who had previously never gone to church ; but their main influence was among the urban lower middle class. Edward's *Gangraena*, published in 1646, is a hysterical but reasonably accurate denunciation of the errors of the sectaries. Many of the heresies he pilloried are as political as ' Further error No. 52—By natural birth all men are equally and alike born to like property, liberty and freedom.' The idea of a single state Church was so deeply embedded in most men's thought that freedom to choose one's religion seemed in itself subversive. All respectable citizens knew that it was the duty of heads of households to bring up their servants in sound religious principles. But if apprentices and journeymen might go to a different church from their masters, who knew what nonsensical notions they might not hear, or even preach ? There could be no good order under such a system. Most sects elected their own ministers and discussed church business in a democratic manner; they formed schools of self-government. The theological starting-point of, say, the Baptists, was subversive of a state Church. For adult baptism meant that each individual, when he reached the years of discretion, decided for himself what Church he would belong to. It denied that every child born in England automatically became a member of the Church of England. So no Baptist could logically pay tithes voluntarily. In general the sects seem especially to have appealed to women, to whom some of them gave equal rights. Again this seemed to conservatives subversive of natural subordination, and productive of nothing but family strife. Women gained immeasurably in status during this period, thanks not only to the greater equality they enjoyed in sectarian congregations but also to economic activities forced on them by the absence of husbands on military service or in exile.

There was a lunatic fringe of self-appointed Messiahs, like Lodowick Muggleton, who damned his rivals with cheerful gusto, and John Robins, who believed he was God Almighty and proposed to lead 144,000 men to reconquer the Holy Land. There were Ranters, some of whom believed that God's grace had made them incapable of sin, and acted upon that belief. But there were also very many who described themselves as Seekers, who tried all Churches and were satisfied with none, men like the Leveller William Walwyn who specialised in Socratic questioning. Seekers and Ranters were not very numerous outside London and the Army, but they seemed to prove the point so laboured by conservatives, that toleration could only lead to scepticism, atheism, and debauchery. Calvinist theology taught that the mass of mankind was sinful : unless preached at and disciplined by their betters they were bound to go astray. Democracy must lead to heresy. ' That the major vote of the people should ordinarily be just and good is next to an impossibility,' wrote Richard Baxter in 1659. ' All this stir of the Republicans is but to make the seed of the Serpent to be the sovereign rulers of the earth.' The greatest heresy of all was that Christ died for all men, that all had a spark of the divine in them, and so, that all men were equal. The Quakers were more interested in religion than in politics ;

but any Justice of the Peace or member of Parliament could
see that to say ' thou ' to social superiors, to refuse to remove
one's hat to constituted authority was neither *merely* religious
nor a harmless eccentricity in the explosive political atmosphere
of the sixteen-fifties. ' His tenets are dangerous,' a major
wrote of another rank in 1657, ' maintaining perfection in this
life.' [1] Pacifism and abstention from politics became dominant
in the Quaker movement only after 1660.

The most obviously political religious group was that of the
Fifth Monarchists, who believed that the reign of Christ upon
earth was shortly to begin. This view was held by many
respectable Independent divines, who drew no directly political
conclusions. But for less-educated laymen, under the economic
stress of the revolutionary decades, especially after the defeat
of the Levellers and the dissolution of the Barebones Parliament, Fifth Monarchy became a desperately held hope. Only
Christ's second coming could achieve what political action
had failed to win. The duty of the elect was to eliminate
hindrances to Christ's rule on earth. This often, in political
terms, became ' overturn, overturn, overturn ', a doctrine of
political anarchism. The existing state and its rulers were bad
and must be rejected. In December 1653 Vavasor Powell
told his congregation to go home and pray, ' Lord, wilt thou
have Oliver Cromwell or Jesus Christ to reign over us ? ' In
1657 and 1661 Fifth Monarchist risings, headed by the wine
cooper Thomas Venner, threatened to overthrow the government. The sense of the imminence of a new spiritual epoch,
in which God's people should be free in a new way, was one
of the many Fifth Monarchist concepts which the Quakers
took over.

Not all Puritans expected the millennium in the immediate
future. But the essence of Puritanism as a revolutionary
creed lay in the belief that God intended the betterment of
man's life on earth, that men could understand God's purposes
and co-operate with Him to bring them to fruition. So men's
innermost wishes, if strongly enough felt, could be believed
to be God's will. By a natural dialectic, those who were most
convinced that they were fighting God's battles proved the
most effective fighters : because they trusted God they took

[1] *Thurloe State Papers*, vi, 162

the very greatest care to keep their powder dry, and were ready to accept a discipline that was effective because self-imposed.

'The godly being in league with God,' wrote the Puritan Thomas Gataker in all simplicity in 1626, 'may have all his forces and armies for their help and assistance, whensoever need shall be.' 'Our duty,' wrote Hugh Peter twenty years later, 'will be only to look to the duty which is ours, and leave events to God, which are his.' [1] 'We cannot limit God to this or that,' Ireton admitted, 'but certainly if we take the most probable way according to the light we have, God gives those things' their success. So men followed their consciences, with grim conviction. Many men agreed that it was their conscientious duty to oppose Charles I and Bishops : and this agreement increased their confidence that their cause was God's. But 'liberty hath a sharp and double edge, fit only to be handled by just and virtuous men', said Milton. 'The Providences of God are like a two-edged sword, which may be used both ways,' a member of Parliament agreed in 1654. After victory agreement among the godly ceased. 'All [God's] communications are reasonable and just,' said the Leveller Overton ; but these communications seemed different to rich and poor. The riot of conflicting sects is the measure of this tendency of the Protestant emphasis on the individual conscience to degenerate into anarchy.

There is another paradoxical element in the Puritan moral compulsion. Men fought for God's cause, and expected it to prevail because it was God's. This confidence helped to bring victory, and victory reinforced the conviction that the cause was indeed His. The humbler the agents of divine Providence, the more manifest God's favour in their success. The democratic implications of this are clear. But the doctrine could turn into one of justification by success : Cromwell and Milton came near to this at times. As divisions set in, not all were equally successful ; as the divisions increased, ultimately the whole cause fell in ruins. So first the radicals, and then all the Puritans, had to ask themselves whether justification by success also meant condemnation by defeat. After the failure

[1] T. Gataker, *Certaine Sermons*, p. 33 ; H. Peter, *Gods Doings and Mans Duty* (1645), p. 6

of the Levellers, the radical sects in their desperation first became wilder and more millenarian (Fifth Monarchists, early Quakers) and then gradually concluded that Christ's kingdom was not of this world.

After 1660 the quietist, pacifist tendency increased as Puritanism turned into nonconformity. The collapse of all his hopes forced Milton to wrestle with God in the attempt to justify His ways to man. The products of this anguish were *Paradise Lost* and *Samson Agonistes*. The former, emphasising God's justice in spite of everything, appears to end on a note of quietism and resignation : ' A Paradise within thee, happier far ' was a moral, not a political aim. But *Samson Agonistes*, with its emphasis on man's integrity, shouts defiance in God's face for deserting His people, and ends in reconciliation only after God has aided Samson to avenge the oppressed on the Philistines. ' Calm of mind, all passion spent ' is attained only after we have envisaged God's (and Milton's) cause as an undying Phoenix.

TOLERATION OR DISCIPLINE?

Most Puritan ministers had adopted the traditional view that God's elect were a minority, and the mass of men predestined to eternal damnation. A coercive state existed to keep the reprobate in subjection. But in order to encourage their congregations and save them from despair, they had also taught that anyone who seriously worried about his salvation probably already had sparks of divine grace at work in him. It was a short but momentous step—and to Calvinist ministers a monstrous step—to proclaim that all men were equally eligible to receive divine grace. Walwyn and Winstanley, like Bacon, thought the Fall of Man retrievable on earth by man's efforts to master his fate : the conclusion of *Paradise Lost* suggests that man could rise to greater heights here than Adam before the Fall. Men of property had hitherto tacitly assumed that the laws which restrained the ungodly had been drafted by godly men, and were administered by godly men. But the Levellers and Diggers thought the corruption of fallen man was equally obvious in the old ruling classes and in those who replaced them during the Civil War. A wider suffrage, annual elections, and the unchangeable 'fundamentals' of the Agreement of the People were designed to preserve rulers from the tendency of power to corrupt.

Far-reaching consequences followed. If there is a spark of the divine in all men, preaching should not be a clerical monopoly. No spoken or printed word should be suppressed, lest God's truth be lost. If all men were equal before Christ, should they not also be equal before the law? Should they not have the vote? Parliament had appealed to public opinion by the Grand Remonstrance in 1641; the Independent dissenting brethren in the Westminster Assembly had used the press to appeal to Parliament and public in 1644; three years later the Levellers appealed from 'the degenerate representative body, the Commons of England . . . to the body represented, the free people'. Where was this to stop? Was toleration to extend ' to debar any kind of restraint on anything that any will call religion?' Ireton asked. If not—who was to decide where the lines were to be drawn?

The power of the Church had broken down with the abolition of the High Commission. Church lands were taxed in the same way as lay property; Church courts ceased to function. In 1650 compulsory attendance at one's parish church was legally abolished, provided one attended at some place of worship. The proviso was unenforceable. This recognised a major achievement : liberation of the common man from parson and squire. It marked a quite new type of freedom for those hitherto unaccustomed to freedom of any sort. It was too good to last.

Religious toleration, then, posed in a new form the problem of discipline. The Presbyterians and their supporters had not abolished Church courts in order to set natural men free to follow their sinful impulses, but in order to submit them to a more effective control. Yet the Presbyterian disciplinary system was never effective. Cromwell's state Church had a system of Triers and Ejectors of ministers, who, Baxter said, ' saved many a congregation from ignorant, ungodly, drunken teachers'. But it had no discipline, no courts. A horrid vacuum remained. There was grave danger that the lower orders might be able to do what they liked, within the limits of the common law. When Bishops had been closely connected with the government in Laud's time, the hierarchy of Church courts had acted as a link between central and local government. The Major-Generals restored such a link, attempted to fill the vacuum, to re-establish some standards of conduct. We should not exaggerate this part of their activities : they were far more often concerned with security than godliness when they prohibited race-meetings or cock-fightings at which Cavaliers might foregather, or when they closed disorderly ale-houses. When they enforced, for example, Sabbath observance they were only putting into effect Parliamentary legislation of the sixteen-twenties which Stuart governments had ignored. The idea that they imposed gloomy godliness on a merrie nation is a post-Restoration myth.

But there was a vacuum. In the sixteen-fifties groups of ministers got together to build up a Presbyterian system from below, within the framework of the Cromwellian state Church. We know from Baxter, the moving spirit in Worcestershire, that their main motive was concern about the behaviour of the lower orders. But a disciplinary system without state power behind it was about as effective as voluntary main-tenance of ministers. Here is one powerful reason why con-servatives supported the restoration of episcopacy in 1660. Bunyan learnt from Justices of the Peace and judges in 1660 that for them the Restoration meant that tinkers and other mechanic laymen should return to their callings and leave divinity to the clergy. In 1640 Baxter had wanted episcopacy to be abolished. But in April 1660 he told the House of Commons, ' The question is not, whether Bishops or no, but whether discipline or none.' He was not alone in this view. Throughout this period the Commons always opposed tolera-tion fiercely. When the Quaker James Nayler symbolically rode into Bristol in 1656 with women strewing palms before him, Parliament imposed savage penalties on him. Not only Nayler, not only the Quakers, but toleration itself (and the Major-Generals themselves) was on trial. The episode was an essential preliminary to the restriction of toleration and restoration of Parliamentary monarchy by the Petition and Advice.

The tolerance of even a Cromwell or a Milton did not extend to Papists. For this the reasons were largely political.

Papists were regarded as agents of a foreign power. They had solidly supported Charles in the Civil War, and after the capture of the King's papers at Naseby he was known to have planned Irish intervention on a large scale. This helps to explain, though not to excuse, the Commonwealth's savagely repressive policy in Ireland, which only Levellers opposed. Hostility to Papists was not a monopoly of the Puritans. In 1640 a group of condemned men in Newgate gaol had conscientious scruples about being hanged unless seven condemned priests whom the King was trying to save were hanged with them.[1] The Parliamentarians also refused toleration to 'Prelatists', for similar political reasons. The vast majority of ministers accepted the ecclesiastical changes and retained their livings throughout the forties and fifties : the small minority of Laudian clergy formed one of the main Royalist resistance groups. The future Bishop Jeremy Taylor wrote a moving plea for toleration in 1647 ; but this doctrine was not acted upon when the Anglican hierarchy was restored in 1660.

POLITICAL IDEAS

The influence of the radical Protestant tradition spread far beyond circles which could in any doctrinal sense be called Puritan. An appeal to Scripture or to conscience could be used to call any authority in question. 'Every man, nay, every boy and wench that could read English,' wrote Hobbes, 'thought they spoke with God Almighty, and understood what he said, when by a certain number of chapters a day they had read the Scriptures once or twice over. . . . This licence of interpreting the Scripture was the cause of so many several sects as have lain hid till the beginning of the late King's [Charles I's] reign, and did then appear to the disturbance of the commonwealth.' The Bible could be put to endless destructive use. Its text was inspired ; it contained all that was necessary to salvation ; therefore anything not specifically mentioned in it was at best indifferent, at worst sinful. The Presbyterians found no Bishops in the Bible. Milton wrote, 'Let them chant while they will of prerogatives, we shall tell them of Scripture ; of custom, we of

[1] C. V. Wedgwood, *The King's War* (1958), p. 44

Scripture ; of acts and statutes, still of Scripture.' Colonel Rainborough remarked at Putney, 'I do not find anything in the Law of God, that a lord shall choose twenty burgesses, and a gentleman but two, or a poor man shall choose none.' Therefore, he concluded, God wanted an extension of the franchise. It was in the Bible that Milton found the arguments which led him to justify the execution of Charles I.

Conservatives did not fail to point out that there was no real distinction between the appeal to Scripture and the appeal to conscience. The Bible is a large book, in which men can find a text to prove whatever they want to prove. After the censorship was lifted in the sixteen-forties, lower-class Englishmen discovered in the Bible and in their consciences things which appalled university-trained divines. The censorship collapsed with the hierarchy. The years after 1641 were unique in that they saw cheap newspapers published of every political colour. In 1645 there were 722 of them. There was also a fantastic outpouring of pamphlets on every subject under the sun, at an average rate of three a day for the twenty years, though much faster between 1642 and 1649.[1] Milton saw here a sign of national revival ; abolition of thought-control would liberate men's energies and lead to a great intellectual leap forward. 'A nation not slow and dull, but of a quick, ingenious and piercing spirit, acute to invent, subtle and sinewy to discourse, not beneath the reach of any point the highest that human capacity can soar to. . . . Methinks I see in my mind a noble and puissant nation rousing herself like a strong man after sleep and shaking his invincible locks.' The censorship was restored only with great difficulty in the sixteen-fifties.

The Interregnum saw a great advance in political thinking. The idea of rule by majority gained ground. Before 1640, though votes were taken in the Commons, the House had always wished to speak to the outside world with a single voice. Swords were drawn in the House over printing the Grand Remonstrance because even the pretence of unanimity was being abandoned, and the majority was forcing its will upon the minority. Laud's protégé William Chillingworth was sent to the Tower for 'reporting we had sides and parts

[1] F. S. Siebert, *Freedom of the Press in England, 1476–1776* (1952), pp. 191, 203

in the House, which was but one body, so to set a division amongst us '. But as Parliament became an effective sovereign assembly, majority decision was a necessary means of settling disagreements. Divisions on party lines in the sixteen-forties foreshadowed the rise of a party system a generation later. Majority government, like religious toleration and Hobbes's political theory, recognises that society is a group of atoms : it abandons the fiction of a one-minded community.

The doctrine of the sovereignty of Parliament (even without the King) emerged only after civil war had begun. Parliament told the Earl of Essex that he was commanding its armies in order ' to secure His Majesty's person . . . out of the hands of those desperate persons ' who had somehow kidnapped him. This claim infuriated Charles, who knew that he had not been kidnapped : but it perhaps symbolically recognises the fact that more than personal issues were at stake. Only a desperate revolutionary like Oliver Cromwell declared that if he met the King on the battlefield he would shoot him like anyone else. But as the war proceeded, political thinkers like Prynne, Hunton, Parker, slowly worked out a theory of Parliamentary sovereignty. If men were to be asked to fight and die in the struggle against the King, they must have a respectable rival authority. They fought, of course, for religion ; but they were also urged to fight for King and Parliament, or even for Parliament alone. Thomas Hobbes had published his first political writings between the meeting of the Long Parliament and the outbreak of civil war ; and they clearly found attentive readers. When in 1651 he published in English the final formulation of his theory of sovereignty, *Leviathan*, political events had predisposed men to accept it. Sovereignty, said Hobbes, must be absolute and unlimited. The sovereign may be a man or a body of men, his right may be derived from remote antiquity or recent conquest ; all that matters is that he can protect his subjects and that his authority is generally recognised. Hobbes followed the logic of his own theory by returning from exile and accepting the authority of the Commonwealth. By 1653 the republican Albertus Warren could state as a matter of course, ' The question never was whether we should be governed by arbitrary power, but in whose hands it should be.'

Sovereignty and political obligation were based on expediency.
Divine Right was dead.

During the Civil War men naturally asked from what
Parliament's authority was derived. The easy answer was,
' Parliament represents the people of England '. But it was
too easy. The Royalist Sir Robert Filmer had great fun
demonstrating that the House of Commons was elected by
less than one-tenth of the people of England. But on the
opposite wing the Levellers suggested that Parliament should
be made representative of all the free people, and of all who
had fought for it. So sovereignty of Parliament led to the
proclamation of the sovereignty of the people. The Levellers
who proclaimed it were suppressed ; but the idea had come
to stay. As we have seen, the Levellers excluded paupers and
wage labourers from ' the free people ', on the ground that their
economic dependence precluded political independence. This
view had something to be said for it, given a largely illiterate
population, which perforce took its political ideas from parson
and squire, and given open voting by show of hands. Nevertheless, the fact that the most radical political party even
of the revolutionary decades excluded over half the male
population (and all women) from political life tells us much
about seventeenth-century English society. In normal usage,
' the people ' did not include the poor.

A parallel development can be traced in attitudes towards
the law. Coke, Pym, and other Parliamentary leaders had
taught that English law was the foundation of English liberty,
and that its origins, like those of Parliament, went back to
Anglo-Saxon times. After the Norman Conquest bad kings
had tried to override the law and representative institutions :
Englishmen had fought back on behalf of their liberties, and
had obtained their confirmation in Magna Carta and other
constitutional documents. The theory had been useful in the
struggle for independence of judges from the crown, and
for supremacy of common law and Parliament over the
prerogative and its courts. It became an orthodoxy, which
underlay Parliament's reliance on historical and legal precedents in its struggle against James and Charles. The wisdom
of our ancestors had established a perfectly balanced constitution, from which practice might deviate, but which could be

ascertained and restored. The legislation of 1641 was designed to free Parliament and common law from recent Stuart encroachments ; so liberty would be secured for all time.

The complexities of seventeenth-century legal procedure meant that ' an amount of injustice frightful to think of must have been inflicted . . . on obscure persons of whom no-one has ever heard '.[1] For Levellers and Diggers the ' Norman Yoke ' was not just the arbitrary rule of kings. William the Conqueror had had the laws written in French so that ' the poor miserable people might be gulled and cheated, undone and destroyed '. The proceedings of the law courts were still ' locked up from common capacities in the Latin or French tongues '. At the Reformation the Bible had been translated into English, and priests cast down from their seats of power. Now the radicals demanded that all legal proceedings should be in English, and that legal reforms should be introduced to oust the lawyers who imposed an expensive and incomprehensible ritual between ordinary people and justice. Between 1651 and 1660 all courts recorded their proceedings in English ; French and Latin returned with Charles II.

The Levellers and Diggers went further. ' Our very laws were made by our conquerors,' complained Wildman at Putney. The ' main stream of the common law ' was corrupt, Lilburne thought. Even Magna Carta was ' but a beggarly thing, containing many marks of intolerable bondage '. ' The laws of kings,' wrote Winstanley, ' have always been made against such acts as the common people were most inclinable to.' ' The best laws that England hath are yokes and manacles, tying one sort of people to be slaves to another.' And he asked whether ' all laws that are not grounded upon equity and reason, not giving a universal freedom to all, but respecting persons, ought not to be cut off with the King's head ? '

So the extreme radicals saw the law as the enemy, just as the men of property saw in it their protection. The extremists' attack on the law helps to explain the failure of more moderate (and very necessary) schemes for law reform, such as were put forward in many pamphlets and seriously discussed in the

---

[1] Sir J. F. Stephen, *History of Criminal Law in England* (1883), i, 402. For other quotations in this and the following paragraph, see my *Puritanism and Revolution*, pp. 67–87.

Rump and Barebones Parliaments. Some reform there was, in addition to the use of English in courts and law books. Judicial torture apparently ceased after 1640. Judges held office during good behaviour. Real equality before the law was established. The 'High Court of Chivalry', which used to punish those who uttered 'scandalous words' against a gentleman, was abolished. (In 1640 a tailor, who had said he was as good a man as the gentleman who refused to pay his bill, was fined an amount equivalent to what his customer owed him. The Court of Chivalry was restored in 1660, but lost its jurisdiction over such 'scandalous words'.) In the Commonwealth's High Courts of Justice, Clarendon complained, 'the greatest lord and the meanest peasant undergo the same judicatory and form of trial'. Modernisation of the law of debt and contract was proposed in the Barebones Parliament; and also that pickpockets should not be executed for the first offence; that provocation to duels should be punishable; that husband murderers should not be burned; that those who refused to plead should no longer be pressed to death; that justifiable homicides should be acquitted; that persons acquitted should pay no fees. But the lawyers successfully defeated all movements for reform, and also the proposal that English law should be codified on the Dutch model. No 'Code Cromwell' emerged from the English Revolution. In the fifties the radicals came to see 'the corrupt interests of the lawyers and the clergy' as their main enemies, law reform and the abolition of tithes and patronage as the main desiderata. Conservatives rallied to defend the state Church and the law which protected their property, just as the lawyers rallied to defend the legal forms which they had laboriously mastered and knew how to exploit. In so far as the common law was modified, this was done by acceptance of the authority of Coke's writings, and by precedents gradually built up in successive judicial decisions.

The Levellers appealed to Anglo-Saxon against seventeenth-century practice. At Putney they were challenged on their history, and gradually they abandoned the claim to be merely re-asserting Anglo-Saxon liberties. Instead they demanded the inalienable rights of man. 'Whatever our forefathers were, or whatever they did or suffered, or were enforced to yield unto, we are the men of the present age, and ought to be absolutely free from all kinds of exorbitancies, molestations or arbitrary power.' So precedents were thrown overboard : ' reason hath no precedent, for reason is the fountain of all just precedents '. (James I, wisely, had said in 1621, ' Reason is too large. Find me a precedent and I will accept it.') Bogus history was abandoned for political theory based on natural rights : it is a momentous transference.

THE VICTORY OF SCIENCE

In this intoxicating era of free discussion and free speculation nothing was left sacred. ' Why should not that pewter pot on the table be God ? ' we hear one drunken trooper asking. Heaven and hell were declared to be states of mind, not places. The immortality of the soul was questioned. The collapse of the censorship allowed matters to be publicly discussed which had rarely appeared in print before. Hitherto unpublishable memoirs exposed the scandals of Stuart courts. Milton defended divorce and regicide, and attacked all forms of censorship. Francis Osborn wrote sympathetically of Mohammedanism. Hobbes criticised the attribution of the authorship of books of the Bible, the belief in miracles. It is not so very much later that Vanbrugh's Lady Brute, when confronted with the Biblical adjuration to love our enemies, blandly replied, ' That may be a fault in the translation.' The conflicts and controversies, the infinite variety of opinions expressed, ultimately produced a historical scepticism.

In this atmosphere Baconian science came into its own. Harvey's discovery of the circulation of the blood, though published in 1628, obtained no prominence until after 1640. The two sides in the Civil War, Miss Nicolson tells us, correspond to the two camps in astronomy. But by the sixteen-fifties the ideas of Ptolemy were dead, though those of Copernicus and Tycho Brahe still strove for the succession.[1] ' The late times of civil war,' wrote Bishop Sprat later, ' . . . brought this advantage with them, that they stirred up men's minds from long ease, . . . and made them active, industrious and

[1] M. Nicolson, ' English Almanacs and the " New Learning " ', *Annals of Science*, iv

inquisitive.' This led to 'an universal desire and appetite after knowledge '. Royalists were purged from Oxford, and a group of Baconians, the nucleus of the later Royal Society, moved into the university behind the Parliamentary armies. Wilkins, Cromwell's brother-in-law, became Warden of Wadham; Goddard, Cromwell's physician, Warden of Merton; Wallis, who had decoded Royalist cyphers during the Civil War, Professor of Geometry; Petty, Commonwealth surveyor of Ireland, Professor of Anatomy. For the first time in its history (and the last until very recent years) Oxford became a leading centre of scientific activity. These scholars, who valued ' no knowledge but as it hath a tendency to use ', attracted to Oxford men later to become famous, like Christopher Wren, Thomas Sydenham, Thomas Sprat, Robert Boyle, Robert Hooke, John Locke. Even Clarendon had to admit that revolutionary Oxford ' yielded a harvest of extraordinary good and sound knowledge in all parts of learning '.

From 1650 ' self-conscious science began to determine the main direction of technology '.[1] Robert Boyle disposed of the medieval theories of the alchemists, and founded the modern science of chemistry. Whereas before 1640 Bacon's had been a voice crying in the wilderness, by 1660 his was the dominant intellectual influence. To this, given freedom of discussion, Puritanism had continued to contribute. The quest for personal religious *experience*, to which so many Puritan diaries and spiritual autobiographies are dedicated, is closely akin to the experimental spirit in science. Many, like the Leveller Walwyn or the Digger Winstanley, who were Seekers in religion, extended their inquiries into every sphere of human existence. The radicals' abandonment of the dogma of human sinfulness contributed to the Baconian hope of pushing forward the frontiers of learning, to turn men's faces to the future. The Puritans' schemes for applying the spoils of the Church to the advancement of learning (the Baconian phrase was regularly used) were never fully realised : nevertheless the universities were relieved of taxation, heads of Oxford and Cambridge colleges received augmentations to their stipends, new schools were founded.

Professor Jordan observes that 'in 1660 educational

[1] C. Singer, *Technology and History* (1952), pp. 6, 16

opportunities were more widespread and stronger than they had ever been before or were ever to be again until well into the nineteenth century '. The decades 1601–60 had been decisive in establishing these opportunities. By 1660, in the ten counties Professor Jordan studied, there was a school for every 4,400 of population, and few boys indeed lived more than a dozen miles from a grammar school which offered free education. This great educational expansion had been achieved with little positive encouragement from the monarchy. But the state's attitude changed during the revolutionary era. ' The first organised movement for a system of national education in Wales ' dates from the Commonwealth, when it was ' a state undertaking '. At least fifty-nine new schools were established there between 1651 and 1653.[1] Educational reformers like Dury, Hartlib, and Winstanley wanted to liberate schools from the tyranny of Greek and Latin, to make curricula more modern and utilitarian. A lively discussion anticipated many ideas which had to be painfully rediscovered later. Petty in 1648 applied the philosophy of the New Model Army to education, wishing none ' to be excluded by reason of the poverty and inability of their parents : for hereby it hath come to pass that many are now holding the plough that might have been made fit to steer the state '.

Discoveries in anatomy and astronomy killed traditional ideas that the head is ' nobler ' than the heart, the sun ' nobler ' than the moon, just at the same time as the political revolution killed the idea of hierarchy in law and politics. Yet problems remained. In a hierarchical society each man had his place, and was punished if he left it. How was a society of equal and competing atoms to be kept at peace ? The problem was first clearly stated by Hobbes, who had been Bacon's amanuensis, and saw himself as the Euclid of a new science of politics. ' Geometry is demonstrable, for the lines and figures from which we reason are drawn and described by ourselves ; and civil philosophy is demonstrable because we make the commonwealth ourselves.' God made the universe but man made the state : so politics was taken away from the theologians and became a matter of empirical investigation and rational

[1] Jordan, *Philanthropy in England*, pp. 48, 283–91, 385–7 ; W. A. L. Vincent, *State and Education under the Commonwealth* (1950), pp. 21, 135

discussion. In the debates on the Agreement of the People
the novel phrase ' to make a new constitution ' was actually
used ; and in practice constitutions were made in abun-
dance. It was impossible to return to the belief that every detail
of the established order had been ordained of God from the
beginning.

James Harrington, whose merchant brother became a
Fellow of the Royal Society, was also deeply influenced by the
scientific movement, and hoped to base a science of politics
on the study of history. From history, he thought, one could
derive laws relating to the behaviour of human beings in the
mass, and draw conclusions like that expressed in his theory
of the balance of property. When possession of political
power coincides with ownership of property, government is
' legitimately founded ' ; when this balance is upset, ' government . . . must of necessity be founded upon force, or a standing
army ', and cannot be stable. In England, he suggested, the
traditional balance between crown, aristocracy, and ' people '
had been altered by transfers of land from the first two to the
third ; this was the ultimate cause of the Civil War. The
war had then transferred political power to those who already
possessed economic power (whom Harrington calls ' the
people ', though he means the propertied commoners). This
transfer, he thought, could not be reversed ; even a restoration
of the monarchy would not be a restoration of the pre-1640
régime. Whatever we think of Harrington's explanation of the
Civil War, his is an impressive advance towards what we
may begin to call social science : a study of society based
on the Baconian method of observation, collection, and analysis
of facts, whose ultimate object is making generalisations which
can be applied in practice and so subjected to experimental
proof. Together with Petty, founder of the science of statistics,
Harrington may be claimed as one of the ancestors of Adam
Smith and the science of political economy.

THE ARTS

Bacon's philosophical belief that things are more important
than words, his suspicion of logical disputation which had no
counterpart in tangible reality, implied a theory of prose style :

it should be as concrete as possible. Trends in Puritanism worked in the same direction. The battles of the Civil War were prefigured in a rivalry of sermon styles. Bishop Lancelot Andrewes and his school preferred an elaborate, scholastic, learned, and highly ornate style ; the Puritans demanded plain sermons, addressed to the understanding not of scholars but of ordinary men. The object of the Puritan preachers was not to impress, not to delight, but to convince. In the revolutionary decades, political pamphleteers were writing for a new public, of insatiable curiosity, but lacking the intellectual and cultural standards, and the pedantry, of the select and secluded audience for Jacobean and Caroline prose. The pamphleteers' public was that for which hitherto the broadsheet and the ballad had sufficed, and their approach had the liveliness of this popular literature.

Both pulpit orators and political pamphleteers thus had to cultivate the virtues of clarity and directness, straightforwardness and simplicity. Their prose was functional rather than learned and allusive ; its object could no longer be fine writing for its own sake. Prose was shorn of its florid circumlocutions, and a direct, racy, sinuous, conversational style began to emerge. First the Bible in English, then the laws in English ; then prose in English. University education, as Defoe was to say, ruined English prose style by making men think in Latin ; the speech of ordinary men had to break through this academic barrier, and it did so during the Interregnum. In periods of civil war, Thomas Sprat observed in 1667, ' all languages ... increase by extraordinary degrees ; for in such busy active times there arise new thoughts of men, which must be signified and varied by new expressions '. So the English language during the Interregnum ' was enlarged by many sound and necessary forms and idioms which before it wanted '.[1] A great deal too much is made in some histories of literature of the ' purification ' of English prose style by ' French influences '. The *émigré* Royalist gentry may have learned in France how to write their own language with the elegant simplicity that we find in Restoration comedy. But they could have discovered how to write equally well if they had stayed at home with

[1] This point is elaborated by F. W. Bateson in *English Poetry : a Critical Introduction* (1950), chaps. 3 and 8.

Pepys and Dryden and Marvell and witnessed the incursion of ordinary speech into written prose.

An economic phenomenon adds to the significance of the Interregnum as a watershed in literary history. Before 1640, and to an almost equal extent after 1660, the hope of a budding author without means was to win the patronage of some aristocrat, to be taken into his household as tutor or chaplain, to be presented to a living, or at least to enjoy financial largesse in exchange for adulatory dedications. Except in the heyday of the popular theatre there was no living to be made by writing alone. Even Ben Jonson told Drummond of Hawthornden that poetry had beggared him ; far better to take up law, medicine, or commerce. But after 1642 many patrons found themselves in exile. The Cavendish family could no longer maintain Hobbes. Of those aristocrats who remained in England many were in financial difficulties. So the patron, although he by no means ceased to exist, no longer occupied the centre of the author's attention. ' Dedications,' Thomas Fuller noted in 1647, ' begin nowadays to go out of fashion.' But authors still had to live, and many Royalist writers had lost their independent means because of their political loyalty.

Two alternatives offered themselves. One was to earn a living as a literary free-lance—a possibility opened up by the easing of the censorship and the expansion of the literary market. Journalists like Marchamont Nedham and James Howell may have managed this. The profession of letters was only just beginning ; but it offered new prospects of freedom for the author who could hit the taste of the public. New forms of collective patronage were evolved. John Taylor the Water-Poet, finding in 1649 that ' too many masters made me masterless ', collected subscriptions in advance for his doggerel verse. Between 1644 and 1658 the Polyglot Bible appeared, the first serious book in England to be published by subscription. The second possibility was the more hopeful : to enter the public service, whose expansion was offering new opportunities to able men.

> The forward youth that would appear
> Must now forsake his Muses dear,
> Nor in the shadows sing
> His numbers languishing.

Marvell left a tutor's post to join the state service as assistant to Milton. Dryden was secretary to Cromwell's Chamberlain. George Wither held various posts under the Parliament. Edmund Waller was a Commissioner for Trade. Pepys entered the civil service before the Restoration. The new civil service was in process of formation, its dialect not yet cluttered up with jargon. Here too Marvell, Dryden, and Pepys may have learned to aim at convincing, to write functional prose.

Historians are now beginning to realise that the Interregnum was no artistic wilderness. Music and books on the theory of music were published in far greater profusion than before or later ; the first performances of opera in English, and the first appearance of women on the public stage, date from the late fifties. Cromwell was a lover and patron of music, and was painted ' warts and all '—i.e. in a style deliberately different from that of the courtly Sir Anthony Van Dyck. Indeed these years saw the national tradition in painting, submerged by the more famous foreigners whom the court had patronised, flourish again. A ' Royalist ' painter like William Dobson (' the most excellent painter that England hath yet bred ', Aubrey rightly called him) quite clearly has an English and insular style, no less than Robert Walker, the favourite portrait painter of the Parliamentarians. It was during the Interregnum that Samuel Cooper began to achieve the fame which later made him ' esteemed the best artist in Europe ' in miniature painting. Artists also shared in the opportunities offered by the expanding literary market ; from the sixteen-fifties books with engraved plates began to be published in increased numbers. During the Interregnum too Sir Roger Pratt built at Coleshill one of the most beautiful English country houses, in an insular version of Inigo Jones's Classical style. (It was destroyed by fire in 1952.) The Palladian style of inward-turning courtyard house, which had been favoured by men who hoped to entertain the royal court, did not survive the disappearance of that court. It was succeeded by houses built in a solid square or rectangular block by gentlemen who had no wish to pay so heavily for court favour. These houses looked outwards across the broad acres their owners dominated, or wished to dominate. The new ' artisan mannerism ' which triumphed during the Interregnum has been described as ' the last English style in which influences circulated in the impenetrable anonymity of masons' yards and joiners' shops '.[1]

The Restoration brought back the domination of foreign painters. Lely had indeed come to England in the sixteen-forties, but under Charles II (who knighted him) his vogue at court drove native practitioners like John Riley and his school to function ' at a lower level than the great foreign rivals '. Edward Pierce, who made busts of Cromwell and Milton, had to work mainly as mason and carver after 1660. Expanding demand for church monuments and chimney-pieces may have given more craftsmen a chance of economic independence ; but at a higher level the Restoration was disastrous for the native tradition in art. In architecture court fashions mattered less, the taste of the landed class more : the great architects of the second half of the century are all British—Pratt, Wren, Hawksmoor, and Vanbrugh, an Englishman despite his Flemish father.[2]

[1] Summerson, *Architecture in Britain, 1530–1840*, p. 97
[2] Whinney and Millar, *English Art, 1625–1714*, pp. 188, 253–5

11 Conclusion, 1640-60

The meanest of men, the basest and vilest of the nation, the
lowest of the people, have got the power into their hands ;
trampled upon the crown ; baffled and misused the Parliament ; violated the laws ; destroyed or suppressed the nobility
and gentry of the kingdom.

Denzil, Lord Holles, Memoirs (1649, published 1699)

When the people contend for their liberty, they seldom get
anything by their victory but new masters.

George Savile, Marquis of Halifax

WHEN we try to summarise the effects of the decades 1640–60,
two apparently contradictory points have to be made. First,
that a great revolution took place, comparable in many
respects with the French Revolution of 1789 ; secondly, that
it was a very incomplete revolution, as can be seen as soon as
the 1789 parallel is considered.

A great revolution. Absolute monarchy on the French
model was never again possible. The instruments of despotism, Star Chamber and High Commission, were abolished
for ever. Strafford has been described as a frustrated
Richelieu ; the frustration of all that Strafford stood for was
complete and final. Even James II in his wildest moments
never forgot what had happened on 30th January 1649; nor
did his ministers or his subjects. Parliamentary control of
taxation was established, as far as legislation could establish it.
Ecclesiastical courts lost their teeth. The Clarendon Code
after 1660 could not destroy the nonconformist sects. Bishops
never again controlled governments. The country had managed
to get on without King, Lords, and Bishops ; but it could
never henceforth be ruled without the willing co-operation
of those whom the House of Commons represented. After
1640 it was impossible for long to disregard their views,

whether on religion or foreign policy, taxation or local government. Nevertheless, an incomplete revolution. The Army
was not used, as Hugh Peter wished, 'to teach peasants to
understand liberty'. A society of the career open to the talents
was not established. There was no lasting extension or redistribution of the franchise, no substantial legal reform. The
transfers of property did not benefit the smaller men, and movements to defend their economic position all came to nothing.
Tithes and a state Church survived; religious toleration
ended (temporarily) in 1660. Dissenters were driven out of
political life for a century and a half.

Between 1640 and 1660 there had been two revolutions, of
which only one was successful. In 1641 Sir Thomas Aston
defined 'true liberty' as meaning 'that we know by a certain
law that our wives, our children, our servants, our goods,
are our own, that we build, we plough, we sow, we reap, for
ourselves'. It meant the assertion of the rule of 'the free'
against threats either from would-be absolutists or from 'our
servants', the democrats. And this was achieved. In local
government Justices of the Peace not only freed themselves
from paternalist interference from above but also defeated
Leveller attempts to make their offices democratically elective.
The common law triumphed alike over prerogative and
Church courts and over radical attempts to reform and
rationalise it. Feudal tenures were abolished, yet the movement to protect copyholders and check enclosure was defeated.
The next century sees agricultural prosperity and an extension
of the cultivated area; it also sees the disappearance of the
small cultivator working on his own land. In industry,
monopolies and government interference were ended: craftsmen were left at the mercy of employers. The rise of a landless
proletariat was a long-drawn-out process; but henceforth it
was an inevitable one. The big company merchants and
the City of London won the foreign policy they wanted, and
overcame the movement for complete free trade. In religion,
the high-flying Laudians were never again a political menace;
yet the radical sectaries who played so decisive a part in
winning the Civil War failed to end the union of Church and
state, and failed to substitute a system of democratic voluntarism.

By the compromise of 1660 the idealists on both sides

were sacrificed. Vane and Harrison were publicly dis-
embowelled, Quakers and other sectaries were driven into a
harried underground existence : while on the other hand
many of the smaller Cavaliers got no compensation for their
losses and sufferings. Those who inherited the earth were
hard-faced business men like George Downing, who betrayed
his comrades to the executioner's knife and got a baronetcy ;
stolid professionals like George Monck who became Duke of
Albemarle ('some men will betray three kingdoms for filthy
lucre's sake', a minister said to his face) ; ex-Presbyterians like
William Prynne, who said, 'If Charles Stuart is to come in, it
were better for those that waged war against his father that
he should come in by their votes' ; ex-Royalist ex-Cromwellians like Sir Anthony Ashley-Cooper, an affluent member
of Committees for Plantations before and after 1660. 'The
corrupt interests of the lawyers and clergy' proved too strong
for the radicals, and the ultimate victors in 1660 were those
conservatives who had been united against Laud and Strafford
in 1640–1 and who came together again in face of a new
threat to liberty and property, this time from the many-headed
monster and the Army of the sectaries. The gentry were able
to reunite in 1660 because the lines of civil-war division were
drawn within a class which had cultural ties and social prejudices in common despite differing political, religious, and
economic aspirations. When in January 1660 the diarist
John Evelyn tried to persuade the Parliamentarian Governor
of the Tower of London to declare for the King, he noted
that his negotiation was ' to the great hazard of my life ; but
the Colonel had been my schoolfellow and I knew would not
betray me'. This early appearance of 'the old school tie'
was symbolic.

One lasting legacy of the Interregnum was a hatred of
standing armies among the men of property. Before 1640
they had feared that the monarchy might use an army to win
independence of Parliament ; after 1646 their own Army
threatened to deprive them of the fruits of victory. The
doctrines of the Agitators seemed to threaten social stability
and the liberties of the ' free '. Cromwell's Army had as little
respect for the sovereignty of Parliament as Charles I, and
far more strength ; the Major-Generals had invaded the holy

of holies, local government and Parliamentary elections. Never again !

A great revolution in human thought dates from these decades—the general realisation, which the Levellers, Hobbes, and Harrington summed up, that solutions to political problems might be reached by discussion and argument ; that questions of utility and expediency were more important than theology or history, that neither antiquarian research nor searching the Scriptures was the best way to bring peace, order, and prosperity to the commonwealth. It was so great an intellectual revolution that it is difficult for us to conceive how men thought before it was made.

So although the Puritan revolution was defeated, the revolution in thought could not be unmade, nor the revolution in science led by the men who were to form the Royal Society after the Restoration, nor the revolution in prose which the same Royal Society was to consecrate. Even the ideas of men who would not compromise in 1660, of Milton and the Levellers, these ideas were driven underground but could not be killed. ' Give me the liberty to know, to utter and to argue freely according to conscience,' Milton had said. ' Truth is strong next to the Almighty ; she needs no policies, nor stratagems nor licensings to make her victorious ; those are the shifts and the defences that error uses against her power. Give her but room, and do not bind her when she sleeps. . . . If it come to prohibiting, there is not aught more likely to be prohibited than truth itself ; whose first appearance to our eyes bleared and dimmed with prejudice and custom is more unsightly and unplausible than many errors.' Such words could not be forgotten. The Levellers came nearer to oblivion, but their ideas continued to circulate underground. A century after the Restoration, Goldsmith's Vicar of Wakefield cried, ' I would have all men kings. I would be a king myself. We have all naturally an equal right to the throne : we are all originally equal.' This, he added, ' was once the opinion of a set of honest men who were called Levellers '. Through the writings of Catherine Macaulay and others the ideas of the Levellers passed into the radical tradition of the seventeen-sixties, and played their part in preparing the American and French Revolutions.

PART THREE

1660–88

12 Narrative of Events, 1660-88

> The Commons succeeding in the property of the peers and Church . . . have inherited likewise, according to the course of nature, their power. . . . You must either bring property back to your old government, and give the King and lords their lands again, or else you must bring the government to the property as it now stands.
>
> Henry Nevill, *Plato Redivivus* (1681)

CHARLES II officially dated his reign from 30th January 1649. An Act of 1st June 1660 declared the Long Parliament fully dissolved, and the existing Convention a legal Parliament even though it had not been summoned by the King. Another Act arranged for continuity of judicial proceedings started before the King's return, and confirmed all legal decisions of the Interregnum, subject to a right of appeal. So the constitutional niceties were preserved. The abolition of the Court of Wards and of purveyance was confirmed by statute : Charles was compensated for loss of revenue by the grant of £100,000 a year from an excise on beer, cider, and tea. A revised version of the Navigation Act was passed on 4th September. Nearly £1 million was voted to pay off the Army. An Act of Indemnity pardoned all offences arising from the hostilities of the preceding decades, but excepted fifty-seven persons, mostly regicides. Thirty of these were condemned to death, of whom eleven were executed. A land settlement, ambiguously promised in the Declaration of Breda, proved difficult. Church, crown, and confiscated Royalists' lands were (in theory at least) restored ; lands sold privately during the Interregnum were not. In Ireland the Act of Settlement (1661) and the Act of Explanation (1665) left adventurers and soldiers with two-thirds of their estates ; several thousand Catholics failed to recover land which they had held in 1641.

At least two-thirds of the good cultivable land in Ireland was now owned by Protestants, many of them absentees. In England extruded ministers were restored to their livings, but no Act was passed to implement the promise of religious toleration made at Breda. On 25th October the King issued a Declaration granting a purely temporary liberty, pending the decisions of a national synod which never met. There had been no religious settlement when the Convention Parliament was dissolved on 9th December.

Its successor, which met on 8th May 1661, and lasted for eighteen years, was the Cavalier or Pensioner Parliament. It passed a series of severe statutes known as the Clarendon Code (Corporation Act, 1661 ; Act of Uniformity, 1662 ; Conventicle Act, 1664 ; Five Mile Act, 1665). Their object was to exclude nonconformists from any share in central or local government. Church courts were restored, with the all-important exception of the High Commission. The Triennial Act (1664) demanded Parliaments every three years, though it had none of the automatic sanctions laid down in the Act of 1641. In May 1662 Charles married Catherine of Braganza, who brought Tangier and Bombay in her dowry. In the same year Dunkirk was sold to France. This helped to make Lord Chancellor Clarendon unpopular in the country. He was already losing influence at court, despite the marriage of his daughter to the King's brother, James, Duke of York, in 1660. Clarendon opposed the Second Dutch War (1665–7), yet was blamed when it brought a series of disasters which coincided with the Great Plague of 1665 and the Fire of London in 1666. In June 1667 the Dutch fleet sailed up the Thames and destroyed English ships in the Medway. England was forced to make peace. A combination of Clarendon's enemies brought about his impeachment in November 1667. He fled from the country, to die in exile.

The administration which succeeded him became popularly known as the Cabal, from the initial letters of the five principal ministers—Clifford, Arlington, Buckingham, Ashley, Lauderdale. Under this government the King carried on a dual foreign policy. England formed a triple alliance against France with the Netherlands and Sweden in 1668 ; but in 1670 Charles signed a secret treaty at Dover with Louis XIV,

by which he promised to declare himself a Catholic when the affairs of his kingdom permitted. In return he received a French subsidy. Despite a state bankruptcy in 1672 (the Stop of the Exchequer), in March 1673 Charles entered upon the Third Dutch War in alliance with France. Two days before war was declared he issued a Declaration of Indulgence for Roman Catholic and Protestant dissenters. Parliament attacked this use by the King of the prerogative to suspend the operation of Parliamentary penal statutes, and reaffirmed its policy of narrow Anglican exclusiveness by the Test Act (1673). This insisted that the holder of any civil or military office should take the sacrament according to the rites of the Church of England, should take the oaths of supremacy and allegiance, and make a declaration against the Catholic doctrine of the mass. In consequence the Duke of York resigned as Lord High Admiral, Clifford as Lord Treasurer. With the dismissal of Ashley, now Earl of Shaftesbury, the ministry collapsed.

Clifford was succeeded as Treasurer by Sir Thomas Osborne, soon to be Earl of Danby. The Dutch war was brought to an end in 1674, and Danby set about building a Parliamentary majority by bribery and distribution of offices. During most of his administration (1674–9) Parliament was prorogued, and Charles relied on subsidies from Louis XIV. Danby himself, however, was anti-French, and in 1677 he brought off a marriage between the Duke of York's eldest daughter, Mary, and the Protestant William of Orange. But in the country at large fear was growing of the suspected pro-French and Papist leanings of the King and his entourage. In 1678 the adventurer Titus Oates denounced an alleged Popish Plot to assassinate the King and to promote a massacre of Protestants and a French invasion of Ireland. The Justice of the Peace to whom Oates had made his depositions was found murdered in October 1678 ; and panic began. On 31st October the Commons resolved ' that there has been and still is a damnable and hellish plot, contrived and carried on by popish recusants for the assassinating and murdering the King, and for subverting the government and rooting out and destroying the protestant religion '. Many Papist suspects were executed. When the Duchess of York's secretary, Coleman, was arrested, he was found in fact to have been engaged in a Papist conspiracy. Meanwhile the English Ambassador in Paris, Ralph Montagu, denounced Danby for obtaining subsidies from France in order to dispense with Parliament, and in December Danby was impeached. A movement to exclude the Catholic James from the succession and replace him by Charles's illegitimate son, the Duke of Monmouth, was started. On 24th January 1679 Parliament was dissolved. Charles signed a declaration that Monmouth was illegitimate ; the Duke of York went into voluntary exile in the Spanish Netherlands.

Three Parliaments came and went in rapid succession. The first sat from March to July 1679. Danby's impeachment was revived. The King announced that he had given him a pardon under the Great Seal. The Commons voted the pardon illegal, and Danby was committed to the Tower of London. Shaftesbury was made Lord President of the Council in a reconstructed ministry. This Parliament passed the *Habeas Corpus* Amendment Act, and was at work on an Exclusion Bill (to prevent James's succession) when it was first prorogued and then dissolved. Shaftesbury was dismissed. In September Monmouth was sent into exile (to Holland) and the Duke of York returned to rule Scotland.

The next Parliament met in October 1679, but was immediately prorogued. A new ministry of courtiers— Sunderland, Godolphin, Lawrence Hyde, ' the Chits '—was formed. Parliament remained in recess for a year. When it met again the Commons passed a second Exclusion Bill, which was defeated in the Lords only by the efforts of the Marquis of Halifax. In January 1681 the Commons resolved that no further supply should be granted until the Exclusion Bill was passed ; and Parliament was dissolved. It was during the recess of this Parliament that new party labels began to occur. Opponents of the court had organised petitions against proroga-tion or dissolution ; their opponents expressed abhorrence of the petitions. The names Petitioners and Abhorrers desig-nated the two parties later to be known as Whig and Tory.

In March 1681 Charles summoned his last Parliament to the Royalist stronghold of Oxford. The Commons brought in another Exclusion Bill, and Parliament was dissolved after a week. Charles was driven back to financial dependence on

France. In the spring of 1682 the Duke of York returned to England; Jeffreys was made Lord Chief Justice and a Privy Councillor. Sunderland, dismissed in January 1681 for temporarily supporting exclusion, returned to office. A reign of legal terror against Whigs and dissenters began. Shaftesbury was arrested on a charge of treason, but was acquitted by a London jury. He fled to the Netherlands, where he died in 1683.

In the years 1682–3 the government tried to get city and borough charters surrendered or forfeited. They were then remodelled so as to produce Parliamentary electorates and juries favourable to the court. Under the new charter forced on London in 1683 no Lord Mayor, sheriff, or recorder could be appointed without royal approval. In the same year the Rye House Plot to seize the King led to the arrest and trial of many leading Whigs. Monmouth went into hiding, the Earl of Essex committed suicide in the Tower; Lord Russell and Algernon Sydney were executed, though neither had been active in the plot. Sydney was convicted only of defending the view that governments might be resisted in certain circumstances: this too in an unpublished treatise. In 1684 Oates was imprisoned and Danby and a number of Roman Catholic peers were released. Under the Triennial Act a Parliament should have met in 1684, but Charles called none before he died in February 1685. On his death-bed he proclaimed himself a Papist.

James II succeeded peacefully. Thanks to the remodelling of borough charters the Parliament which met in May 1685 was more favourable to the court than any since 1661. It voted James an income of nearly £2 million, almost twice what had been granted to Charles at his accession. While Parliament was still sitting two risings took place. The Earl of Argyll invaded Scotland; and in June 1685 Monmouth landed at Lyme Regis. Neither revolt lasted more than a few weeks. Both leaders were executed and savage reprisals followed. Judge Jeffreys' Bloody Assizes in the south-west after Monmouth's defeat at Sedgemoor became notorious. James used the occasion to demand a permanent standing army. 16,000 men were concentrated just outside London. Some of the army officers were Papists, although

legally they were disabled from serving by the still unrepealed
Test Act. In October 1685 Halifax was dismissed for refusing
to be a party to the repeal of the Test and Corporation Acts.

James threw down the gauntlet at an unfortunate time.
In the month of Halifax's dismissal the culmination of a long
persecution of French Protestants came when Louis XIV
revoked the Edict of Nantes. Parliament suggested that, instead
of a standing army, the militia should be reorganised. James
prorogued Parliament, and it never met again. In a collusive
legal action (*Godden versus Hales*) the judges affirmed the
King's right to dispense with the Test Act. In 1686 the Papist
Earl of Tyrconnel was made Lord Lieutenant of Ireland,
where a Catholic army was also in process of formation. (In
1688, 3,000 Irish troops were sent to England.) In 1686 the
navy too was entrusted to the command of a Catholic admiral,
Sir Roger Strickland. A Jesuit, Edward Petre, was made a
Privy Councillor. The Lord Privy Seal was a Catholic, Lord
Arundell of Wardour. The chief minister, Sunderland, did
not proclaim himself a Catholic until June 1688, but he
certainly had no Protestant scruples. A papal nuncio was
publicly received. Houses of Franciscans, Dominicans, and
Benedictines were opened in London. A Court of Commissioners for Ecclesiastical Causes was erected, which was
indistinguishable from the High Commission, declared illegal
in 1641. This court was used to force Roman Catholics upon
Oxford and Cambridge colleges. The resistance of Magdalen
College, Oxford, led to the dismissal of twenty-five Fellows
before the subservient Samuel Parker, Bishop of Oxford, was
elected President, followed shortly by one of the papal Vicars
Apostolic.

In April 1687 James issued a Declaration of Indulgence,
which suspended the tests and granted liberty of public worship
to Protestant and Roman Catholic dissenters. He declared
that he did not doubt the concurrence of Parliament with this
Declaration when it should meet. To ensure that his next
Parliament was even more subservient than its predecessor, the
remodelling of town corporations was continued. James made
preparations to influence even county elections, though with
little success. In May 1688 he issued a second Declaration of
Indulgence, and promised that a Parliament would meet not

later than November. Bishops were ordered to have this Declaration read in every church in the kingdom on two successive Sundays. Seven Bishops, led by Archbishop Sancroft, petitioned the King to withdraw the order, since they thought he had no right to dispense with the statutes which denied toleration to dissenters. The Bishops were sent to the Tower and prosecuted for seditious libel. In June they were found not guilty. In the same month James's Queen bore him a son, James Edward. This proved the last straw. An invitation was sent to William of Orange to invade England, signed by seven Englishmen, including the Bishop of London, Danby, a Sydney, a Russell, and a Cavendish.

As William made his preparations for invasion James backed down hastily. He announced that Catholics would remain incapable of sitting in the House of Commons when the promised Parliament met. A Protestant was put in command of the fleet. All municipal charters granted since 1679 were annulled. The Ecclesiastical Commission was abolished. Some Papist Lords Lieutenant were dismissed; the Fellows of Magdalen were restored. But it was too late. William's invasion was long delayed, but on Guy Fawkes Day he landed at Torbay with 11,000 foot and 4,000 horse. Slowly the peerage and gentry rallied to this formidable force, which accomplished the last successful invasion of England. Danby seized Yorkshire, Lord Delamere rose in Cheshire, the Cavendish Earl of Devonshire in Nottinghamshire. James's supporters deserted *en masse*, led by his daughter, Princess Anne, and her favourite, Lord Churchill. James packed his wife off to France, and tried to follow himself, after first giving orders to disband the army—unpaid. Anarchy threatened in London, and a group of peers invited William to advance with his army and maintain order. James was inconveniently captured by Kentish fishermen and brought back to London; but he was allowed to escape again, and was in France by the end of the year.

13   Economics, 1660-88

> The thing which is nearest the heart of the nation is trade
> and all that belongs to it.
>
> Charles II to his sister, 14th September 1668

THE LAND

IN JANUARY 1660 Monck expressed the view that those who
had bought land during the revolutionary period formed so
significant an interest that their anxieties could not be disregarded in any settlement of the nation.   The Declaration of
Breda promised that all things relating to grants, sales, and
purchases of land should be determined in Parliament, ' which
can best provide for the just satisfaction of all men who are
concerned '.   Eventually a compromise was reached.   Church,
crown, and Royalists' confiscated estates were to be restored,
but not lands sold privately by Royalists.   In practice this
meant that a great deal was left to private negotiation.   Even
Oliver Cromwell's son, Henry, was able by various devices to
keep or to sell most of the estates which had been granted to
him.   It was not thought worth the trouble of taking legal
action to dispossess the purchasers of Henrietta Maria's dower
lands ;   the Queen Mother was given compensation instead.
Any purchaser who had made himself conspicuous in bringing
about the Restoration had a good chance of a long lease on
favourable terms.   Such leases were ' never denied to any of
the Coldstreamers ' (Monck's troops).   The revenue expected
from crown lands in 1663 was half the estimate of 1660.

Many who had bought Royalists' lands were no less fortunate.
' The Act of Oblivion proved a great hindrance and obstruction
to . . . all the royal party,' complained the Duchess of Newcastle.   Her husband got a special Act of Parliament to restore

his lands, but even so he failed to recover some of them. So we can imagine the difficulties facing lesser Royalists who lacked the credit and political influence of a duke. Many ran badly into debt in the effort to recover their lands, and some families may never have recovered from their financial embarrassments. The Restoration land settlement, Roger L'Estrange said, ' made the enemies of the constitution masters, in effect, of the booty of three nations '. ' For some Royalists the real cost of the Civil War was poor marriages for their daughters,' wrote Professor Habakkuk. Gentlewomen with meagre dowries could hardly compete in the marriage market with rich merchants' daughters.

The Duke of Newcastle sold lands worth £56,000 in order to pay debts. Then, like many other returned Royalists, he turned improving landlord. The agricultural writer Houghton spoke of ' the great improvement made of lands since our inhuman civil wars, when our gentry, who before hardly knew what it was to think, . . . fell to such an industry and caused such an improvement, as England never knew before '. The economy of the market-place was extended into regions where hitherto more feudal, patriarchal relations had prevailed. Selden observed that in the days when tenants performed military service for their lords it was reasonable that their rents should be light ; but now ' 'tis vanity and folly not to take the full value '.

' Let no man's love, friendship or favour draw thee to forgo thy profits,' the Royalist Sir John Oglander advised his descendants. ' Serve God and make much of your own,' the ex-Parliamentarian Edward Moore similarly urged his son in 1668 ; ' and as these new leases fall out, raise your old rents, . . . that you may have something to live on like other neighbour gentlemen.' Like other neighbour gentlemen : Moore's harshness was not individual, it was forced on him by society. Even Bishops, traditionally the most conservative of landlords, consulted together to work out ways of extracting the maximum rent or succession fines from their tenants. Bishop Cosin of Durham, who closely followed his land agent's dealings with his tenants, used to quote the practice of other Bishops and to suggest that he would be liable to criticism if he violated their agreed policy.

After 1660 the landowning class was secure against social revolt from below. Henceforth a major pre-occupation of governments was to stimulate production and to protect the producer, no longer to safeguard the consumer or to protect the subsistence farmer. This marks a decisive change in outlook. Parliament did much to help the improving lessee, for example by authorising the crown to enclose forest lands for cultivation. Regrating and engrossing (buying corn in the open market and storing it for re-sale when scarcity had raised prices) were permitted under an Act of 1663, whose object was to stimulate cultivation of waste land by giving ' sufficient encouragement . . . for the laying out of cost and labour '. By the end of the sixties corn import was virtually prohibited, so as to keep home prices high. From 1673 to 1681 bounties were granted on exported wheat—a ' revolution in our fiscal policy ', Professor Hughes calls it. Bounties were discontinued during the period of personal government ; they returned with the Liberator in 1689. Protection against imports, and this export bounty, steadied wheat prices and greatly reduced the speculative element in agriculture. Production was stimulated. After the nineties there were no more famines, and a rise in living standards is suggested by the widespread substitution of wheat for rye.

As division of labour and regional specialisation increased, the demand for food from London and other urban areas made enclosure for intensive crop cultivation even more profitable than enclosure for sheep-grazing. Large-scale market-gardening and dairy-farming prospered ; there were experiments with hothouse fruit. Most of the new crops which were to be important in England's agricultural history over the next century had been started experimentally during the Interregnum : beans, peas, lettuces, asparagus, artichokes, sainfoin, clover. Sir Robert Walpole's father was growing turnips, clover, and artificial grasses in the sixteen-seventies. ' " Turnip " Townshend and Coke of Holkham in the eighteenth century,' Dr Plumb observes, ' were mere publicists of a system of agriculture already well established in Norfolk.' Root crops and grasses permitted the abandonment of the system of crop rotation in which land was rested and lay fallow for a year. More cattle could be kept alive in winter. More fresh meat and vegetables must have improved the national health, though meat would have been cheaper still if the landed interest had not secured prohibition of the import of Irish cattle. The great age of English stock-breeding dates from the middle years of the century. Samuel Pepys told his parents in 1663 that it was ' not good husbandry to such a family as yours to keep either hogs, poultry, sheep, cows, . . . there being meat of all sorts, milk, butter, cheese, eggs, fowl and everything else to be had cheaper . . . at the market '. When Bunyan's Mr Badman asked, ' Who would keep a cow of their own that can have a quart of milk for a penny ? ' we may deplore the attitude towards holy matrimony which he was advocating ; but we note that he confirms Pepys's view of the cheapness of dairy produce.

The post-Restoration atmosphere was conducive to capital investment and scientific experiment. The Royal Society made suggestions for agricultural improvement, ' by which means parks have been disparked, commons enclosed, woods turned into arable, and pasture lands improved by clover . . . so that the food of cattle is increased as fast if not faster than the consumption '. Racking of rents was justified because having to pay more to landlords encouraged tenants to work harder and to grow new crops. One argument in favour of fen drainage was that it not only rendered fresh land available for cultivation but also forced poor squatters to ' quit idleness and betake themselves to . . . manufactures ', thus reducing unemployment. Fortrey argued in 1663 that ' as many or more families may be maintained and employed in the manufacture of the wool that may arise out of 100 acres of pasture, than can be employed in a far greater quantity of arable '.[1] Industry could now absorb a greater proportion of those evicted ; this helped to generate opinion favourable to enclosures.

Meanwhile the abolition of feudal tenures, and the failure of copyholders to win legal protection, increased the profitability of capital investment in agriculture. A rise in dowries, forced by the competition of merchant wealth on the marriage

---

[1] J. Houghton, *A Collection of Letters for the Improvement of Husbandry and Trade* (1727), p. 82 ; *Husbandry and Trade Improved* (1728), p. 56 ; Fuller, *History of Cambridge* (1655), p. 71 ; S. Fortrey, *England's Interest and Improvement* (1663), pp. 18–20

market, widened the gap between big and small landowners. The legal device of the 'strict settlement', evolved in the fifties in order to prevent heirs breaking up estates, enabled families to concentrate land and capital into large units. Younger sons now received their patrimony in the form of a capital sum, not in land : they were thus impelled to seek a career elsewhere, and turned to the expanding professions and the civil service. Since honours were no longer publicly sold, the peerage tended to become a closed oligarchy. Rich landowners invested in production rather than in peerages. 'The liquidation . . . of scores of ancient families, lesser gentry and freeholders, and the rise . . . of vast new agglomerations of landed estates' constituted 'a basic social revolution in the century after the Restoration '.[1]

INDUSTRY AND THE POOR

'The constitutional order established at the Restoration,' wrote Mr Lipson, 'and consolidated by the Revolution of 1688 created the framework within which a capitalist society could work out its destiny unhampered by the control which the crown had hitherto endeavoured to enforce.' The Restoration saw no attempt to revive the authoritarian régime in industry. When in 1664 a Bill before Parliament proposed to revive the pin monopoly, at a meeting of wire-drawers one of them was heard to declare that the late King had lost his head for granting such patents. The Bill was allowed to drop ; and it is significant of the decline in the royal prerogative that it was a Bill. Parliamentary statutes were now sovereign, and there was no Star Chamber to enforce monopolies.

The Cromwellian ordinance authorising disbanded soldiers to practise trades to which they had not been apprenticed was re-enacted in 1660 ; the attitude of the now triumphant common-law courts ensured that restrictive gild and apprentice regulations were never again effectively enforced except in agriculture. An Act of 1663 threw the linen industry open to

[1] Habakkuk, 'Marriage Settlements in the Eighteenth Century ', *T.R.H.S.* (1950), pp. 18–20 ; E. Hughes, ' The Professions in the Eighteenth Century ', *Durham University Journal* (New Ser.), **13**, 47–8

all. In 1669 a draper said of the Elizabethan Statute of Apprentices that 'though not repealed, yet [it] has been by most of the judges looked upon as inconvenient to trade and to the increase of inventions'. The Privy Council accepted his contention. In 1685 the courts ruled that apprenticeship was necessary only for servants hired by the year, thus exempting most wage labourers from it. In 1689, of 200 towns in England, only a quarter had any organised gilds at all. The prosperity of Birmingham and its industries in the later seventeenth century is attributed to the fact that it was not a chartered borough : it had no gilds, and its many dissenters were free from the restrictions imposed by the Clarendon Code. The clothing industry benefited especially from the new freedom. Within a few years of the Restoration the object of Cokayne's Project was attained : dyeing and dressing of cloth in England became the rule, and the quantity of undressed cloth exports fell sharply. In 1666 came the famous statute enacting that the dead were to be buried in woollen, and not in imported textiles.

The price-revolution boom was over. The disbandment of 50,000 soldiers, the Plague, the Fire of London, the Dutch fleet in the Medway—all these shook the economy. So industrial expansion at first was slow if steady. Coal shipments from Durham and Northumberland, which had advanced fourteen and a half times between 1550 and 1640, increased by only fifty per cent between 1640 and 1690. But the rebuilding of London after the Great Fire stimulated industry, and ended the monopoly of the building trade hitherto claimed by the Masons' Company. There was general agreement among contemporaries that the country was prospering, especially after about 1674. And the political and legal conditions for further advance had been created. The abolition of prerogative courts and changes in the interpretation of common law worked to the advantage of landlords. Before 1640 the Fletcher family in Cumberland had been prevented from developing its coal property by the rights of freeholders : by 1680 they were exporting coal on a large scale. 'At the end of the seventeenth century,' Professor Nef says, 'there remained few wastes in which the lord's power to mine, or to lease his coal, was seriously restricted.' The failure of copyholders to win legal security of tenure was as beneficial to landlords opening up coal deposits as to enclosers. The sales of Church property during the Interregnum had led to the development of coal-bearing areas hitherto unworked, e.g. in South Wales.

In 1696 Gregory King estimated the number of cottagers and paupers at one-quarter of the population, labouring people and out-servants at another quarter. Both groups, he thought, had to spend more than they earned. Modern research confirms this gloomy picture. At least one-third of the households of England were exempt from the Hearth Tax on grounds of poverty. After 1660 the great impetus of private charity fell off, and there followed a more effective administration of the Poor Law by rulers of the localities, no longer at loggerheads with the central authority in attitudes towards the development of capitalism. In Charles II's reign the sum raised by the poor rate was estimated at nearly half the entire revenue of the crown. Even this was only 3d per week for each pauper and cottager.

It is difficult to generalise about the position of wage labourers. If we look only at figures, real wages are rising. But a greater proportion of labourers, having lost their plots of land, now had no subsidiary earnings to cushion them against unemployment. For those entirely dependent on wages it remains true, in Mr Ogg's words, that ' neither contemporary nor modern economists can explain how they lived '. In the early eighteenth century men worked thirteen and a half hours a day, six days a week, in the ironware factory of the philanthropist, Ambrose Crowley. Industrial craftsmen under the putting-out system also had to work extremely long hours in their own houses, with their whole families. They were as economically dependent on their employers as were wage labourers, and their employment was less continuous.

Contemporaries now saw the main problem so far as labour was concerned as one of organisation, not of surplus population. ' Fewness of people is real poverty,' Petty exclaimed in 1662. ' The hands of men employed are true riches,' said the historian of the Royal Society. England, Fortrey thought in 1663, could support twice its population, ' were they rightly employed '.

The problem was to find the right form of organisation. It was assumed that the poor would work only to avoid starvation : this was one reason for encouraging corn export, in order to keep wheat prices high. Landlords benefited doubly, by high rents from prosperous farmers and easily obtained labour from people who had to work for dear life. One effect of the Restoration, indeed, was to strengthen the position of the employing classes. ' We find the unreasonableness of servants' [i.e. wage labourers'] wages a great grievance,' said the Grand Jury (i.e. chief landowners) of Worcestershire in 1661 ; ' servants are grown so proud that the master cannot be known from the servant.' In order to put the lower orders back in their place, the Jury added, the authority of Justices of the Peace should be enhanced.

The 1662 Act of Settlement, passed partly to solve the problem set by masses of disbanded soldiers seeking work, authorised Justices to send back to his last place of domicile any newcomer to a parish who seemed likely to become a charge on the rates. Thus only persons of some standing could move, even to look for work, without the consent of the Justices. In Thorold Rogers's words, the Settlement Act made the labourer ' a serf without land '. The assumption behind the statute was that a pauper was idle, vicious, and rightless. The impotent poor received relief in their parish of settlement, at minimum rates. Workhouses were deliberately made unpleasant in order to discourage applicants for relief ; so they helped to keep down wages outside. This harsh code was more effective in villages than in towns. Hence the drift to the greater freedom and economic opportunity of the cities, where a mass of casual labour prevented wages rising too rapidly and began to form that new phenomenon, the mob.

We have little evidence of what the poor themselves thought. The Restoration confirmed the defeat of democratic movements in London. Before the end of the century the small masters in most City companies had lost all influence in running their affairs ; everywhere oligarchy ruled. Industrial struggles began to take more modern forms. There were strikes and mutinies in the dockyards in the sixteen-sixties, and combinations to secure higher wages. In 1670, when London was being rebuilt after the Great Fire, the

sawyers tried to form a craft trade union, to keep out casual
labour and so prevent wage-cutting. If they succeeded, the
master craftsmen said, their combination would bring the
building trades to a standstill. Sometimes industrial action
took the form of machine-breaking. In 1675 the ribbon-loom
weavers of London, 'good commonwealth's men',[1] two or
three hundred in a company, broke into houses in order to
seize and burn looms for weaving ribbons, which were putting
them out of employment. There were weavers' riots in
Colchester in 1676, in Trowbridge in 1677. A combination
of journeymen cloth-workers in London refused to work for
less than 12s a week. We know too little about such movements, since our information almost invariably derives from
hostile sources. But we can see the shape of things to come
when London printers in 1663 made the essential distinction
between labour and capital. 'Having the clothier,' they
asked, 'what need (necessarily) is there of the draper? . . .
And having the printer there is no fear of wanting books,
though there were no booksellers.'

The trend of economic development, then, was in the
direction of sharper differentiation between classes: a landless working class dependent on wage labour increased, the
yeomanry and small masters declined. Large numbers of
households still preserved a precarious independence by
agriculture or domestic handicrafts, or by a combination of
both. But workers in domestic industry were steadily coming
under the control of the merchants who employed them, and
the division between substantial farmers and 'the poor' in the
villages was becoming more marked. The payment of rates
gave a man the franchise in local government; receipt of
poor relief put him outside the pale. There was a tendency
to oligarchy everywhere in this period. The administration
of the parochial rate had long tended to concentrate power in
the hands of those who paid most; now the exclusion of
nonconformists from local government further narrowed its
basis. England was rapidly becoming a two-class society,
divided into the ruling class and the masses. Most economists
saw a large population working for subsistence wages as the
sine qua non of successful conquest of the markets of the world.

[1] Shadwell, *The Virtuoso*, Act V (*Works*, ed. Summers, III, p. 168)

TRADE AND FOREIGN POLICY

After 1660 governments concerned themselves steadily with the furtherance of trade. A number of measures of the revolutionary decades were re-enacted. Thus the legal rate of interest was again fixed at six per cent (1651 : re-enacted 1661). Tobacco planting was prohibited in England in the interests of colonial production (1652 : 1660). One of Charles II's earliest acts was to establish a committee of the Privy Council to collect information and offer advice about the colonies. It continued to exist in various forms down to William III's Board of Trade. Noel, Povey, and Drax, experts in high favour with Cromwell, were influential after 1660 ; Modyford, Restoration Governor of Jamaica, had greatly influenced the Protector's Western Design. The termination of proprietary rule in the Caribbean in 1663, the retention of Jamaica under direct government control, were evidence that the Interregnum policy of subordinating colonies to rule from Whitehall was to be continued ; Ashley-Cooper personified the continuity.

The most obvious outward sign of continuity in policy was the Navigation Act of 1660. This laid down the principle that no African, Asian, or American goods might be imported into England or Ireland except in ships belonging to Englishmen, Irishmen, or English colonists, and manned by crews at least seventy-five per cent English. No goods might be imported to or exported from English colonies except in ships owned by Englishmen or Irishmen. Alien merchants and factors were excluded from colonial trade, and from the coastal trade of England and Ireland. Regulations aimed against the Dutch carrying trade excluded (or subjected to double customs dues) various commodities unless they were imported in English ships or ships of the exporting country manned by seventy-five per cent English crews. These commodities included naval stores, wines and spirits, oils and salt—in all about half the value of England's European imports. The import duty on Dutch fish was doubled. Enumerated articles produced by English colonies—sugar, tobacco, raw cotton, ginger, indigo, and dye-woods—were to be shipped only to England, or English possessions, so that England became the *entrepôt* for these goods.

The Navigation Act declared its object to be ' the increase of shipping '. The tonnage of English merchant shipping in fact doubled between 1660 and 1688. The code took time to reach its full effect. In the early sixties dispensations had to be given to foreign-built ships. But their numbers dropped rapidly after 1662, despite high constructional costs which would have militated against English shipbuilding without the protection of the Act. Giving English seamen a monopoly of English trade seems also to have raised their wages. Since merchant shipping was one of the three or four largest employers of wage labour, this must have helped the slow upward trend of wages.

But the Act had wider objects. The Venetian Ambassador summarised the Speaker's arguments when presenting it to Charles II : if it had the effect intended, Charles would ' be in a position to give the law to foreign princes, this being the true way to enlarge dominions throughout the world, the most easy for conquests and the least costly for appropriating the property of others '. In the first instance the Act was directed against the Dutch. Josiah Child said frankly in 1672 that, ' This kingdom being an island, the defence of which has always been our shipping and seamen, it seems to me absolutely necessary that profit and power ought jointly to be considered, and if so, I think none can deny but the Act of Navigation has and does occasion building and employing of three times the number of ships and seamen that otherwise we should or would do.' Without the Navigation Act, ' you should see forty Dutch ships at our own plantations for one English '. Most contemporaries would have agreed with this analysis.

The Dutch were completely driven out of England's trade with the Baltic. The annual average of English ships passing through the Sound after 1660 was nearly twice what it had been before 1650. Although the bulk of this trade passed not to English ships but to those of Baltic countries, still England was saved from dependence on Dutch merchants for the vital naval stores from which she had nearly been cut off during the First Dutch War. The Second and Third Dutch Wars were due, among other things, to the renewal of the Navigation Acts. War was ' much desired by the City of London ', the Duke of York had said in 1662. ' What matters is not this or that reason,' added the Duke of Albemarle. ' What we want is more of the trade the Dutch now have.' War was provoked, among a host of other quarrels, by two British acts of aggression against the Dutch in 1664, springing from calculated imperial policy. One was the seizure of stations on the West African coast, by controlling which the Dutch had established a monopoly of the slave trade. At the end of hostilities England retained only two of these stations, but the Dutch monopoly was broken ; the future prosperity of Bristol and Liverpool was assured.

The other act of aggression was the seizure of New Amsterdam (later New York) in 1664. The aim was to exclude the Dutch from trade with the North American colonies. Despite its recapture in the Third Dutch War, England insisted on retaining New York at the Treaty of 1674. Under Charles II England was unable to mobilise sufficient striking power to beat the Netherlands to their knees. That was done for us by Louis XIV of France. The Anglo-French maritime treaty of 1677 allowed English ships to carry Dutch cargoes whilst France and the Netherlands were at war, and so England could cut in on the Dutch carrying trade, especially in the Mediterranean.

But the main point of the Navigation Acts was a deliberate policy of developing the production, and monopolising the export, of colonial commodities like tobacco, sugar, cotton, dye-woods. The labour of the colonists, Davenant thought, was ' probably six times more profitable than labour at home ', thanks to slavery. In 1640 colonial goods imported and then re-exported accounted for a bare five to six per cent of England's trade ; by the end of the century, with a very different fiscal policy, they were well over twenty-five per cent. By 1686 forty-four per cent of English ships were engaged in trade with America and India.[1] The Acts created monopoly conditions of trade with the colonies, and so increased the profits of English merchants. They mark a decisive turning-point in England's economic history. Whereas down to 1640

[1] C. Davenant, *On the Plantation Trade* ; K. G. Davies, *The Royal African Company* (1957), pp. 170, 174 ; R. Davis, ' Merchant Shipping in the Economy of the Late Seventeenth Century ', *Econ. H.R.* (2nd Ser.), **9**, 70. All my subsequent references to the Royal African Company are drawn from Mr Davies' valuable book.

wool and cloth had for centuries been almost the sole English exports, by the end of the century cloth formed less than fifty per cent of exports. By then forty per cent were either re-exports of non-European commodities, or exports to India and America. This greater diversity of English exports had a stabilising and stimulating effect on the economy. Unemployment in the clothing industry was no longer the national disaster it had been under James I.

Exports and imports increased by some fifty per cent between the Restoration and the end of the century, from roughly £4 million to £6 million a year each. These statistics ignore those English interests outside Europe which were not reflected in customs figures, for example, the slave trade and the Newfoundland fishing, which Mr Davis thinks may have exceeded £500,000 a year by 1688.[1] Tobacco, sugar, and calico were hardly re-exported at all before the Navigation Acts. By the end of the century they formed two-thirds of England's imports from outside Europe, and nearly two-thirds of English re-exports to Europe. Retail prices of these commodities (and of other re-exports, such as Indian silks and pepper) fell steeply during these decades. The rapid expansion of English trade resulted not only from monopoly but from cheapness due to 'mass production'. In this respect what Mr Davis calls the 'commercial revolution' can be compared with the eighteenth-century industrial revolution. Before 1650 Dutch merchants had looked like winning the monopoly for themselves. Thanks to the Navigation Acts and sea power they were ousted by English traders.

This was a transition to a new type of economy. For the colonies, or rather their white populations, offered a protected market for English manufactures, as well as cheap sources of raw materials, and so stimulated home production. Slaves from West Africa were paid for by English manufactures. A whole series of refining and finishing industries sprang up, in London and elsewhere, for the home market and for re-export. So for England at all events a way was found out of the mid-century crisis. Between the sixteen-sixties and 1700, manufactures (other than cloth) exported to Europe expanded by

[1] R. Davis, ' English Foreign Trade, 1660–1700 ', *Econ. H.R.* (2nd Ser.), 7, 150–63

eighteen per cent ; similar exports to the colonies by over two hundred per cent, even though such exports still amounted only to eight per cent of the total in 1700. But their protection allowed English industries to develop to the point at which, in the eighteenth century, they could compete in European markets. Nineteenth-century industrialism, Mr Davis suggests, might well have been impossible without the Navigation Acts. Colonial trade prepared for the industrial revolution, just as the political revolution had made possible the use of full state power for the capture and retention of monopoly colonial trade. The policy of Hakluyt, Ralegh, and Pym had triumphed at last.

But the short-run effects of the commercial revolution were the opposite of its long-term stimulus to industry. The Navigation Act's indirect subsidy to shipping, and the great profits of the colonial re-export trade, diverted capital from investment in heavy and capital goods industries. Long voyages had to be financed, overseas fortifications built and maintained, native rulers bribed. Davenant, assessing the annual addition to the national wealth at £2 million, thought that seventy-five per cent of this came from colonial and East Indian trades. Only in time would the profits made through the slave and fishing trades, through shipbuilding, through re-export and the industries working for it, spill over into general industrial investment. Meanwhile the steam engine was not developed, coke was not substituted for charcoal in the iron industry until more than a century after it had been used for drying malt.

Industrial monopoly had been abolished during the Interregnum : commercial monopoly survived. But the companies engaged in European trade soon lost their privileged positions in face of the competition of interlopers and Parliament's hostility to monopolies. The fortunes of the Merchant Adventurers fluctuated with the political situation. Under pressure from the Cavalier Parliament trade in their area was thrown open. In 1683, in the absence of Parliament, the Company was restored to its full privileges ; from 1689 the trade was permanently opened. In 1671 the Eastland Company refused to lower the admission fine which had kept it so exclusive. Thereupon Parliament established free trade in the

Baltic and opened the Company to all on payment of £2. There was no need to abrogate the Company's charter after 1688 ; it had ceased to exist as a separate monopoly. The Greenland trade was thrown open by statute in 1671.

The monopolies of these companies had indeed become superfluous once the navy had established adequate protection against rival powers and pirates in European waters. But other companies engaged in long-distance trade more than held their own. The restored monarchy no longer played fast and loose with them. In this new atmosphere of security, the East India Company built up a permanent fund which it used for fortifications and defence, and so laid the foundations of its future military conquests. The East India and African Companies, indeed, were essential instruments for defeating the Dutch, and enjoyed the peculiar patronage of the government. Both Companies were allowed to set up courts, whose authority was exercised against interlopers by virtue of the royal prerogative alone. Judges nominated by the Companies were thus given power over the property of English subjects. Interlopers, on the other hand, looked to Parliament for protection and support. The Royal African Company was saved only by the dissolution of Charles II's third Parliament in July 1679.

The East India Company offended against the canons of contemporary financial orthodoxy by exporting bullion to pay for its purchases. Sir Josiah Child defended the Company with the argument that four-fifths of its imports were re-exported, ' by the returns of which more than treble the bullion is imported ' ; and in fact bullion exported to India bought goods that were subsequently exchanged for the African gold which gave its name to the guinea. In 1663 the ' bullionist ' enemies of the Company were defeated by the Act legitimising the export of foreign coin, gold, and silver, ' a historic change in English monetary policy ', Mr Lipson calls it. But the Company continued under attack. In 1668, in the case of *Skinner versus the East India Company*, the House of Lords awarded heavy damages to an interloper ; and in 1684 Chief Justice Pollexfen laid it down that interlopers infringed no law since the Company was not established by Act of Parliament. Both the East India and Royal African Companies were thus deeply involved in politics. They were pressed to lend money on a large scale to the government, in return for the privileges and protection they received. The East India Company's new charter of 1657 had narrowed its governing body, and it was now run by a group of extremely rich capitalists, who dismissed the arguments of their enemies as 'levelling' complaints. Under James II Whig members of the Company were forced to sell their stock.

Merchants profited greatly by the trade boom. Between 1660 and 1688, apart from paying large dividends, the East India Company doubled, and the African Company quadrupled, its nominal capital. The Hudson's Bay Company tripled its capital between 1670 and 1688. The only conspicuous failure among the new companies was the Royal Fishing Corporation, which was composed of courtiers and aristocrats after the fashion of the pre-1640 industrial monopolies, with the King as 'Protector' and the Duke of York as Governor. It proved unable to do business and collapsed in a reek of scandal. But in general the companies of the Restoration were run by merchants, not aristocrats. Sir Josiah Child, whom the gentlemanly Evelyn thought 'most sordidly avaricious', made enough from the East India trade to marry his daughter to the heir of a duke 'with £30,000 portion at present, and various expectations'. 'He is a bad merchant,' it was said in 1674, 'that cannot make six times as much of his money by trade as he can by land.'[1]

Charles II's reign opened with harmony between traders and the crown. The Portuguese marriage confirmed the Cromwellian alliance of 1654. Tangier gave England a naval base in the Mediterranean, Bombay a foothold in India, though the King valued them so lightly that he abandoned the former and rented the latter to the East India Company for £10 a year. Merchants remained influential, and their interests affected policy. The 1667 treaty with Spain insisted that colonial and East India goods should be admitted to Spain as though products of England. But Charles II's hostility towards the Dutch, so popular with the East India Company, was not based on purely commercial considerations. Neither Charles nor James shared the fear of France which

[1] *H.M.C., Fifth Report, Appendix*, p. 375

the business community began to feel from the sixteen-seventies, and in consequence their governments gradually lost the confidence of the commercial classes. The disasters of the Second Dutch War, the failure even to provide convoys to bring coal from Newcastle, reminded men how much better trade had been protected under Cromwell.

In the late seventies England prospered by being at peace, whilst the Netherlands and France, its two main rivals, continued at war. But the City does not seem to have been as grateful as some historians think it should have been. In 1676 Charles told the French Ambassador that if Louis XIV seized English ships coming from the Mediterranean it would be almost impossible to deal with the outcry among the merchants who were ' masters of London ' and supported in all things by Parliament. The statute of 1678, excluding the principal French products, an adaptation of an Act of 1649, was passed by a Whig majority. It was repealed in James II's reign ; it was the Tories who were for ' free trade '. A prohibitive tariff was renewed in 1689. As in the earlier years of the century, the constitutional struggle meant that from 1674 to 1688 governments could not afford an effective foreign policy.

FINANCE

The Interregnum transformation in the system of taxation was not reversed. What remained of crown lands was indeed restored in 1660, but they were now a relatively insignificant source of revenue. Charles II sold lands to the value of £1,300,000 in the seventies, and the remainder went soon after 1688. The £100,000 a year which the government received in return for feudal tenures and purveyance was a bad bargain : it barely covered the loss from purveyance. But for the landed classes the bargain was far better than the abortive Great Contract of 1610 : they reduced their own share of taxation at the expense of the poorer consumers on whom the burden of the excise mainly fell. An observer wrote at the beginning of the Cavalier Parliament, ' 'Tis the general opinion of some that this Parliament, being most of all landed men and few traders, will never take away the excise, because their own burdens will thereupon become greater.' ' The acceptance in the seventeenth century,' writes the historian of taxation, ' of the doctrine that the poor should pay taxation is one of the landmarks in English political opinion.' [1] The doctrine that landed proprietors should also pay a fair share of taxation was more popular with traders (as with Cromwell's Army) than with those whom the House of Commons represented. The last of the old Parliamentary subsidies was voted in 1663. After that date Parliamentary taxation did indeed take the form of a land tax, but it was at the reduced rate of 2s in the pound. ' The nobility and gentry are the necessary if not the only support of the crown,' said Sir John Holland whilst attacking the land tax in 1668, ' if they fall that must.' The excise was much preferred by the court party. James II, ' like a true English king ', regarded a land tax as ' the last resource if God Almighty should afflict us with a war '.[2] Only after the true English king had been replaced by a Dutchman was the fiscal revolution completed, and the land tax became a regular feature of English finance.

With the King no longer even expected to live of his own, the possibility arose of establishing a fixed and regular income for the crown's ordinary expenditure; this was something of which ministers since Robert Cecil had dreamed, but which lack of confidence between government and taxpayer had prevented. Parliament in 1660 voted the King a revenue of £1,200,000 a year—half what Cromwell had spent, but twice Charles I's income. But the revenue had been overestimated, perhaps not without some intention of keeping the government dependent on Parliament. Receipts fell £250,000 short of what had been voted. To bridge this gap Parliament voted in 1662 a tax of 2s on every hearth. Although the very poor were exempt, the Hearth Tax, like the excise, fell heavily on small property owners, thus helping the downward march of yeomen and artisans. The Whigs always hated it, and it was abolished after 1688. Its collection was bitterly attacked as

[1] E. Hughes, *Studies in Administration and Finance* (1934), p. 124; W. Kennedy, *English Taxation, 1640–1799* (1913), p. 67
[2] Ed. C. Robbins, *The Diary of John Milward* (1938), pp. 25, 202–3, 311; ed. W. E. Buckley, *Memoirs of Thomas Earl of Ailesbury* (1890), i, 105

an invasion of the Englishman's privacy, though it may be noted that Parliament in 1671 cheerfully allowed any Justice of the Peace to empower the gamekeeper of any lord of a manor (of the rank of esquire and upwards) to search the houses of suspected poachers. The protection of game was a more serious matter than the collection of taxation !

The bulk of the regular revenue came from customs and excise. So governments had every interest in furthering trade. Both excise and customs expanded rapidly after the depression of the sixties. Thanks mainly to this, from 1673 Charles began to receive the full £1,200,000 voted at the Restoration. The practice of leasing (' farming ') the collection of customs dues to private individuals (who made a profit) had been abandoned in 1643 ; it was resumed in 1662. Petty estimated that owing to false declarations, to the cost of collecting, and to the profits of the farmers, the government received only half of what was paid. But gradually merchants, better placed for advancing money, extruded the gentry from the farms. The Cavalier Parliament lost its enthusiasm for farming taxes. From 1671 the customs farm was abandoned. The excise followed in 1683, and, after a number of experiments, the Hearth Tax was taken over by the government in 1684. Leases of farms had been used to compensate ex-Cavaliers for their losses ; they expected more compensation when farming was given up. They often got it in the form of secret-service money. ' The key to the whole problem of corruption under Charles II is to be found in the single word " compensation ",' wrote Professor Browning.

The abandonment of tax-farming, a ' revolution in fiscal policy ', had long-term effects. A new branch of the civil service began to be formed, and expanded rapidly. In 1671, when farming was abandoned, 763 customs officers were added to the national service. There were 10 customs officers at Exeter in 1646, 71 in 1685. Here was an important new source of full-time and well-paid employment, both for younger sons of the gentry, driven from the land by the ' strict settlement ', and for sons of the developing commercial and professional middle class. Sir Richard Temple could never have paid off his debts in the seventies if it had not been for his Commissioner-ship of the Customs, and his loss of government salary between

1685 and 1689 had disastrous effects on his finances.[1] The state machinery was thus strengthened and brought into closer connection with business life, at the same time that individuals and families profited. Their profits, unlike those from monopolies, were not a parasitic burden on the national economy. But many, like Sir Richard Temple, must have learnt the hard way that, in the modern state that was beginning to emerge, patronage had become too important a matter to leave at the arbitrary disposal of an irresponsible sovereign : it must be brought under the control of ministers who could be called to account.

Bankers, said Clarendon, ' were a tribe that had risen and grown up in Cromwell's time, and never were heard of before the late troubles '. Charles I's seizure of bullion in the Tower in 1640, a severe shock to credit, had encouraged deposit banking with goldsmiths. The latter had also benefited by the dangers of private hoarding during the Civil War. In the sixteen-fifties the creation of a national bank was frequently mooted. But the Restoration government was opposed to such a bank, which might well have become too powerful. In 1666 ' the unsafe condition of a bank under a monarchy, and the little safety to a monarch to have any ' were explained to Pepys. Bankers, said a member of Parliament in 1670, were ' the Commonwealth's men who destroy the nobility and gentry '. Nevertheless, they proved necessary to Charles II and James II. Debarred from any form of un-Parliamentary taxation, Charles systematically anticipated revenue by borrowing, and this proved a decisive factor in the evolution of a banking system. Confidence in the government was rudely shaken by the Stop of the Exchequer in 1672, which led to a number of failures among bankers and naturally caused a rise in the rate of interest the government had to pay in future. Though the legal rate of interest was six per cent, Charles was paying ten per cent by the mid-seventies. King and kingdom had become ' the slaves of the bankers '.[2] There was no possibility of creating a funded debt until full

---

[1] Hughes, *Studies in Administration and Finance*, pp. 123, 138–67 ; W. B. Stephens, *Seventeenth Century Exeter* (1958), pp. xxiv, 90 ; E. F. Gay, ' Sir Richard Temple . . . 1653–75 ', *Huntington Library Quarterly*, **6**, 270–6

[2] Anon., *The Mystery of the New-fashioned Goldsmiths or Bankers* (1676), p. 3

confidence had been established between crown and business community.

From 1665 onwards the House of Commons tried to appropriate their grants of taxation to specific uses. This device originated with the ex-Cromwellian Sir George Downing, and was intended to facilitate government borrowing as well as to control expenditure. The Commons repeatedly protested against the government's practice of anticipating customs revenue as a means of avoiding Parliamentary control. The opposition had reason to be worried, since part at least of the increased expenditure went on bribing members as the Cavalier Parliament became the Pensioner Parliament. In 1673-5 pensions cost the government over six times as much as in 1661-3. Between 1676 and 1679 Danby's secret-service fund averaged £84,000 a year. Charles was helped in the seventies by French subsidies. But his salvation came, after the deadlock which followed the dissolution of the Cavalier Parliament, by the improvement of the excise and customs consequent upon the expansion of trade. £1 million of debt was paid off between 1679 and 1682. In James's reign, customs and excise alone brought in as much as the total revenue allotted by Parliament to Charles II—an average of over £600,000 a year each. James's total revenue averaged over £2 million a year. He was thus relatively independent of French subsidies, and could afford to raise his army to four times the size of his brother's.

So the government slipped from under the financial yoke which Parliament had intended to place upon it, thanks to the country's prosperity. The gentlemen's agreement of 1660 failed to establish that confidence between crown and business community for which the latter had been looking throughout the century. In its attempt to escape from control, the government was driven into a pro-French policy, to the neglect of what were regarded as England's political and economic interests. The very prosperity accidentally produced by this policy in the late seventies and eighties roused alarm, because it obviated the necessity for Parliaments ; and the lack of confidence itself set limits to economic expansion. The Stop of the Exchequer, a contemporary tells us, caused greater consternation than did the presence of the Dutch fleet in the

Medway. There was a crisis of confidence in 1682, the year
of the attack on the City's charter, a disturbance of credit in
1685 ; and in the winter of 1688 James seemed deliberately to
be aiming at disrupting social stability by his actions on the
eve of his departure. There were many reasons why the City
welcomed the Liberator, under whom £1,300,000 was at last
repaid to Charles II's bankers.

14 Politics and the Constitution 1660-88

> I think his Majesty that now is, is King upon the best title under heaven, for he was called in by the representative body of England.
>
> Henry Marten, on trial as a regicide in 1660

THE RESTORATION OF PARLIAMENT

THE Restoration of 1660 was a restoration of the united class whom Parliament represented, even more than of the King. The Convention Parliament was not summoned by the King ; it summoned him. 'It is the privilege, . . . the prerogative of the common people of England,' Clarendon told the Lower House in 1661, 'to be represented by the greatest and learnedest and wealthiest and wisest persons that can be chosen out of the nation. . . . The confounding the Commons of England . . . with the common people of England was the first ingredient into that accursed dose . . . a commonwealth.' 'Without the safety and dignity of the monarchy,' Charles II said twenty years later, 'neither religion nor property can be preserved.'

A pamphlet of 1660 succinctly stated the position : 'This island . . . is . . . governed by the influence of a sort of people that live plentifully and at ease upon their rents, extracted from the toil of their tenants and servants, each . . . of whom within the bounds of his own estate acts the prince. . . . They sit at the helm in the supreme council ; they command in chief at sea and land ; they impose taxes and levy it by commissioners of the same quality. Out of this rank select we sheriffs, Justices of Peace and all that execute the authority of a judge ; by the influence of which powers they so order all elections, to Parliament or otherwise, that the whole counties follow their respective factions, and the commonalty in the votes are managed by them as the horse by his rider.' Parliamentary elections throughout the kingdom, Petty confirmed, ' are governed by less than 2,000 active men '.[1] Acts of 1661–2 put the local levies of the militia under the King's control, but he had to act through Lords Lieutenant, who were of course the aristocracy. The latter nominated the leading county gentry as officers. The duty of supplying horse and foot for the militia was based on a property qualification, higher in the case of cavalry. This ensured that the militia remained ' the fortress of liberty '.[2] It had done much to restore Charles II in 1660 ; its defection to William of Orange in most areas was decisive in 1688. Charles II once pointed out to a Quaker that the soldiers who attacked Quaker meetings in London were not his troops but those of the Lord Mayor. It was through the militia that many of the chief borough-mongers exercised their influence.

The restoration of the House of Lords and Bishops served the same social purposes. In 1675 Shaftesbury, in Harringtonian vein, claimed that, ' There is no prince that ever governed without a nobility or an army. If you will not have the one, you must have the other, or the monarchy cannot long support or keep itself from tumbling into a democratical republic.' Peers, Shaftesbury implied, were cheaper as well as nicer than rude mercenaries. It was perhaps in recognition of this useful social function that none of the many peers convicted of murder between 1660 and 1702 suffered any penalty.[3] But although the Upper House was restored, its position in the constitution could never be the same. Clarendon blamed the negligence of the King, his excessive reliance on the loyalty of the Cavalier Lower House, and the laziness and selfishness of the peers themselves, for the Lords' loss of reputation. Resolutions of the Commons in 1661, 1671, and 1678 finally established their right to initiate money Bills and appropriate supplies ; and denied the power of the Lords to amend such Bills. In the case of *Skinner versus the East India*

---

[1] Anon., *A Discourse for a King and Parliament* (1660), pp. 1–2 ; ed. Lansdowne, *Petty Papers* (1927), i, 7

[2] *Thurloe State Papers*, i, 54

[3] D. Ogg, *England in the Reigns of James II and William III*, p. 107

Company (1668), the Lords' claim to exercise original jurisdiction in civil cases between commoners was finally defeated ; but the Upper House retained its appellate jurisdiction.

The social panic of 1660 partly explains why the King was not bound by specific conditions. But there were plenty of unspecified restrictions. Moreover, the prerogative courts were not revived ; without them the Privy Council lost its power of interfering in local affairs against the wishes of the ' natural rulers '. It also lost its criminal jurisdiction, and abandoned any attempt to legislate or tax independently of Parliament. The Book of Rates of 1660 was passed as a Parliamentary statute. The abolition of military tenures and the sale of nearly all crown lands transformed the nature of the monarchy's power. It was no longer, in the medieval tradition, based on land, on personal relations between King and subjects, and on the crown's ability to inflict economic harm. The court in the sense of the royal household ceased to be the centre of real power. Royal patronage henceforth was exercised almost solely through appointment to state offices ; control of such appointments passed slowly into the hands of ministers.

But the greatest change of all was in the minds of men. The execution of Charles I, Mr Ogg rightly argued, was the most important political event of the century. Almost as significant was the experience in government gained during the Interregnum. For nearly twenty years, Committees of Parliament had controlled Army, navy, Church, and foreign trade, and more efficiently than the old government had ever done. No longer could these be treated as ' mysteries of state ', into which subjects must not pry. City merchants had served on committees for finance, trade, and colonies. A new civil service had arisen which was far too useful to be scrapped. The returned Royalists could not command the navy without the help of ' tarpaulin ' captains who had served their apprenticeship under the Commonwealth. The Duke of York, Burnet tells us, disliked tarpaulins, who ' hated Popery and loved liberty '. He started training and promoting ' young persons of quality '. But the naval code of discipline published in 1661 and the military code of 1666 were substantially those of the Commonwealth.

Twelve out of thirty of Charles II's Privy Council in 1661 had been in arms against his father. The Committee for Trade and Plantations of July 1660 included only two former Royalists out of ten members. Downing—soon to be reputed the richest man in England—was indispensable in the sphere of finance and economic planning, and developed a completely new system of book-keeping in the Treasury. Samuel Pepys, himself an old Cromwellian, tells us that in January 1668 ' all the Cavalier party were not able to find the Parliament 9 Commissioners [for Accounts], or one Secretary, fit for the business ', and they were ' fain to find out ' old-fashioned men of Cromwell's ' to do their business for them '. Even in the militia there were ' few of the old stock of people left who knew which way to go about it '. The Act of Oblivion and Indemnity came to be called an Act of indemnity for the King's enemies and of oblivion for his friends. 'Presbyterians for their money must be served,' grumbled a Bishop, ' while the royal party, that have endured the heat of the day and become poor, be put off with inconsiderable nothings.' [1]

THE LAW

The common-law courts had emerged victorious over their rivals.[2] The King's Bench succeeded to most of Star Chamber's jurisdiction. King's Bench and Parliament inherited the general supervision of legal processes which the Privy Council had previously exercised ; this prevented the growth of any system of administrative law. The prohibition of martial law brought all cases of riot and rebellion to the ordinary courts, so that the ' state of siege ' is practically unknown in England. Parliament succeeded to Star Chamber's control of the press. Church courts returned, but with depleted powers ; henceforth their subordination to the common-law courts was accepted. The latter also took over much commercial jurisdiction from the Admiralty court. Governments once again

[1] H.M.C., Fifth Report, p. 195 ; A. Wood, Life and Times (1891), i, 333
[2] For the following paragraphs, see R. Robinson, Anticipations under the Commonwealth of Changes in the Law (1869) ; T. F. T. Plucknett, A Concise History of the Common Law (1956), passim ; Sir W. Holdsworth, A History of English Law (1923-56), esp. i, v, vi

occasionally employed torture against political prisoners, but furtively and shamefacedly.

The common law whose supremacy was now established was not the common law as interpreted by Charles I's judges, but as interpreted by Coke and his Parliamentarian successors, like Rolle and Hale, the latter of whom long survived the Restoration. During Coke's lifetime the last three parts of his *Institutes* were forbidden publication : they were printed only in the revolutionary year 1641, by order of the Commons. But henceforth Coke was regarded as ' a second father of the law, behind whose works it was not necessary to go '. This attitude towards Coke's *Reports* and *Institutes* had the effect of concealing such medieval precedent as was inconvenient ; so legal continuity was preserved by wholesale suppression.

Common-law supremacy led to considerable modifications in the law of libel and slander. Chancery—the equity court— began to evolve its own system of consistent law and precedent. The practice of choosing a common lawyer as Lord Chancellor continued, and Lord Chancellor Clarendon himself tacitly accepted some of the Commonwealth reforms. Under Hale and ' the Father of modern Equity ', Lord Nottingham, himself a common lawyer, equity ceased to be ' mysterious ' and ' the measure of the Chancellor's foot '. Many laws passed during the revolutionary decades, though formally annulled in 1660, were re-enacted before the end of the century. The Statute of Frauds (1677), whose main object was to give creditors better remedies against their debtors' land, was possibly planned during the Interregnum. Legal continuity at the Restoration included continuity of personnel. Roger North complained bitterly of the Parliamentarian sympathies of the mass of the legal profession.

Under the Commonwealth, judges had held office ' during good behaviour '. After the Restoration, they once again held ' during the King's pleasure ', and this lasted until the Act of Settlement re-established Parliamentary control in 1701. In 1665 a statute insisted that jurors should possess freehold land worth at least £20 a year. Three years later the House of Commons voted that it was illegal for judges to menace, fine, or imprison juries. The Recorder of London fined a jury for acquitting two Quakers in 1670 ; but the Court of Common

Pleas reversed this, and the principle was established that juries are immune from fines for their verdicts.

KING AND COMMONS

Former Parliamentarians were at first little less determined than former Cavaliers that there should be no more trouble from the lower orders. The Act against Tumultuous Petitioning of 1661 forbade the collection of more than twenty signatures to a political petition to King or Parliament, ' unless the matter thereof have been first consented unto or ordered by three or more Justices of that county, or by the major part of the Grand Jury ', or in London by Lord Mayor, aldermen, and common councillors. That would prevent anything like Leveller tactics of propaganda. It called the gentry in to redress the balance inside towns. So did the Corporation Act, whose object was nakedly stated : ' that the succession in such corporations may be most profitably perpetuated in the hands of persons well-affected to his Majesty and the established government '. It required all holders of municipal office to renounce the Covenant, and to take an oath of non-resistance and the sacrament according to the rites of the Church of England. The Act gave commissions appointed by the crown absolute power to remove and replace officers of corporations ; and the government chose its commissioners from peers and gentlemen living near the particular corporation due for purging, to the virtual exclusion of townsmen. The Earl of Derby knew from bitter experience who the dangerous men in Manchester were ; and even burghers anxious to take the oaths were in many cases turned out and replaced by loyal nominees.

Purging corporations helped to ensure favourable elections of borough members to the House of Commons ; both Charles I and Cromwell had tried it. But Charles II and his brother found the policy more necessary now, since Parliament could not be dispensed with, and since after 1673 the crown was compelled to abandon its claim to create new Parliamentary boroughs. The government had wanted the commissions appointed under the Corporation Act to be permanent ; Parliament limited their period of authority to fifteen months.

Members of Parliament did not want to give the crown a free hand to gerrymander the bodies which elected them. For the next eighteen years there were continual attempts to remodel town charters so as to give the crown the right to nominate officials, or at least exercise a veto, and to restrict the Parliamentary franchise in towns to officials recommended by the King. The more drastic interference in the affairs of corporations between 1681 and 1688 was thus not a new policy but the more vigorous application of an old one. It had the additional advantage for the government that corporation officials nominated juries, and so their selection could be influenced even if jurors could no longer be intimidated.

Relations between government and House of Commons were indeed paradoxical. Clarendon was regarded by many ex-Royalists as too lenient with Presbyterians. The government was compelled by the Commons to abandon its attempt either to include Presbyterians within the Church of England or to dispense with the penal laws, and much of the ' Clarendon Code ' was forced on it. Loyal though they were, the Commons took full advantage of the new position in the constitution which the events of the preceding decades had won for them. Clarendon's fall was due (over and above his loss of the King's confidence) to his failure to build up a party of supporters in the House of Commons, or to accept the fact that, in his own outraged words, ' the House of Commons was the fittest judge of the necessities and grievances of the people '. Henceforth no chief minister survived for long who could not command a majority in the Lower House.

Macaulay wrote of the Cavalier Parliament, ' The great English revolution of the seventeenth century, that is to say the transfer of the supreme control of the executive administration from the crown to the House of Commons, was, through the whole long existence of this Parliament, proceeding noiselessly but rapidly and steadily.' In 1665 the principle of appropriation of supply, opposed by Solicitor-General Finch as ' introductive to a commonwealth ', was accepted ; in 1667 the first Parliamentary Committee of Public Accounts was established. In the same year the sentence pronounced against Eliot, Holles and Valentine in 1629 was declared illegal, because an infringement of the right of free speech in Parliament. So the Cavalier Parliament condemned Charles I. In 1676 the Privy Council committed a man to prison for a mutinous speech, and refused either to grant bail or to bring him to trial. The Whigs retorted in 1679 by passing the *Habeas Corpus* Act, forcing governments to give their prisoners speedy trial. An Act of 1641 had insisted that a writ of *habeas corpus* should be issued ' without delay upon any pretence whatsoever ' when demanded on behalf of anyone arrested on warrant from the King or Privy Council. The Act of 1679 defined the existing procedure, and so confirmed one of the principles fought for since the sixteen-twenties. When Charles II wished to punish a country gentleman for words spoken in a Parliamentary debate, he had to hire thugs to slit the man's nose ; and times had so changed that the King had to assent to an Act of Attainder against his bravos, which expressly denied him any right to pardon them.

After Clarendon's fall the King's government was run by an unholy alliance of ex-Cromwellians, future Whig exclusionists, and Papists. It split on the French alliance formed in the secret Treaty of Dover. In 1673 Charles was compelled to abandon the Declaration of Indulgence, after proclaiming his determination to stick to it ; and to give up his pro-French policy and the financial independence which it promised. He had to accept the Test Act, which drove Papist and Protestant dissenters out of public life again, and so laid a secure basis for Danby's rule through the gentry. Danby accepted more whole-heartedly than Clarendon the necessity of support in the House of Commons. His party was based on the old Cavaliers and Anglicans ; but he also took over from Arlington new methods of management. Offices and pensions were distributed with a view to influencing members of Parliament ; and the holders were organised and disciplined in the House. Systematic pressure was brought to bear on constituencies, sheriffs, returning officers ; direct bribery was employed in the House of Commons. A pamphlet of 1679 listed 214 members alleged to be taking government money in one form or another. The story of the Secretary of State's remark to a Cornish member in James II's reign may be apocryphal, but it illustrates what had by then become accepted practice. ' Sir ! ' he cried, as the member voted against the court. ' Have

you not got a troop of horse in His Majesty's service?' 'Yes,
my lord,' was the reply, 'but my brother died last night and
has left me £700 a year.' That was the price of political
independence.

But Danby had to work within clearly defined limits. He
himself accurately reflected the views of his gentry supporters
in opposing acceptance of money from Catholic France. The
Commons' first step at the new session of October 1673 had
been to order the solemn observance of the anniversary of
Gunpowder Plot. There is a direct connection between the
revelation of Charles II's dependence on France and the
hysteria over the Popish Plot. The traditional fear of a too
strong centralised government would apply even more to a
King with a French or Irish army behind him than to the
Major-Generals. Danby wondered in 1677 whether 'a small
insurrection' might not be desirable as an excuse for obtaining
money and arms for the government. Even the opposition
leaders were astonished by the completeness of the court's
defeat when a general election at last came in 1679.

The impeachment of Danby showed how even a minister
who originally owed his position to a Parliamentary majority
could not survive once he had lost the confidence of the
Commons, and that not even bribery could keep the confidence
of the House for a man against whom public opinion outside
had decisively turned. Since Danby's fall sprang from the
government's foreign policy, the Commons' effective control
of this hitherto sacrosanct sphere was again demonstrated.
The Cavalier Parliament in 1678 passed an Act which for
sheer offensiveness to the ruling monarch has perhaps never
been equalled. It said that Papists should be permitted to
come into the presence of the King or Queen only if they
first procured 'licence so to do, by . . . warrant under the
hands and seals of six or more Privy Councillors, by order
of His Majesty's Privy Council, upon some urgent occasion,
therein to be expressed, so as such licence exceed not the space
of ten days, and that the said licence be first filed and put
upon record . . . for anybody to view without fee or reward,
and no person to be licensed for above the number of thirty
days in any one year'.

By 1678 three factors had transformed the political situation from that in which Charles had been so joyfully welcomed. First, a large number of by-elections had diluted the original Cavalier element, over-represented in the enthusiasm of 1661 : the House of Commons became more representative of the long-term views of the propertied class, though even so Charles's advisers rightly supposed that they would never again have so favourable a House. Secondly, the pro-French foreign policy of the King and rumours of the secret Treaty of Dover had given rise to alarm. In 1673 Charles had to deny that ' the forces I have raised in this war were designed to control law and property '. Then, thirdly, the Popish Plot seemed to corroborate the worst fears of the opposition, and played into their hands. The most memorable remark of Nell Gwyn, Charles II's actress mistress, was her rebuke to a hostile mob which had mistaken her coach for that of the Duchess of Portsmouth, the French and Papist royal mistress. ' Be silent, good people,' cried Nell, ' I am the *Protestant* whore ! ' The crowd roared its approval of her theological patriotism.

How then did Charles not only survive the crisis of 1678–81, but defeat the Exclusion Bills and emerge in a strong enough position to defy the Triennial Act ? Charles was as intelligent, if as lazy, as his grandfather James I. But he had also learnt political prudence and a hard cynicism in his years of exile, when he had resolved never to go on his travels again. Unlike his brother, he had no principles to which he would sacrifice his convenience. On his death-bed he acknowledged himself a Papist, and the secret Treaty of Dover probably represents the policy which he would ideally have wished to pursue. But it would not have been a realistic policy : in the last four years of his reign Charles achieved a relative political independence by the closest collaboration with the Tory-Anglican gentry.

Their favourite political theorist, Filmer, once spoke of monarchy being crucified between two thieves, Popery and the people. Certainly that was the fate of the Tory gentry. Shaftesbury had countered Danby's court party by organising a country party based on the old ' Presbyterian ' interest and City merchants, with the dangerous support of dissenters and London populace. By economic reprisals against persecutors, merchants made the Test and Corporation Acts unworkable in many towns. The Green Ribbon Club, established in London in 1675, may be regarded as the first party headquarters. Its green colours were those of the Levellers. The ghosts of the Interregnum were walking again. Whig electioneering and rabble-rousing tactics were too successful. In Buckinghamshire it was the yeomen who were most vociferous for exclusion ; not the gentry, who normally gave the lead. In 1679 a Whig government was forced on the King, and the Commons refused to accept the royal nominee as Speaker. But Charles retained his old civil servants, and the Whig aristocrats themselves were not prepared to face civil war. They did not need to be reminded by Halifax that ' the most forward in the Long Parliament were soon turned out by others ', and that in 1681 too ' the gentlemen, the knights of the shires, may be kicked out by mechanics, by citizens and burgesses, for he who practiseth disobedience to his superiors teacheth it to his inferiors '. With Tory support Charles was therefore able to call the Whigs' bluff at the Oxford Parliament. The Rye House Plot completed their discomfiture by apparently associating them with republican desperadoes.

But the King's triumph of 1681-5 was not a personal triumph. Nor, close though relations were with France, was it an unqualified victory for Louis XIV. Charles survived only because of his complete surrender to the Tory and Anglican gentry. His purge of local government in these years was made in the closest agreement with them. ' How complete a monopoly of local administration the Tories now won,' Dr Feiling wrote, ' was amply shown four years later by King James's herculean efforts to reverse it.' The victor was not military absolutism but the Tory gentry. ' I will stick by you and my old friends,' Charles told the Tory Reresby in 1680, ' for if I do not I should have nobody to stick to me.' The King had no prerogative courts, and dared not even repeal the *Habeas Corpus* Act.

PARTIES

The history of parties in this period is highly controversial. Two terminal points are clear. Between 1640 and 1660 there was a civil war : so the existence of at least two parties can be assumed then. By 1760 party labels had lost almost all political significance. What happened in between?

Civil-war animosities survived the Restoration : the Clarendon Code was a straightforward Cavalier-Anglican party measure, designed to exclude their rivals from political office. But the men of property on both sides were anxious to avoid another civil war. In 1662 a Londoner expressed the hope that 'all the gentry in the land would kill one another, that so the commonalty might live the better'. Consciousness of this deep hostility lies at the back of gentry political thinking, though it is rarely openly discussed. For example, Baxter wrote on the eve of the Restoration, 'The rabble hate both magistrates and ministers.' A letter-writer at about the same time agreed that between the gentry and ' the ordinary sort of people ' there was ' a natural animosity, of late years infinitely increased '.[1] Edward Chamberlayne fifteen years later spoke of ' most of the tradesmen and very many of the peasantry ' as ' hating, despising or disrespecting the nobility, gentry and superior clergy '. The prosperity of some dissenters, and the pacifism of others, blunted the edge of their discontent. But the sharpening class divisions of the later seventeenth century increased the restlessness of the poor, and this made Parliamentary leaders think twice about pushing their quarrels too far. The Popish Plot stirred up wild passions in London, but the extent of Shaftesbury's reliance on the populace in the end proved fatal to his cause. The men of property rallied to the crown in fear of civil war.

This is the essential if usually unspoken background to late seventeenth-century politics. The propertied classes could not forget the lesson they had learnt in 1646–60, just as kings did not forget the lesson of 1649. So political opposition was never pushed to extremes ; if it was, it tended to disintegrate. The House of Commons might criticise, but did not fundamentally oppose government, so long as government did not attack the interests of those whom the members represented. So the government, the court, always exercised a strong influence, cutting across political parties. This arose in part from its dispensation of patronage, but also from deeper considerations of its contribution to social stability, to the

[1] *Middlesex County Records*, iii (1888), 326 ; *Thurloe State Papers*, vii, 704

system from which both Whigs and Tories benefited. 'What does it matter who serves His Majesty,' Sunderland used to ask, ' so long as His Majesty is served ? ' He might have added, ' What does it matter which majesty one serves, so long as there is a majesty to serve ? '

JAMES II

So the prospects seemed hopeful for James II. When Parliament finally met in 1685, 200 members (out of 513) were directly dependent on the King for their livelihood. 400 had never sat in the House before. The increased income voted him by this Parliament, plus the rising revenue from customs and excise, left James better off than any of his predecessors. The Tory-Anglican theory of passive obedience, used against the Solemn League and Covenant and preached tirelessly in the early sixteen-eighties, when Filmer's tracts circulated most widely, sounded like an invitation to despotism. Monmouth's revolt seemed to make James's position impregnable. For it split the Whigs. Few of the hereditary landowning Whig aristocracy joined the bastard usurper ; it was the small men of the south-western counties who rallied to his support. We can see this from the fact that Sedgemoor was an infantry battle : the cavalry which had been the strength of Cromwell's Army was not there. James's victory was complete ; henceforth the Good Old Cause was dead. There was to be no organised democratic movement in England for many generations.

Yet the triumph of 1685 was illusory. The rank and file of the Somerset militia had proved unreliable, and James's victory was won by his small professional army. Monmouth's revolt seems to have decided James that he must increase this army ; that it must be largely officered by men in whom he had confidence, mainly Catholics ; and that he must build up another army in Ireland. James thus faced in an exaggerated form the dilemma from whose horns his brother had never been able to escape. Normally the staunchest supporters of the monarchy were the Tory gentry. But their loyalty was to Church as well as to crown. A Catholic policy could hope to succeed only if the gentry's power in the country was counter-

balanced by a Catholic-Nonconformist alliance. Charles II
had flirted with such an alliance, but had always been forced
to draw back. James tried but never had a chance. Protestant
dissenters were politically weaker than a generation earlier.
The aftermath of the Popish and Rye House Plots and of
Monmouth's rebellion had taken heavy toll. Such accessions
of numbers as they had received came largely from the middle
and lower classes; their thought now tended away from
politics and towards pacifism. Dissenters who had supported
Shaftesbury and Monmouth could hardly be won overnight
for a King who was all too plainly using them in his own
interests. William Penn and other Quakers appear to have
taken James's intentions at their face value; the Quakers had
suffered most of all the sects from Tory-Anglican persecution.
As long as the heir to the throne was a Protestant, dissenters
might take comfort from James's age; but the birth of his son
—another of his seeming triumphs—must have aroused the
gravest misgivings among those whose support James was trying
to woo.

James moreover had all the stupid obstinacy (or high
devotion to principle) of his father: and the gentry thought
the religion to which he was devoted was the wrong one.
His actions did everything to unite the propertied class against
him and to heal the split between Whigs and Tories which
had appeared to threaten civil war in 1681. First, the defeat
of Monmouth's rebellion relieved the right-wing Whigs of their
radical allies: henceforth there was little danger that 1640
would lead to 1649. Secondly, Jeffreys' barbarities in the
Bloody Assizes offered a magnificent propaganda platform, and
played the same part in the mythology of 1688 as the Marian
persecutions did in Elizabethan propaganda. The Bloody
Assizes and the Revocation of the Edict of Nantes in France
in the same year fitted perfectly into the traditional legend, for
cruelty was one of the things Protestants were most taught
to abhor in Papists, whether it was the burning of the
Marian martyrs, the Spanish Inquisition, the ill-treatment of
American Indians by Spaniards, the Gunpowder Plot, or
the Irish massacres of 1641. Nor is it to the discredit of
English Protestants that they disliked cruelty. The brutal
and bullying Jeffreys tried the accused at the rate of 500

a day; James's Queen made profits out of transporting condemned rebels. (See Plate 10, facing page 197.)

Thirdly, most Tories were alarmed by the introduction of Roman Catholic officers into James's army. This was indeed the point at which the hitherto docile Parliament dug in its toes, and had to be prorogued and finally dissolved. For three long years James tried to cajole or bully the gentry into accepting repeal of the Test Act, the rock on which their supremacy had been built. Then, with the 'heat' which had led Charles to prophesy that his brother 'would never be able to hold it out four years to an end', James sacked his Tory ministers, and started to attack the privileges of the Anglican universities and the freehold tenure of fellows of colleges. In *Godden versus Hales* he won legal sanction for the employment of Roman Catholic officers in the army; and in Ireland he was known to be building up a strong and entirely Papist army, under the command of the terrifying and anti-English Tyrconnel. Worst of all, in renewing Charles's attack on borough charters, he allied with the Tories' bitterest enemies, the radical dissenters, so painfully weeded out of governing positions in their natural strongholds, the towns, over the preceding twenty-five years.

The relationships of patronage between loyal gentry and their local boroughs were broken overnight. The Parliamentary franchise and administration of justice in many towns was handed over to republicans, dissenters, and Papists, men who themselves had for years been virtually outside the law. An Anabaptist became Lord Mayor of London, soon after Sir Henry Vane's son joined Father Petre on the Privy Council. At Bedford, where several members of Bunyan's congregation were made aldermen and common council men, reforms were instituted reminiscent of the rule of the Major-Generals: previous mayors who had pocketed moneys belonging to the town's charitable foundations were ordered to disburse them. In the counties, the last holy of holies, 'the prime of the gentry' were dismissed from the commission of the peace and Deputy Lieutenancies unless they would pledge their support for repeal of the Test Act. And who replaced them? 'Ordinary persons both as to quality and estates (most of them dissenters). . . . Neither of them have one foot of freehold

land in England,' said Sir John Reresby of new Justices of the
Peace in Yorkshire. This was something very like a social
revolution, as bad as the rule of the Major-Generals, who
had been installed because the government had found
the militia unreliable. It was too much even for Tory
loyalty. Lord Keeper Guilford had given a clear warning in
1684 of the ' reasons against tolerating Papists '. It would
' discontent the gentry '. If the gentry would not serve cheerfully, then ' the whole use of the law is lost ; for they are
sheriffs, etc. If the gentry are discontented, the rabble will
quickly be poisoned by preachers, etc. And then what will
force signify ? '

Moreover, the rank and file of the army concentrated on
Hounslow Heath to overawe the City, indulged in political
discussions and the reading of pamphlets, and recalled the
New Model Army by their excessive interest in Magna Carta
and similar unsuitable subjects. Their applause at the acquittal
of the Seven Bishops echoed the applause of Lilburne's guards
at his acquittal in 1653. This was an army very unlike the
well-to-do farmers and citizens of the militia whom James so
despised. The eventual disintegration of this army in 1688,
from on top, is evidence of the reluctance of its propertied
officers to face civil war. The difference between supporters
of Monmouth and William was comparable to that between
' Independents ' and ' Presbyterians ' in the Civil War : a
foreign army enabled the latter to avoid putting arms into
the hands of the common people.

For a generation the Church of England had taught that
resistance to the Lord's Anointed could in no circumstances be
justified. When Monmouth claimed to die a Protestant of the
Church of England, a divine told him, ' My lord, if you be of
the Church of England, you must acknowledge the doctrine of
non-resistance to be true.' The parsons and the squires had
gladly repeated these phrases. But they were thinking of the
common people's duty of passive obedience to established
authority. They had assumed that the Lord's Anointed would
never attack their supremacy, nor that of their Church. Bishop
Morley, one of the makers of the Restoration, had warned James
that ' if ever he depended on the doctrine of non-resistance he
would find himself deceived. The clergy might not think

proper to contradict their doctrine in terms, but he was very
sure they would in practice.' [1]

There is great symbolic significance in the fact that it was
Bishops who gave the signal for resistance to the royal prerogative. Some of the Seven held their convictions so dear that,
even though they stood trial rather than yield to James, they
resigned rather than accept 1688. But can we imagine Laudian
Bishops behaving as they did ? Or enjoying such popularity
with the people of London and the rank and file of the army ?
For all its cult of King Charles the Martyr, the Church of
England had advanced farther with the times than it realised.
' If the King can do no wrong,' Defoe sneered, ' somebody did
the late King a great deal of wrong.' James would have
heartily agreed. He was flabbergasted and outraged by the
failure of Tories and Anglicans to live up to their principles.

The Tories, then, were badly confused and rattled in 1688.
Lord Willoughby summed up their difficulty when he said,
' It was the first time any Bertie was ever engaged against the
crown and it was his trouble ;—but there was a necessity either
to part with our religion and properties, or do it.' General
dissatisfaction ' with the present conduct of the government
in relation to . . . religion, liberties and properties ' was the
first point made in the letter of invitation sent to William of
Orange in 1688. Religion, liberty, and property : we have
heard of them before. Religion and property were ' the two
things men value most ', James himself stated in the Declaration
of Indulgence issued in 1687. He added, in so many words,
that ' although the freedom and assurance we have hereby given
in relation to religion and property might be sufficient to
remove from the minds of our loving subjects all fears and
jealousies in relation to either, yet we have thought fit further
to declare that we will maintain them in all their properties
and possessions, as well of church and abbey lands, as in any
other their lands and properties whatsoever '.

James protested too much. His protestations could hardly
undo the effect of his actions. In *Godden versus Hales* the judges
had laid it down that ' there is no law whatsoever but may be
dispensed with ' by the King, for reasons of which he is sole
judge. That had been royal doctrine in the Ship Money case.

[1] E. H. Plumptre, *The Life of Thomas Ken* (1890), i, 298

The Seven Bishops' council said, ' If the King may suspend the laws of our land which concern our religion, I am sure there is no other law but he may suspend ; and if the King may suspend all the laws of the kingdom, what a condition are all the subjects in for their lives, liberties and properties ! All at mercy ! ' ' It amounts to an . . . utter repeal of all the laws,' Justice Powell told the jury. ' If this be once allowed of, there will need no Parliament ; all the legislature will be in the King, which is a thing worth considering, and I leave the issue to God and your consciences.' (The judges were under great popular pressure in this trial, and yielded to it to such an extent that their dicta caused some embarrassment to later commentators.)

There are two points to make here. First, James had a strong legal case in *Godden versus Hales* and in his interference in the Magdalen College election. But this was irrelevant since, as in the sixteen-thirties, the King was flying in the face of the opinion of those who mattered in the country. James's habit of ' closeting ' the judges was something even Charles I had not resorted to. Four judges were dismissed before *Godden versus Hales* came up for trial : Powell and another judge who summed up in favour of the Seven Bishops were also dismissed. James needed to protest that property was not endangered by judges interpreting the law under such pressure : for this was the point on which Whig propaganda had long concentrated. Yet his protests were not believed. Or rather, there was enough doubt in the minds of the Tory gentry to undermine their absolute loyalty. Their devotion to Church and King had worn thin when Charles II had pursued a Catholicising policy. It snapped under a King whose openly Papist policy affected not only religion but also their jobs in central and local administration. Nothing else could have driven the Tories to see at long last that *their* position could not be secure unless the supremacy of Parliament was established. This contradicted their traditional Royalist political theory ; but theories proved weaker than facts when it came to the point. Even some English Catholics abandoned James. His most trusted advisers were Irishmen and priests ; the main body of Catholic peers were horrified at the recklessness of his advance towards an absolutism of the French type, which would no

longer have been so dependent on the direct support of the
landed class. This was a further source of weakness : the main
English agent of James's schemes was Sunderland, a man to
whom religion meant nothing, and who delayed his ' con-
version ' until a son had been born to Queen Mary and the
Catholic succession seemed to be assured.

Even James's close relations with Louis XIV were not a
source of strength to him, though they did him great harm
with his subjects. At Charles's death-bed James had asked
the French Ambassador to ' assure your master that he shall
always have in me a faithful and grateful servant '. He
abjectly apologised for summoning a Parliament without his
French cousin's permission : ' I hope that he will not take it
amiss that I have acted without consulting him. He has a
right to be consulted ; and it is my wish to consult him about
everything.' Louis XIV helped to persuade James to take
Sunderland into his service. Yet, despite James's appeals,
he obtained much less financial help from France than his
brother had done—some £125,000 in all, about one-eighth of
a year's revenue. James's foreign policy, wavering between
submission to Louis and fitful revolt, managed to get the
worst of both worlds. In 1688 Louis was unprepared to give
him overwhelming military and naval support ; and anything
else, as James realised, would do more harm than good.

So James ran through the whole gamut of Stuart policy.
He began with the traditional dependence on the Anglican
gentry, the policy of Hyde and Danby. He flirted, as Henrietta
Maria and Charles II had flirted, with the idea of imposing
despotism with French support ; but he was less skilful than
Charles II in extracting the maximum from the bargain and
drawing back from any dangerous commitment. Then, and
too obviously merely as a gambit, he revived the Indulgence
policy of his brother, the alliance of Protestant and Roman
Catholic dissenters against the Anglican supremacy, and
again lacked Charles's wisdom in deciding when to retreat.
Finally, after his desperate attempt to resuscitate the Anglican-
Tory alliance had failed, he lost his head completely.

Charles I saved the Stuart monarchy by proclaiming that
he died a martyr for religion, law, and property. James damned
it for ever by an apparent attempt to appeal to anarchy. He

departed without handing authority over to any government. He destroyed the writs summoning Parliament, and threw the Great Seal into the Thames in the vain hope of preventing one being called. He ordered the disbandment, unpaid, of the terrible army on Hounslow Heath. The navy, in which the seamen were discussing politics no less than in the Army, was ordered to sail to Tyrconnel in Ireland. Riots in London and other towns united the men of property in submission to William the Liberator. By James's absence, the loyal Sir James Bramston summed up, 'it became necessary that government should be by somebody, to avoid confusion', and to prevent 'the rabble from spoiling and robbing the nobility and wealthy'. Continued non-resistance to James would defeat its object—the maintenance of social subordination.

15 Religion and Ideas, 1660-88

> *Christian* Did you not know about ten years ago one Temporary in your parts, who was a forward man in religion then ? . . . All of a sudden he grew acquainted with one Save-self, and then he became a stranger to me.
>
> Bunyan, *Pilgrim's Progress* (1672)

> If our Church should be an enemy to commerce, intelligence, discovery, navigation, or any sort of mechanics, how could it be fit for the present genius of this nation ?
>
> Bishop Sprat, *History of the Royal Society* (1667)

PARLIAMENT AND THE CHURCH

ALTHOUGH they had played an ignoble role during the Inter-regnum, and had contributed little to the Restoration, Bishops came back in 1660, recovered their lands, and returned to their seats in the House of Lords. The old Prayer Book services were restored. 1,760 ministers and 150 dons and schoolmasters were ejected as dissenters, with none of the compensation given to ejected Royalists in the sixteen-forties. But the Church did not regain its old position. Parsons were restored to their benefices by Act of Parliament, with exceptions which were laid down in the Act : the supremacy of Parliament over the Church could hardly have been more clearly declared. Bishops did not recover their dominance in politics. Archbishop Sheldon was an important figure so long as Clarendon held office ; after Clarendon's fall no Bishop was ever again a significant member of a government, except the diplomat John Robinson, Bishop of Bristol and London, who was made Lord Privy Seal by the Tory government in 1711—an appointment that was regarded as highly provocative.

Laud's economic programme for the Church was abandoned. So was his social programme. Ecclesiastical authorities no longer inquired about enclosure or the decay of tillage. Following Interregnum precedent, the clergy were taxed together with the laity by Parliament and voted in Parliamentary elections, though still incapable of sitting in the House of Commons. Even in the Lords churchmen counted for less. At the beginning of the century Bishops formed nearly one-third of its members, by the end one-eighth. With taxation, Convocation lost most of its *raison d'être* and rapidly sank into insignificance. The medieval conception of the clergy as a separate estate finally vanished ; they became one of many professions, much the worst remunerated. The Act of 1661 which restored ecclesiastical jurisdiction insisted that nothing therein should be ' construed to extend . . . to abridge or diminish the King's Majesty's supremacy in ecclesiastical matters '. The *jure divino* authority of Church courts had gone for ever ; and political events soon transformed the supremacy of the King over the Church into the supremacy of Parliament.

The High Commission was not restored. So Church courts slowly lost their power. Prohibitions were frequent as a means of asserting the now unchallenged overriding control of the common-law judges. In 1666 the Archdeacon of Durham reported ' general complaint of ministers and church-wardens that they cannot get any sesses [assessments] for reparation of churches ' because they had no coercive powers ; and Justices of the Peace in Quarter Sessions refused to assist. Bishop Burnet, after some years of experiment, gave up hope of doing any good through his Consistorial Court and stopped going to it. In 1678 Parliament abolished ' all punishment by death in pursuance of any ecclesiastical censures ', and limited the power of Church courts in cases of heresy to the imposition of spiritual penalties. Churchwardens concerned themselves mainly with regulating the morals of the lower orders and harrying nonconformists. ' Churchwardens' presentments [of offenders] are but laughed at,' we hear from Lancashire in 1669. In 1670 a vicar found it necessary to remind the gentry of the horrors of the Interregnum, when they were slaves to their own tenants and might themselves have to wear a white sheet on the stool of repentance. But even he argued for the use of the secular arm against nonconformity, because Church courts would make themselves too unpopular by prosecuting it.[1] In the long run Justices of the Peace were residuary legatees of the Church courts as disciplinary agents for the lower ranks of society.

The Clarendon Code was imposed by Parliament and enforced against dissenters by the secular arm. It aimed more at reducing the influence of opposition politicians than at re-establishing the unity of the national Church. Persecution imposed by Parliament, moreover, could be removed by Parliament. The Toleration Act of 1689 finally killed the old conception of a single state Church of which all Englishmen were members. The parish became more exclusively a local-government area, whose officers regarded themselves as responsible to secular rather than to ecclesiastical authority. The attempt to punish ' sin ' by judicial process was virtually abandoned. The laity had won its centuries-long struggle against the Church courts. In this respect the Middle Ages were over.

In 1660 the Church had a wonderful opportunity to solve its economic problems. Almost all leases on Bishops' and Dean and Chapter lands had fallen in during the Interregnum. Burnet calculated that some £1½ million were raised in fines demanded for renewal of these leases. If this sum had been used for purchasing impropriated tithes, or glebes for poor vicarages, Burnet suggested, ' a foundation had been laid for a great and effectual reformation'. Instead Bishops pocketed the fines themselves. Bishop Cosin left his family over £20,000. Samuel Butler attributed the ' general ill-will and hatred ' which Bishops had contracted in part to their greed and lack of charity. Lesser clergy of the re-established Church lost the additional revenues voted to them by the Long Parliament, or settled on them at the expense of delinquent Royalists ; and no doubt many laymen who had made voluntary contributions to ministers during the Interregnum would transfer them to nonconformists extruded by the Act of Uniformity. So, though individual Bishops helped individual clergymen, the mass of the lower clergy were probably worse off immediately after the Restoration than at any time during the century. In

---

[1] B. Nightingale, *Early Stages of the Quaker Movement in Lancashire* (1922), p. 72 ; [T. Pittis], *A Private Conference between a Rich Alderman and a Poor Country Vicar* (1670), pp. 131, 232–8

1670 John Eachard published his *Grounds and Occasions for the Contempt of the Clergy*, and gave poverty as a main reason.

DISSENTERS

After 1660 (and again after 1688) there was much discussion of broadening the Church of England in order to comprehend Presbyterians, the most conservative of the dissenters, and so to divide them from the rest of the sectaries. This suggestion was opposed not only by high-flying Episcopalians but also by all the other sects, who realised that ' comprehension ' would mean intensified persecution for those excluded. Charles II took advantage of the failure of ' comprehension ' to pursue his own scheme of granting toleration as an act of royal grace, dispensing with Parliamentary penal statutes. Thus the monarchy succeeded to Cromwell's policy of being demonstrably more tolerant than Parliament. The Declarations of Indulgence of 1662, 1672, 1687, and 1688 made a bid for the support of all those shut out from the state Church. But Charles and James were more genuinely interested in the welfare of Roman Catholic than of Protestant dissenters ; their offers of indulgence were therefore naturally regarded with suspicion by most Protestants. James's real intolerance to Protestant dissenters was notorious and made nonsense of the liberal-seeming phrases of his Declarations. Moreover, Charles II, unlike Cromwell, had no army to enforce toleration ; and the army which James tried to build up was too obviously Papist-controlled to be popular with Protestant dissenters.

In opposing the Declaration of Indulgence of 1662, Archbishop Sheldon appealed against the King's policy to the ' law established ' by Parliament. But whenever the crown co-operated with the Tory gentry, the Church was its staunchest supporter against the Whigs. In 1683, for instance, the royal declaration alleging Whig complicity in the Rye House Plot was read twice in every parish church, with great political effect. Nevertheless, the fact that there were two policies with regard to dissent had important consequences. Nonconformists suffered severely under the Clarendon Code, which excluded them from political life, municipal administration, and the universities, and tried to prevent them developing their own independent educational system. It rendered them liable to heavy fines and periods of imprisonment in unhealthy prisons merely for worshipping in the way they thought right. Bunyan wrote *Pilgrim's Progress* during a twelve years' sojourn in Bedford gaol. The law was not always enforced in its full rigour, thanks to the goodwill of constables and Justices in many towns ; but there was an arbitrary uncertainty in the very irregularity of its enforcement. Exchequer processes against Quakers for absence from worship amounted to as much as £33,000 in May 1683. The Presbyterian minister, Oliver Heywood, was excluded from his parish church because excommunicated, and yet fined for non-attendance. In consequence of all this, Protestant dissenters gladly availed themselves of the Declaration of Indulgence of 1672. They emerged from underground to take up royal licences to worship in such numbers that their complete suppression was clearly out of the question.

1688 registered Parliament's victory over the monarchy on the constitutional issue ; but in the Toleration Act Parliament took over something very like the royal indulgence policy. Even a High Tory Anglican like Sir John Reresby recognised in May 1688 that ' most men were now convinced that liberty of conscience was a thing of advantage to the nation '. The Toleration Act itself stated its function with brutal clarity. There are no high-flown passages about liberty such as had appeared in James's Declaration of Indulgence. Instead the preamble declared that ' some ease to scrupulous consciences in the exercise of religion may be an effectual means to unite their Majesties' Protestant subjects in interest and affection '. The Toleration Act served a *political* purpose : it was necessary for national unity and the safety of the régime that dissenters should be allowed freedom of worship. But they remained excluded from political life.

The permanent existence of dissenting sects meant that the monopoly of the established Church gave way to consumers' choice in religion. The sentence of excommunication lost much of its efficacy. Nonconformity might even have its uses in enabling a man to avoid unwanted municipal office. Multiplicity of alternatives in religion naturally helped to spread a spirit of scepticism. The association of ' enthusiasm ' with radical politics led to a reaction which contributed to the growth of rational religion and deism. ' There is nothing that can prevail more to persuade a man to be an atheist,' Samuel Butler thought, ' as to see such unreasonable beasts pretend to religion.' Individualism was curbed by ' good taste ', as a re-united society re-imposed standards. Aubrey, who regularly cited the Interregnum as a turning-point in social customs and intellectual habits, tells us how superstition declined. ' When I was a child and so before the civil wars, the fashion was for old women and maids to tell fabulous stories, night-times, of spirits and of walking of ghosts, etc. . . . When the wars came, and with them liberty of conscience and liberty of inquisition, the phantoms vanish. Now children fear no such things.' Persecution of witches declined rapidly after the mid-century. When an astrologer offered his services to Charles II, the Merry Monarch took him to Newmarket and asked him to spot winners.

SCIENTIFIC AND POLITICAL IDEAS

Before 1640 the court would have none of Bacon's theories. After 1660 the scientists ejected from Oxford were powerful and skilful enough to obtain royal, aristocratic, and episcopal patronage. ' This wild amazing men's minds with prodigies and conceits of Providences,' Sprat wrote, ' has been the most considerable cause of those spiritual distractions of which our country has been the theatre.' The Royal Society would help to prevent their recurrence. Science, like Hobbism, became fashionable at Charles II's court, even though distinctions of rank were ignored at the Society's meetings. The Royal Society in its early years stimulated agricultural improvements, and its investigations contributed to advances in navigation and the manufacture of precision instruments. Its encouragement of Graunt's *Observations upon the Bills of Mortality* spread interest in scientific attempts to estimate the size of the population from the number of registered deaths. Such attempts had also been aided by the more accurate assessment of taxable wealth made during and after the Interregnum. Great progress was made in chemistry (Boyle), botany (Ray, Sloane, Grew), geology (Woodward), medicine (Sydenham and Morton), mathematics and astronomy (Wallis, Halley, Hooke, Flamsteed).

But we must not exaggerate the intellectual liberalism of the Restoration atmosphere. New ideas had invaded the court ; but for the mass of the population there was far less intellectual freedom than there had been in the forties. The Baconians were ejected from Oxford and Cambridge, and the universities ceased to be centres of science. The scientists themselves were so anxious to cover up their revolutionary past that they flooded the Royal Society with dilettante aristo-crats who hated soiling their hands with experiments ; the close connection with industrial crafts and agriculture which had been the Baconian heritage soon lapsed. After the initial impetus in the age of Hooke (1635–1703), the application of science to technology was to proceed very slowly until the end of the eighteenth century, when a new advance coincides with a new revolutionary age. It is the same in chemistry, where Boyle (1626–91) trembled on the verge of discoveries which were not in fact made until the epoch of the French Revolution, after which progress quickens again. As the older generation of Parliamentarian scientists died off in Restoration England, science became a fashionable adornment to gentlemanly conversation rather than an aid to production. Sir Isaac Newton is the only great scientist of the second generation, and Newton himself ultimately abandoned science for the Wardenship of the Mint and the study of Biblical prophecies. Newton's subjects were practical enough—astron-omy was the basis of navigation and geography, mathematics of surveying ; but his theory of universal gravitation raised these sciences to a level of abstraction which made them acceptable even in eighteenth-century Cambridge, the uni-versity which in 1669 had presented Cosimo de' Medici with a treatise condemning the Copernican astronomy.[1]

Under the Licensing Acts (1662–95) a rigid censorship was re-established. All books dealing with history or affairs of state had to be licensed by a Secretary of State ; books of divinity, philosophy, or science by the Archbishop of Canterbury, the Bishop of London, or the Vice-Chancellor of Oxford or Cambridge. The only newspapers to appear

[1] For Newton, see below, pp. 305–6

between 1660 and 1679 were official government sheets. ' A
public mercury should never have my vote,' declared the
editor of one of these in 1663 ; ' it makes the multitude too
familiar with the actions and counsels of their superiors. . . .'
Sir Roger L'Estrange added, significantly, ' You shall sometimes find a seditious libel to have passed through so many
hands that it is at last scarce legible for dust and sweat, whilst
the loyal answer stands in a gentleman's study as clean and
neat as it came from the press.' Secretary Jenkins described
printing as ' a sort of appeal to the people '.

The temporary and partial lifting of the censorship after
the expiry of the Licensing Act in 1679 released a flood of
Whig newspapers and pamphlets ; but they were soon suppressed by judicial action. In 1680 Chief Justice Scroggs
notified printers and booksellers that ' to print or publish
any news books or pamphlets of news whatsoever is illegal '.
So was the publication of Parliamentary debates until the
second Exclusion Parliament ordered its proceedings to be
printed week by week under the supervision of the Speaker.
Justice Allybone declared in the Seven Bishops' Case that
' no private man can take upon him to write concerning the
government at all '. By that time there was again only one
newspaper, the official *London Gazette*.

The political atmosphere thus imposed limitations on
freedom of thought. Hobbes was afraid the Bishops might
try to burn him; and his *Behemoth* was withheld from publication
until a pirated edition appeared in the year of liberty 1679.
Waller refused to praise Hobbes in print because he too feared
ecclesiastical penalties. Aubrey was worried in 1683 lest, if
his *Lives* should fall into the wrong hands, he might be charged
with *scandalum magnatum*, libel upon superiors. In the same
year the University of Oxford officially condemned and burnt
most of the great treatises on political theory which
seventeenth-century England had produced—Hobbes, Milton,
Baxter. Coffee-houses, which dated from the sixteen-fifties,
were suppressed in 1675 as ' the great resort of idle and
disaffected persons, . . . tradesmen and others '. It is a sign of
the secularisation of the times that coffee-houses and clubs were
succeeding sectarian congregations as the centres of sedition.
The men who drummed James II out of his kingdom did not

sing psalms but a popular song-hit written by an atheist peer—
' Lillibulero '.

One can imagine the stultifying effects of this repression
on the ' unfree ', whose brief period of liberty had ended in
1660. The Restoration indeed was a tragedy for popular
education. Ecclesiastical control was re-established. In
Dr Schlatter's words, ' the Established Church was foremost
in stifling a movement which would have given the power of
knowledge to the lower classes '. All but one of the newly
founded schools in Wales were dissolved. Grammar schools
were widely held to have caused the Civil War by educating
too many people above their proper station : they were
justified only in so far as they served the needs of the professional classes. For others, the study of Latin might lead
to hankerings after ancient republicanism, Hobbes thought.
Equality of educational opportunity, as advocated by Parliamentarian theorists, would divert ' those whom nature or
fortune had determined to the plough, the oar, or other
handicrafts, from their proper design. . . . The multiplying
of these foundations [free schools] is represented as dangerous
to the government '.[1] The Act of Uniformity (1662) subjected schoolmasters to episcopal licence and imposed oaths
of non-resistance on them. The Corporation Act forbade
dissenting ministers to keep schools or teach in them. Nevertheless, despite the persecution, a few Dissenting Academies
were started.

The success of propertied classes and ecclesiastical hierarchy
in suppressing or driving underground revolutionary and
democratic ideas is very remarkable. They were helped by
pacifist and quietist trends of thought among the dissenters.
' We do not think religion will so soon cause another war,'
wrote Pepys in 1667. This is often spoken of as ' the separation
of religion from politics '. But it would be more accurate to
say that revolutionary politics ceased to be expressed in
religious form : the restored Church of England certainly
continued to perform political functions. The very widely
read *Whole Duty of Man* told the poor man to ' be often
thinking of the joys laid up for thee in heaven ; look upon that

[1] C. Wase, *Considerations concerning Free Schools* (1678). Wase did not
accept the views he was reporting. Contrast Petty, above, p. 181.

as thy home, on this world only as an inn, where thou art fain
to take up thy passage. And then, as a traveller expects not
the same conveniences at an inn as he hath at home, so thou
hast reason to be content with whatever entertainment thou
findest here, knowing thou art upon thy journey to a place
of infinite happiness, which will make an abundant amends
for all the uneasiness and hardship thou canst suffer in the
way.' ' When men are gazing up to heaven,' Winstanley had
complained in 1652, ' imagining after a happiness or fearing a
hell after they are dead, their eyes are put out, that they see
not what is their birthrights, and what is to be done by them
here on earth while they are living.' The contrast between
these two passages neatly illustrates the advantage to the
propertied classes of the restoration of ecclesiastical censorship
and of a state Church.

This is not an impressive period in the history of political
thought. The seminal works of Hobbes, Filmer, Harrington,
Milton, the Levellers, and Winstanley had all been written
before 1660. The influence of Hobbist ideas spread rapidly if
furtively. Those of Harrington came to be almost orthodox
in Whig circles, aided by the popularisation of Henry Nevill
in *Plato Redivivus* (1681). But the sense of historical change, so
powerful and original in Harrington, was not recaptured in the
more static society of the Restoration. Harrington was
influential mainly through his emphasis on the necessity of the
rule of property. He had no successor in the philosophy of
history until the rise of the Scottish school in the second half
of the eighteenth century. The ' Trimmer ' Halifax combined
Harrington's respect for property (Halifax was very rich) with
Hobbes's respect for power to justify a deeply cynical conservative scepticism. He jeered at theories of fundamental law
or fundamental rights : ' " Fundamental " is a word used by
the laity, as the word " sacred " is by the clergy, to fix everything
to themselves they have a mind to keep, that nobody else may
touch it.' Filmer's posthumously published *Patriarcha* (1680)
became the Bible of non-resistance High Tory Anglicans. Its
theory that royal authority descended from that of Adam and
the patriarchs, ludicrous though it seems today, had its point
in seventeenth-century society. For the head of the family
still exercised great authority, not only over his wife and

children, but also over apprentices, journeymen, and servants : the household was still the most significant unit in the economy.

LITERATURE AND SOCIETY

In literature too this age is transitional. Its greatest figures (for us, but not for contemporaries) are Milton and Bunyan, who transmit to posterity much that was noble in defeated Puritanism. Bunyan, with his vivid characterisation, his psychological insight, and his perfect ear for spoken prose, links the pamphlet literature of the forties with the novels of Defoe. The Royal Society set the seal of its approval on the Interregnum development of prose by ' preferring the language of artisans, countrymen and merchants before that of wits or scholars '. The distinction between prose and poetry became sharper. Milton's uniquely elevated and dignified style, perfect for his high purposes, established the deplorable ' poetic diction ' of the eighteenth-century poetasters. Dryden and Waller perfected the rhymed couplet, whose studied antitheses and balanced rhetoric reflected the greater stability towards which society was moving, and its fear of ' enthusiasm '. Their flowing numbers contrast markedly, both in form and content, with the earlier ' metaphysical ' lyric of internal conflict. The theatres reopened in 1660, but no dramatists were found to equal the great tragedians of James I's reign, whose plays had expressed the first stirrings of the conflict of the epoch. Even drama abandoned blank verse for the heroic couplet (tragedy) or prose (comedy). Tragedy and comedy, which Shakespeare had integrated in his plays, are now as sharply distinguished as prose and poetry, as pure and applied science.

This tendency to subdivide, to label and pigeon-hole, is typical of the age, which was very conscious of ' the rules ', such as the dramatic unities which Shakespeare had disregarded.

> Late, very late, correctness grew our care,
> When the tired nation breathed from civil war.

So Pope thought, looking back from the eighteenth century. Fear of the vulgar, of the emotional, of anything extreme, was deeply rooted in the social anxieties of Restoration England.

Enthusiasm was associated with lower-class revolution : the propertied classes had learned the dangers of carrying things to extremes, and were learning the virtues of compromise. Halifax saw God Almighty as a Trimmer too, ' divided between his two great attributes, his mercy and his justice '.   In this cult of the golden mean something vital was repressed from poetry, which was recaptured only a century later by the Romantic movement, when political radicalism also revived.

Too often the Restoration attitude is regarded merely as a reaction against Puritanism.   It was that ; but Restoration comedy, a comedy of manners, also comments sceptically on a world in which aristocratic standards were adjusting themselves to a society dominated by money.   Hence the dramatists' obsession with the relation of the sexes.   For in England ' the law of marriage . . . is almost the groundwork of the law of property '.[1]   *Paradise Lost* (1667) is a great hymn to wedded love :   Restoration comedy discusses the relation of the sexes among those classes whose marriages are property transactions and therefore exclude love ;   and tilts against the potential hypocrisy in sentimental idealisation of marriage.

All roads in our period have led to individualism.   More rooms in better-off peasant houses, use of glass in windows (common for copyholders and ordinary poor people only since the Civil War, Aubrey says) ;   use of coal in grates, replacement of benches by chairs—all this made possible greater comfort and privacy for at least the upper half of the population. Privacy contributed to the introspection and soul-searching of radical Puritanism, to the keeping of diaries and spiritual journals, to George Fox and Samuel Pepys.   Possibly even the mirror may have aided self-consciousness.   The defeat of Puritan political hopes turned men's aspirations to seek a Paradise within.   Bunyan's Christian abandoned even his family to save his soul.   Earlier in the century the popularity of portrait-painting, of the drama, of the ' character ', had revealed a growing interest in individual psychology to which Burton's *Anatomy of Melancholy* bears witness.   Now through Bunyan this blossomed into the novel, the most individualistic of all literary forms.   Bunyan, like Defoe and the eighteenth-century

[1] Robinson, 'Anticipations under the Commonwealth of Changes in the Law ', p. 484

novelists after him, appealed especially to the lower middle class which had previously devoured Puritan sermons and political pamphlets : only now life was a little easier, a little less intense. Women of this class especially had more leisure and wanted to be entertained. Addison and Steele would entertain them as soon as the press was freer.

PART FOUR

1688–1714

16   Narrative of Events, 1688-1714

> With a Queen so devout,
> And a people so stout,
> A Parliament that will supply 'em,
> A cause that is right,
> And a King that will fight,
> Our enemies all we defy 'em.
>
> Sir Charles Sedley, *The Soldiers' Catch*

WILLIAM summoned a Convention Parliament, which met in February 1689.   Since James had made himself impossible and William was in command of the situation, Parliament's only problem was to find a suitable form of words.   Finally William and Mary (James's daughter) were accepted as joint sovereigns, and a Bill of Rights stated limitations on their power.   The Mutiny Act, renewed annually from 1689, made the maintenance of an army legal for one year only.   An Act of 1689 gave limited toleration to Protestant dissenters.   Frequent Parliaments were ensured by the Triennial Act of 1694.   The Bank of England was founded in the same year.   In 1695 the Licensing Act ran out and was not renewed ; a relative freedom of the press was established.   The Act of Settlement (1701) fixed the succession (failing heirs to Mary's sister, Anne) in the House of Hanover, descendants of James I's daughter, Elizabeth, and the Elector Palatine ; transferred the right to dismiss judges from King to Parliament ; and declared that no royal pardon should be pleadable to a Parliamentary impeachment.

After 1688 a foreign policy of Cromwellian scope was resumed.   Louis XIV helped James to invade Ireland in the hope of returning thence to England ; the subjugation of Ireland was therefore as necessary for William as it had been for the Commonwealth.   In 1689, as in 1641, a Catholic revolt in Ireland temporarily liberated the country from

English domination. The Patriot Parliament at Dublin restored to Irish landowners estates confiscated during the Interregnum. English power in Ireland was reduced to Londonderry, which endured a grim three months' siege in 1689. In 1690 William himself went to Ireland. His victory in the Battle of the Boyne (July 1690) was nearly as decisive as Cromwell's campaign of 1649. By Acts of the English Parliament all proceedings of the Patriot Parliament were annulled ; Catholics—the overwhelming majority of the Irish population—were excluded from all public offices and from the legal profession. In Scotland Presbyterianism was re-established as the state religion. The failure of the Scottish Darien Company's attempt to establish a settlement on the Isthmus of Panama showed Scottish weakness when competing with England in trade and colonisation. It contributed, together with anxiety lest different sovereigns should succeed in the two countries after Anne's death, to the Union of 1707.

England and the Netherlands were now allied against France. The Anglo-Dutch fleet was decisively defeated off Beachy Head the day before the Battle of the Boyne, and there was a panic fear of invasion. But no attempt was made until May 1692, and by then naval reorganisation enabled the French fleet to be shattered in the Battle of La Hogue. From that time the revolutionary settlement in England was secure. At the Treaty of Ryswick (1697) Louis XIV promised to give no assistance to anyone who might try to challenge William's possession of his kingdoms. Ryswick, however, was only a truce. The great powers were waiting to divide up the Habsburg empire when Charles II of Spain should die. A Partition Treaty of 1699 allocated Spain, the Spanish Nether-lands, and America to the Archduke Charles, second son of the Emperor Leopold. France was to acquire Naples, Sicily, and Milan, the latter to be exchanged for Lorraine. The Emperor refused to accept this treaty. So did Charles II of Spain, who on his death-bed in 1700 made a will leaving the whole inheritance to Philip of Anjou, second son of Louis XIV's heir. Louis repudiated the Partition Treaty which he had just signed, and accepted the will.

For a time it seemed that he might get away with it. The governments of the Netherlands and England recognised the Bourbon Philip as King of Spain. The House of Commons was at first anxious for peace, and the Whig ministers ('the Junto') were impeached for concluding the Partition Treaty without reference to Parliament. But Louis sent French troops into the Spanish Netherlands and expelled the Dutch from the barrier fortresses granted to them at Ryswick. French companies were set up to monopolise American trade and the slave trade ; the export of Spanish wool was restricted to French merchants. All this created great alarm in England. A petition from the Grand Jury of Kent asked the House of Commons to abandon party squabbles and vote supplies so that the government could fight if necessary. Those who presented it were committed to prison by the Commons, who proceeded with the impeachment of the Junto. But the predominantly Whig House of Lords urged William to enter into an anti-French military alliance with the Netherlands and the Emperor, and they acquitted the impeached ministers. The quarrel between the two Houses was ended only by prorogation (June 1701) and dissolution (November). In August England, the Netherlands, and the Emperor signed a Grand Alliance to ensure that France should not dominate the Mediterranean or the Netherlands, that the crowns of France and Spain should never be united, and that France should not possess Spanish America. Nine days later James II died in France, and Louis recognised his son (the 'Old Pretender') as James III, King of Great Britain, in violation of the Treaty of Ryswick. The election of December 1701 showed a swing towards the Whigs. Parliament accepted the Grand Alliance, and voted supply ; an oath repudiating the Pretender was imposed on all members of Parliament and office-holders. When William died in the spring of 1702 the country was on the verge of war, and party divisions had receded into the background.

William had appointed Churchill (later Duke of Marlborough) to command the allied troops, and the war of 1702–13 was his war. Victories at Blenheim (1704), Ramillies (1706), Oudenarde (1708), and Malplaquet (1709), together with British command of the sea (alliance with Savoy and the Methuen Treaty with Portugal, 1703) and a less successful land campaign in Spain, placed Britain in a victorious position. But the government's insistence on the abdication of the

Bourbon King of Spain in favour of the Habsburg claimant wrecked peace negotiations in 1708. A French military revival prolonged the war until 1713. In the Treaty of Utrecht Philip V was left on the Spanish throne, with an assurance that the French and Spanish crowns would never be united. The Dutch recovered most of their barrier fortresses. France abandoned the Pretender and recognised the Hanoverian succession. England gained Newfoundland, Nova Scotia, the Hudson Bay territories, Fort James in Senegambia, Gibraltar, and Minorca. English merchants were to trade with Spain on equal terms with French merchants ; and England gained the coveted *asiento*, the monopoly right of supplying slaves to the Spanish American colonies.

At first the war had been waged by a coalition around Marlborough and Godolphin, but gradually it became preponderantly a Whig ministry, in alliance with these two ministers. But as public opinion wearied of war the Tory leader, Robert Harley, conducted a skilful campaign against it. Queen Anne disliked the Whigs ; she quarrelled with the Duchess of Marlborough, long her favourite. All this weakened the position of the Whig ministry. The occasion of its fall was the Sacheverell Case. In 1709 the High Churchman Dr Henry Sacheverell preached a sermon before the Lord Mayor and aldermen of London in which he violently denied that 1688 had been a revolution, and accused the Whig ministry of hostility to the Church. The government impeached him. But the House of Lords only convicted Sacheverell by the narrow margin of 69 to 52. He was forbidden to preach for three years, and his sermon was ordered to be burnt. This was a moral victory for the Tories. Fortified by it, Harley was able to engineer changes in the government. By 1710 he was at the head of a Tory ministry, and the general election of that year gave him the expected majority in the Commons.

The new government, in addition to opening peace negotiations, passed two Acts against nonconformists. The Occasional Conformity Act of 1711 prohibited the practice whereby dissenters could qualify for state office by taking the Anglican communion on rare occasions. The Schism Act of 1714 aimed at restoring the Church's educational monopoly and destroying nonconformist schools. (These Acts were not

repealed until 1719, but they were effectively nullified by the
Whig governments after 1714.) An Act of 1711 confined
membership of the Commons to those possessing substantial
landed property ; in 1712 a tax on newspapers and pamphlets
aimed at reducing popular discussion.

But the Tory majority split on the succession question.
In 1709 an unsuccessful attempt by the Pretender to invade
Scotland was easily defeated. It demonstrated the success
of the Union of England and Scotland. The French associations
of the Pretender and his refusal to abandon Catholicism made
moderate Tories reluctant to reverse the succession laid down
by the Act of Settlement. Lord Treasurer Harley, now Earl
of Oxford, procrastinated. St John, Viscount Bolingbroke,
intrigued against Oxford without wholly committing himself
to the Jacobites, the supporters of ' James III '. The Schism
Act was a manoeuvre of Bolingbroke's to attract the High
Church Tories against the moderate Oxford. In August 1714
Anne dismissed Oxford, but she died five days later, after
appointing the Hanoverian Duke of Shrewsbury in his place.
Bolingbroke's support of the Jacobite invasion of 1715 was
a gambler's last fling without real hope of success.

17 Economics, 1688-1714

Trade . . . is the creature of liberty : the one destroyed,
the other falleth to the ground.

Halifax, *A Rough Draft of a New Model at Sea* (1694)

TRADE AND FOREIGN POLICY

THE Revolution of 1688 was no less a turning-point in the
economic than in the political and constitutional history of
England. A week before James fled, the secretary of the
Royal African Company was still, as a routine matter, issuing
commissions authorising the seizure of interlopers who had
infringed the charter of 1672. With no recorded decision the
Company abandoned this claim to enforce its monopoly by
coercive measures. Free trade was established formally by
Act of Parliament later ; but the real change was recognised
to have taken place with the fall of James II. Just as 1640
had brought the end of industrial monopoly, so 1688 saw the
end of old-style commercial monopoly. Industrialists now felt
that the existence of monopoly exporting companies, even for
long-distance trades, was a fetter on expansion. Clothiers
and representatives of the outports complained that exports
were artificially restricted by the Royal African Company's
monopoly, and joined the ' Jamaica interest ' in demanding
free trade. Interlopers who had been fined by the Company's
courts for infringing its monopoly now demanded compensation. In the event a compromise was reached in 1698, by
which African trade was opened to all on payment of a ten
per cent duty on exports. In 1712 the trade was finally
thrown open without any restrictions. The overthrow of this
monopoly made possible the development of Jamaica. The
Company delivered 25,000 slaves to Jamaica in fifteen years

of peace ; free trade delivered 42,000 in the ensuing eleven years, of which seven were years of war.

A similar attack was made on the East India Company. In 1693 its charter was forfeited, and in the new charter an obligation was laid on the Company to export English commodities to the value of £100,000 a year. The strength of the clothing interest, which had destroyed the Irish cloth industry in 1699, was demonstrated again the next year, when Parliament excluded eastern printed calicoes and silks from the English market ; they were to be re-exported only. At the same time cloth exports were exempted from all duties. Parliament forced the East India Company to buy out many former interlopers ; from 1698 it was compelled to share its privileges with a rival company. The two carried on a fierce Parliamentary battle; their competition drove up the price of borough seats. But there were still advantages in having a single organ to protect traders in India. As in the sixteen-fifties, the old Company's enemies had no objections to a monopoly in which they shared ; and in 1709 the two Companies united. The East India Company soon ceased to rouse party political passions.

Similar fates befell the other companies. Entrance fees to the Merchant Adventurers, which had been doubled in 1634, were reduced again in 1661, and abolished in 1689. In 1699 the Russian Company's entrance fee was reduced from £50 to £5. (The House of Commons had suggested £2.) The result was a great stimulus to trade with Russia. The Levant Company survived, but in 1694 the Commons condemned a by-law passed to restrict the trade to apprenticed merchants. So by the end of our period there had been a complete reversal of economic policy. The medieval ideas which underlay the great trading companies—restrict output, maintain quality and prices, still accepted at the beginning of the century—had been totally abandoned by the end. They had been abandoned under pressure from manufacturing interests, which preferred a régime of unfettered production of cheaper articles and competitive free trade to dispose of them. ' Trade,' Parliament declared in 1702, ' ought to be free and not restrained.' In 1701 a Chief Justice said that royal grants and charters in restraint of trade were generally void because of

' the encouragement which the law gives to trade and honest industry '. Such charters were ' contrary to the liberty of the subject'. So industry and common law celebrated their joint victory over the monarchy. Taking the whole period 1603–1714, exports and imports probably trebled, and changed markedly in character. In *Absalom and Achitophel* Dryden accused the old Rumper and Whig, Slingsby Bethel, of holding ' that kings were useless and a clog to trade '. Perhaps Bethel was right about would-be absolute monarchs. Customs revenue more than doubled in the quarter of a century after the fall of James II.

The later seventeenth century saw a rapid expansion of western ports, notably Bristol, Liverpool, and Exeter. London's trade was increasing too, but the capital lost the position of absolute predominance which it had held for a century and a half. By 1677 its share of trade had fallen to less than three-quarters ; after 1698 there was a still greater relative decline. The customs of Bristol increased tenfold between 1614 and 1687. Its rise was expedited by its share in the Anglo-Portuguese trade resulting from the treaty of 1654. Improved access to the Midlands by way of the Severn made Bristol a port for textiles and ironware, as well as for lead ; but its main prosperity came from the colonial trades—sugar-refining, tobacco, and the slave trade, the latter especially after Parliament established free trade in slaves. In the same period Liverpool (Parliamentarian during the Civil War) ousted the decaying (Royalist) port of Chester. The rapidly expanding Lancashire textile industry furnished the bulk of Liverpool's exports. But its prosperity too depended on the sugar, tobacco, and slave trades. The rise of these two ports thus resulted directly from the establishment of a British monopoly in colonial trade and from the industrial expansion which took place under the shelter of the Navigation Acts. By 1700 perhaps twenty per cent of English exports went to colonial markets. It was estimated that half the West Indies planters' profits were used to purchase English manufactures : firearms, nails, tools, brass, copper and ironware, glass, pottery, harness, hats, textiles. The proportion was probably even greater in New England.

Quarrels between Stuarts and Parliament had reduced

English foreign policy to virtual impotence ; after 1688 the resources of the nation were once more, as in the sixteen-fifties, devoted to a foreign policy which would benefit England's trading and colonial interests. War with France was fought on a world scale and involved a new imperial strategy. Since France was less dependent on trade than the Netherlands, it could not be hit so hard by naval warfare. French trade suffered many temporary interruptions in consequence of naval defeat, whilst English merchant tonnage probably increased by fifty per cent in the course of the war ; but French fighting power was not significantly affected. Against France an expensive war of attrition, with England subsidising continental armies, set a new pattern for the eighteenth century. This kind of warfare could only be undertaken after the establishment of confidence between government and moneyed interest. During the war England's taxable capacity rose steadily ; that of France declined.

The War of Spanish Succession won the *asiento*. The conquest of Nova Scotia and Newfoundland checked a growing French superiority in the fishing trade. Since trade with Old Spain was no less important than that with the Spanish empire, Cromwell's Mediterranean policy was resumed, his plan of seizing Gibraltar carried out in 1704. Minorca gave a base for British fleets to winter in the Mediterranean. Another Cromwellian echo was the provision in the Treaty of Utrecht that the fortifications of Dunkirk were to be destroyed. The Methuen Treaty completed the alliance of 1654 by giving British manufacturers a virtual monopoly of trade with Portugal and her empire in Brazil, Africa, and the Far East, to the advantage especially of West Country clothiers. The Whigs and the clothing interest managed to defeat the Tory government's project for a commercial treaty with France in 1711-13, since an expansion of trade with France might mean losing that with Portugal. The inadequate commercial treaty which the Tory government had concluded with Spain in 1713 was replaced in 1715 by another which the Whigs negotiated to the greater satisfaction of English merchants. At Utrecht England got all the pickings, at the expense of France and the Netherlands. It was no less dangerous to be England's ally than her enemy. London had succeeded Amsterdam as the centre of world trade. The dream of the men of 1650–1 had been realised.

INDUSTRY AND THE POOR

By 1700 all sections of the population were to some extent cash customers for goods produced outside their areas, and to meet this there was a highly developed regional specialisation. 'There are shopkeepers in every village,' Defoe observed, ' or at least in every considerable market town.' So there was less need for households to feed and clothe themselves. There had been a rapid expansion of the cheap consumer-goods industries—pottery, Midlands hardware, and the like. The home market was variously estimated at from 6 to 32 times the foreign market. Yet before 1688 investment in industrial production had been retarded. The early sixteen-nineties was a period of industrial boom and projecting. Of 236 patents for invention issued between 1660 and 1700, 64 were in 1691–3. Companies were now formed without royal (or Parliamentary) charter, in complete independence of the state. The number of joint-stock companies (i.e. those in which a number of separate individuals bought shares) increased from eleven to about a hundred between 1689 and 1695, almost entirely in the sphere of home production. Foreign trade was depressed in the early years of King William's war, and capital had to seek its outlet at home ; so it was fortunate that many companies now competed for it. Government military contracts and naval construction acted as an ever increasing stimulus. Between 1654 and 1687 the number of workers in naval yards had increased by about twenty per cent ; between 1687 and 1703 by over four hundred and seventy-five per cent. ' The inhabitants of Portsmouth,' said Defoe, ' are quite another sort of people than they were a few years before the Revolution.' The navy was ' in some respects the largest industry in the country '. In 1688 it had 15,000 men on its payroll ; there were three times as many a few years later.[1]

This industrial development was aided by deliberate

---

[1] D. C. Coleman, 'Naval Dockyards under the Later Stuarts', *Econ. H. R.* (2nd Ser.), **6**, 139–41 ; J. Ehrman, *The Navy in the War of William III, 1689–97* (1953), p. 174

encouragement from Parliament, sometimes forced on governments. After 1689 anyone, in any part of England, was authorised to export cloth ; in 1700 cloth exports were freed from customs duties. A statute of 1689 threw open the copper-mining industry. Export of English iron and copper was permitted in 1694 to any country except France. Two Acts of William's reign encouraged landowners to dig for tin, lead, iron, and copper on their estates. In 1710 Parliament forbade agreements among coal-sellers to keep prices up. A number of statutes and judicial decisions further whittled away the Statute of Apprentices, and so opened industrial employment to the whole population. Quarter Sessions virtually ceased to deal with apprenticeship cases. In 1694 the rural woollen and weaving industries were legally opened to the mass of the working class. Parliament and the courts similarly intervened against those privileges of town corporations which hindered free trade.

The Union of England with Scotland, dreamt of by radicals like Protector Somerset in the sixteenth century, and first realised under the Commonwealth, was a most important economic measure. The great majority of the clauses of the Act of Union deal with economic matters. Even before 1707 England had been the largest area in Europe with no internal customs barriers to hinder trade. Access to English markets now sent the price of Scottish cattle soaring. The repayment of the Darien Company's capital gave a fillip to Scottish industry, though in the long run English competition proved disastrous to Scottish clothiers.

By the end of our period large-scale enterprises are found much more frequently. There are examples of sail-cloth makers employing up to 600 persons, a saltmaker employing 1,000, silk manufacturers with up to 700. But there is little evidence that working conditions improved. The development of partnerships and joint-stock companies, with diffused ownership of capital and ownership separated from management, helped to end the patriarchal household system which had for so long humanised some industrial relations. Employment in larger establishments was probably more erratic and more harsh. Employment fluctuated very considerably during the intermittent wars of the reigns of William and Anne. But the relative over-population, from which commentators assumed that England suffered before the Civil War, had ended. The cry now is rather one of shortage of ' hands '. Emigration, transportation of convicts, and kidnapping of labour for the plantations had helped to reduce the surplus population. Far more now served in Army, navy, and mercantile marine. But the economic liberalism which followed the downfall of personal government was the main cause.

So there were changes in attitudes towards the poor. The Act of Settlement (1662) was now criticised because its restrictions on the mobility of labour retarded industrial advance. Few parents can afford to have children, wrote Roger Coke in 1694. It is difficult to find employment in the overpopulated countryside ; they cannot legally be bound apprentice in market towns ; and they cannot build cottages on the waste. He advocated complete freedom of emigration to the cities. ' The poor are imprisoned in their towns [i.e. villages],' wrote Sir Dudley North. ' Men want the work and the work men, and are by laws kept from accommodating each other.' A statute of 1697 permitted greater freedom of movement. But the liberties for which the men of property fought so valiantly during the seventeenth century were not extended to the lower half of the population. For the poor the significance of the *Habeas Corpus* Act was that it allowed them to opt for transportation when condemned to death for stealing goods worth more than a shilling.

In 1696 the Commissioners for Trade and Plantations deplored ' the dearness of labour '. It should be bought as cheaply as possible if English exports were to capture foreign markets against the competition of French and Dutch industry protected by tariffs. Labourers were not free : they stood outside ' the nation '. It was with irony that Bernard Mandeville wrote, ' In a free nation where slaves are not allowed of, the surest wealth consists in a multitude of laborious poor. . . . To make the society happy and people easy under the meanest circumstances, it is necessary that great numbers of them should be ignorant as well as poor. . . . We have hardly poor enough to do what is necessary to make us subsist. . . . Men who are to remain and end their days in a laborious, tiresome and painful station of life, the sooner they are put upon it, the more patiently they'll submit to it for ever after.'

The years after 1688 saw an outburst of trade-union activity. In 1698 journeymen feltmakers of London ' conspired and combined together ' to increase wages. They went on strike, collected funds, took action against blacklegs. In the early eighteenth century there were weavers' unions in Devon, Wiltshire, Somerset, and Gloucestershire. There was also a rise in the number of Friendly Societies, whose object was to provide sick and funeral benefits. One of them was alleged by employers in 1712 to be ' encouraging mutinies and disorders '. Even a group of footmen were said to have ' arrived to that height of insolence as to have entered into a society together and made laws by which they oblige themselves not to serve for less than such a sum '. They had a fund which provided unemployment benefit and financed legal actions.

THE LAND

In 1689 the customs duty on corn export was removed ; the bounty, which had lapsed during the years of reaction since 1681, was restored. Exports soon rose rapidly, with occasional exceptions in years of bad harvest. After 1690 statutes encouraged distillation of gin from English grain : import of French brandy and foreign spirits was prohibited. In the early eighteenth century sixty times as much grain was exported from London annually as forty years earlier. In this favourable atmosphere it became even more profitable to bring new land under cultivation, whether by enclosure of the commons, by disafforestation, or by drainage schemes. But the fate of richer and poorer landowners diverged more than ever. By the early eighteenth century the land tax (aided by bad harvests in the nineties) was completing the discomfiture of the less economically efficient of the smaller gentry, who together with the lesser clergy, hard hit by the same economic processes, formed the basis of the Tory-led country party. Great landlords set standards of building and day-to-day expenditure with which lesser men could not compete ; and the latter benefited less than the former from agricultural improvements. Eighteenth-century enclosure substituted larger for smaller tenants. The greater families now raised long-term mortgages (loans upon the security of their land) and accepted annual interest payments as a standing charge on their estates. There was no attempt by moneylenders to foreclose, because they could always sell the mortgage instead ; it was one of the most popular forms of investment before the development of banks and the National Debt. Sir Dudley North thought land-owners living above their income still remained the chief borrowers. The moneyed interest prospered as the lesser gentry declined. In Gregory King's estimate of 1696, greater merchants already have substantially higher incomes than the lesser gentry. The latter, crippled by war taxation on land, were unable to compete with standards of expenditure and endowment of daughters set by the former.

Increasingly those who purchased land did so in order to acquire power and social prestige. Landlords who leased their estates rather than cultivating them personally, and who were interested in political control of their neighbourhoods rather than in profits, were more divorced than in the earlier seventeenth century from the business world. They might invest in joint-stock companies or government funds, but they took little direct part in trade or industry. Younger sons sought careers in the expanding Army and civil service rather than in trade. The lesser gentry were for the most part debarred from profitable entry into trade or professions by lack of capital.[1] The *rentier* landlord had also more time to pursue an active political career than the man who personally supervised his estates.

FINANCE AND CREDIT

The Second Dutch War had cost about £5 million in three years. William's war cost £5 million and more each year ; in 1709 war cost £9 million. Such vast sums could not have been provided without the drastic reorganisation and redistribution of taxation which 1688 made possible. The various items of revenue were at last consolidated into a single national account. To pay for the wars, after experiments with poll taxes and a tax on servants' wages, reversion was made to the Interregnum system of supplementing customs

[1] Habakkuk, 'English Landownership, 1680–1740', pp. 16–17

and excise by a far heavier land tax. In 1692 there was a new assessment of the 'ratable value' of landlords' estates. After that date 4s in the pound once more, as in the revolutionary decades, regularly took in taxation about one-fifth of the landowners' rental—a prodigious achievement if we recall the laughable proportion paid by landlords at the beginning of the century, when they had possessed a far greater share of the national wealth. 1688 thus reversed the landed class's victory of 1660 : henceforth wars fought in the interests of trade were paid for by the gentry and, through the excise, by the poorer classes who had no vote anyway. But taxation per head of the population was still far lower than in France or the Netherlands.

The establishment of the Bank of England with Parliament's guarantee meant that William could borrow at a lower rate of interest than his predecessors, and that interest rates for the general public came down too. In 1714 the official rate was fixed at five per cent ; it had halved since James I's reign. Accumulation of capital and the circulation of hitherto hoarded wealth was encouraged by the establishment of a confidence impossible when the government might repudiate its debts (as in the 'Stop of the Exchequer'), thus bankrupting goldsmiths and scriveners. The use of paper money enlarged the currency, and cheques came into use. From the middle of the century bills of exchange (written orders to pay a given sum on a given date) had become transferable to other people on the money market by successive endorsement. Under Chief Justice Holt the legality of thus transferring bills of exchange was recognised at common law ; and in 1705 a statute made promissory notes (written promises to pay) negotiable too. Long-distance payments no longer had to be made in coin, with all the dangers of highway robbery. The importance of these changes in facilitating business transactions can hardly be overrated. The Bank of England helped to identify the moneyed classes with the revolution settlement by making it easy to lend to the government on profitable terms. This left Jacobitism politically impossible and further strengthened business confidence. In 1696 there was a re-coinage ; after that the value of money was not allowed to fluctuate.

If we survey the century as a whole we can see significant changes in the roles of money and credit, and in accepted attitudes towards foreign trade. In 1603 England was still in the bullionist phase, when precious metals seemed all-important. Sea-dogs hunted Spanish treasure ships, explorers sought El Dorado. Capital and credit were short. But gradually a new policy began to be advocated, exemplified in the title of Mun's treatise, *England's Treasure by Foreign Trade*, written in the sixteen-twenties. From the Interregnum, governments thought it their duty to stimulate English exports, and by the end of the century the country was indeed being enriched annually by foreign trade. Bullion export was now permitted. Companies no longer restricted output to keep prices high. The economy was geared to the export of large quantities of cheap goods. England had entered the competitive epoch, well ahead of her rivals.

Before 1640 industrial and commercial monopoly restricted the field of investment for savings and drove a disproportionate amount of capital into land, or into the purchase of honours and offices. The Interregnum saw a sudden concentration of capital, a transfer of wealth from unproductive to productive purposes. After 1660 land ceased to be the most easily available investment, or the safest ; but the Navigation Act's indirect subsidy to shipping and the profitability of overseas trade (still monopolised), together with aristocratic building and luxury court expenditure, continued to absorb capital which might otherwise have been invested in the heavy and capital goods industries. From the Interregnum onwards, publicists had called for the stimulation of trade and manufacture by an increase in supplies of money and credit : their propaganda triumphed with the new government policies of the nineties, when there was an outburst of speculative industrial investment. After the establishment of the Bank of England and the National Debt, greater security combined with higher rates of interest could be won elsewhere than in land ; and small sums could be invested for short periods. So a steady flow of capital became available for industrial investment.

Unwin pointed out that King's and Davenant's division between those who increase and those who decrease the wealth of the country was based on contribution to capital investment. The poor were unproductive, the rich alone productive. After 1688 state action again positively fostered national investment, as it had done during the revolutionary decades. An essay of about 1723 said, ' We are greatly beholden to the laws and duties since the Revolution, not for lessening the expenses of our whole people, but for disabling them to increase their expenses equally with their riches. . . . Parsimony was not the virtue of that age [Charles II's reign]. Indeed, it could not be expected men would contract their expenses under no example from the court, under no sumptuary laws, under no taxes on their annual incomes and next to none on their annual consumption,' and when no protective tariff excluded foreign goods.[1] Henceforth a greater proportion of the national income was invested, not consumed. This was an indispensable condition for future industrial expansion.

Other modern financial institutions date from this period. In the sixties and seventies English ships still had to be insured in Amsterdam. Marine insurance developed in England from the eighties ; in 1688 we first hear of Lloyd's. Modern fire insurance dates from after the Fire of London. The Stock Exchange was incorporated in William III's reign. Before the end of the century there was a highly organised stock and share market in London, and newspapers carried stock-exchange news. In 1697 an Act was passed ' to restrain the number and ill-practices of brokers and stock-jobbers '. The science of statistics, developed by Graunt, Petty, and the Royal Society, made life insurance possible ; this in its turn allowed provision to be made for dependants after death without buying land, hitherto the only means.

The moneyed men were in every way becoming the equals as well as the rivals of the landed interest. ' I choose rather to keep my estate in money than in land,' wrote a former landowner as early as 1674, ' for I can make twice as much of it that way, considering what taxes are upon land and what advantages there are of making money upon the public funds.' [2] After 1694 these advantages increased, whilst taxation on land was increasing too. So peers and gentlemen with

---

[1] Quoted in G. N. Clark, *Guide to English Commercial Statistics, 1696-1782* (1938), pp. 120-5. ' Sumptuary laws ' regulated expenditure on dress according to social status.

[2] *H.M.C.*, *Fifth Report, Appendix*, i, 375

money to spare put it into trade, just as merchants who prospered had to buy land if they wanted to count in politics. 'The wealth of the nation,' wrote Swift in *The Examiner*, ' that used to be reckoned by the value of land, is now computed by the rise and fall of stocks.' The two interests were distinct though no longer opposed ; and the moneyed interest was now as clearly the senior partner as the landed interest had been a century earlier.

18 Politics and the Constitution 1688-1714

> They don't so much value in England who shall be King, as whose King he shall be.
>
> George Lockhart to the Duke of Atholl, 1705
>
> Law in a free country is, or ought to be, the determination of the majority of those who have property in land.
>
> Dean Swift, *Thoughts on Various Subjects*

'THE GLORIOUS REVOLUTION'

THE Revolution of 1688 saw a restoration of power to the traditional ruling class, the shire gentry, and town merchants, as well as a change of sovereigns. Borough charters were restored. The militia was returned to safe hands, and was used henceforth chiefly against any threat from the lower classes. William summoned members of Charles II's Parliaments to London in December 1688, but not those elected after the remodelling of corporations. The Convention of 1689 contained more than twice as many knights of the shire from the Exclusion Parliaments as from James's Parliament. In the latter the counties had not been represented by their 'natural rulers'. The Declaration of Rights proclaimed that 'the election of members of Parliament ought to be free', and that juries in treason trials ought to be freeholders.

In 1688 the City of London appeared almost as a separate estate of the realm. The Lord Mayor, aldermen, and fifty common councillors were summoned to sit with the members of Parliament in December to decide on the country's future. In 1660 the City had probably played the decisive part in restoring Charles II ; in 1688 its leading role was formally recognised. The internal constitutional development of the

City closely followed that of the nation. During the Inter-regnum, Common Council had got rid of the aldermanic veto. This veto returned in Charles II's charter of 1683 ; but now the position established under the Commonwealth was restored. Henceforth Common Council was no longer checked by the richer and more conservative aldermen.

The Revolution demonstrated the ultimate solidarity of the propertied class. Whigs and Tories disagreed sharply about whether James had abdicated or not, whether the throne should be declared vacant, whether Mary alone or William and Mary jointly should be asked to fill it, or declared to have filled it. But these differences were patched up, and the Declaration of Rights—as successful a compromise as the Elizabethan Prayer Book—simply stated both positions and left it to individuals to resolve the contradictions as they pleased. One reason for this solid front was the behaviour of James and William. The latter, so far from remaining inscrutably in the background, made it perfectly clear that he was determined to have the title of King. But a second reason for agreement was men's recollection of what had happened forty-five years earlier, when unity of the propertied class had been broken. Like Essex and Manchester in 1644–5, Danby feared too complete a victory for either side. James's attempt to appeal to anarchy had been a warning. The purges and counter-purges of the preceding years had weakened respect for authority. James had remodelled some town corporations three or four times within a year, Maldon six times. Monmouth's rebellion was a sufficiently recent reminder that the Good Old Cause was not dead. So when in November 1689 the republican exile, Edmund Ludlow, returned to England, believing that his day had come at last, the Commons at once asked William to order the seizure of this dangerous radical ; and Ludlow was hustled out of the country.

Nevertheless, if 1642–9 was not forgotten, neither were the mistakes of 1660. The Revolution Settlement set down in writing the conditions which had been tacitly assumed at the Restoration. The House of Commons resolved that, before filling the throne, it would secure the religion, laws, and liberties of the nation. The Declaration of Rights was the result. Nothing could be less satisfactory as a statement of political principles. But such a statement was impossible if unity between Whigs and Tories was to be preserved. Facts were slowly causing the Tories to abandon their high-flying theories ; but they could not yet be expected to admit this formally. The Declaration concentrated on removing specific grievances, such as the King's claim to suspend laws without Parliament's consent; his dispensing power ' as it hath been exercised of late ' ; the Ecclesiastical Commission ; maintenance of a standing army within the kingdom in peace time ; tunnage and poundage without Parliamentary consent ; imposition of excessive bail or fines, and cruel and unusual punishments. Less negatively, freedom of elections to Parliament, freedom of speech in Parliament, and frequent Parliaments were declared to be rights of the subject. There was still some vagueness : ' cruel and unusual punishments ', ' frequent Parliaments '. But the vagueness was a price worth paying for agreement between the two parties. Any future ruler would at his peril defy those whom Parliament represented : no ruler did. The King still retained considerable powers, within the framework of the rule of ' the free '. But the limits to the sovereign's power were real and recognised. William vetoed five Bills before 1696, but they all subsequently became law ; after that date he used the veto no more. Anne's solitary veto in 1708 is the last in English history.

Some of the vagueness of the Declaration of Rights was cleared up by later legislation. The Triennial Act (1694) provided not only that Parliaments should meet every three years but also that they should not last longer than three years. Henceforth Parliament was a necessary and continuous part of the constitution, in closer dependence on the electorate. The Act of Settlement prohibited the pleading of a royal pardon to an impeachment, and so removed the last barrier to Parliamentary control of ministers.

PARLIAMENTARY CONTROL

Parliament's control was exercised through finance. The hereditary revenue of the crown—the main source of income at the beginning of the period—now amounted to very little. William was given £700,000 a year for life, to cover the cost of the court and civil government. Other expenditure was voted *ad hoc*. Even the customs were granted only for a period of years at a time. There was no fear that a king could make himself independent of Parliament or maintain an army against the will of the electorate on £700,000 a year. From 1690 government policy was controlled by specific appropriations. The King, a courtier complained in that year, was kept ' as it were at board wages '. William was compelled to maintain a larger navy and a smaller army than he wished. By the end of Anne's reign the Treasury was as a matter of routine drawing up annual budgets for submission to Parliament. We are in the modern world.

William's wars necessitated the maintenance of an army, and a series of Mutiny Acts was passed to ensure its discipline under Parliamentary control. (The disciplinary code for soldiers was indeed tightened up.) But for three years after 1698 no Mutiny Act was passed, and the Army was progressively reduced, to the King's helpless fury. The navy however was another matter, despite a cost already averaging nearly £2½ million a year in King William's war. By 1713 England was far and away the leading sea power. The number of ships had risen by over forty per cent since 1688 ; tonnage by over sixty per cent.[1]

Since Parliaments sat for such short periods, William's special position as ruler both of Holland and of England, and his unrivalled knowledge of foreign affairs, at first enabled him to make his own foreign policy. But the defeats of the early sixteen-nineties forced Parliament to concern itself with the direction of affairs. In 1701 the Tory majority attacked the Junto for agreeing to the Second Partition Treaty without reference to Parliament. The Act of Settlement contained the first statutory limitation on royal control of foreign policy in its provision that Englishmen were not to be involved by a foreign king in war for the defence of territory not belonging to the English crown. Henceforth William was scrupulously careful to consult Parliament at every point. ' The eyes of all Europe are upon this Parliament,' he said on 31st December 1701. ' All matters are at a stand till your resolutions are known.'

[1] J. Ehrman, *The Navy in the War of William III*, pp. xv, xx

Parliament regularly exercised a right of criticising royal appointments to office. It set up its own commissions for examining public accounts, and took the initiative in establishing the Council of Trade and Plantations. In 1696 the Board of Trade was set up, at Parliament's instance, to promote trade and industry. The royal prerogative of pardon, which, Mr Ogg says, had acted under Charles and James as ' a direct encouragement to crime among the ruling classes ', ceased to be exercised in this manner.

Yet, though in this period the constitution took the form it was to retain throughout the eighteenth century, we must beware of antedating the completeness of Parliamentary control. William himself had high prerogative views and wanted to choose his own ministers : only gradually under pressure of financial necessity did he yield some of his position. Moreover, because 1688 had been a compromise, much of the old constitution lived on. Too many men whose co-operation was essential in 1688 had been associated with James's misdemeanours for the repudiation of the past to be sharp and decisive. Judge Jeffreys was a convenient whipping-boy because he happened to be dead. A few of James's servants were imprisoned for short periods ; none were executed. Whigs chafed at William's employment of the Tories ; but they dared not overthrow him. Tories re-insured their future by entering into negotiations with the exiled James II whenever military affairs were going badly ; but they took no active steps to bring him back. The debts of Charles's and James's governments were honoured. As in 1660, there was virtually complete continuity of administrative personnel, with the exception of a few marked men like Pepys. Already the legend of 1688 as the revolution to end revolutions was forming. A veil ought to be drawn over the episode, said a Bishop in 1689. Danby, now Duke of Leeds, distinguished between revolution and resistance. Resistance was a dangerous and odious word, and ought for ever to be forgotten. Such distinctions played a big part in the Sacheverell affair.

William's employment of Danby and Sunderland ensured that their methods of securing a Parliamentary majority were continued. Many boroughs kept the restricted franchise given by charters of Charles and James ; henceforth the Commons were less enthusiastic about widening the franchise. The arts of Parliamentary management which reached their apogee after the passing of the Septennial Act in 1716 were already a necessary part of the constitution. The crown owed its limited but considerable power of independent manoeuvre to the compromise of 1688, the balance between executive and legislative, the failure to extend the franchise, the monopoly of the spoils of government by a narrow ruling class.

PARTIES

Between 1689 and 1708 party divisions counted for little : there were factions, groups, and individuals trying to re-insure against any eventuality, but all against a background of real, if unwilling, unity. Two clear trends of opinion can be traced in the negotiations of 1688–9, to which we can only give the names of Whig and Tory used by contemporaries. The names continued to be used to the end of our period, and we must use them too. But a subtle change was setting in. Sunderland summed it up neatly when he told William that ' it was true that the Tories were better friends to monarchy than the Whigs were, but then His Majesty was to consider that he was not their monarch '. Despite William's personal predilection for the Tories, and his suspicion of the Junto's attempts to monopolise patronage, he had inevitably to rely to a great extent on the support of the Whigs since they alone were whole-heartedly behind his foreign policy. The nature of the court changed, and with it the nature of party rivalry, as the Tories became the country party, the ' outs ' and not the ' ins '. But relations between court and party changed too. Office, as Macaulay pointed out, was the shortest road to boundless wealth in the late seventeenth century. After 1688 effective patronage slowly but inevitably slipped from the hands of the King into those of his ministers who managed Parliament. Thanks to the expansion of the civil service, there were now far more members of Parliament dependent on the government for their income who could be dismissed at will. Sunderland organised these ' King's Friends '. He had to insist that William ' must take care to make all his servants of a piece ', and that he should speak to the members of

Parliament who depended on their offices ' and let them know his intentions and receive no excuse '.[1] Already ministers were using the King as much as he was using them.

The Tories had always found it difficult to decide whether their loyalty was primarily to monarchy or Church. So long as republicans and dissenters seemed one and the same, there was no problem. But Tory hatred of dissenters survived and indeed increased as the latter grew more respectable. Dissent was an urban phenomenon. Its extension into the villages, under the Toleration Act, threatened the squire's supremacy. ' The Church in danger' was always a good rallying-cry for the backwoods gentry. Most of them accepted toleration only as a temporary political manoeuvre. But the more the Tories' loyalty after 1688 was focused on Church rather than crown, the less chance there was in 1714 of Bolingbroke's persuading them to support a king who resolutely refused to abandon Popery.

As leaders of the new country party, the Tory politicians succeeded to many of the methods of opposition used by the Whigs between 1675 and 1688. They now sponsored Place Bills, designed to prevent holders of paid government office (' placemen ') from sitting in the Commons. (In 1675 a Whig Place Bill had been rejected because it would turn England into a republic !) The Tories now opposed standing armies, impeached royal ministers, and tried to resume grants made to royal favourites, whilst the Whigs elevated the prerogative. The Tories introduced the Act of Settlement, described as ' An Act for the further Limitation of the Crown and better securing the Rights and Liberties of the Subject'. They even used methods of popular agitation and demonstration, as in the Sacheverell affair. The London populace, always anti-government, could be used by Tories when Whigs were in office. In 1710 mobs directed their attention to the dissenting chapels and the Bank of England. All this suggests that constitutional principles are expendable : they can be taken up and discarded to suit men's interests.

When Anne succeeded, the Tories believed they had a sovereign after their own hearts, and that the old slogans of

[1] J. P. Kenyon, *Robert Spencer, Earl of Sunderland, 1641–1702*, pp. 251, 266, 323

Church and crown could be revived. Within limits this was true. But the hard-won unity of 1688 had severed official Toryism from the old Catholic families of the north : the Tories, like the Whigs, abandoned their more extreme wing in 1688-9. Bolingbroke himself said that the distinction between Whigs and Tories was less acute before 1688 than men thought, and that it hardly existed after the Revolution. The Union with Scotland in 1707, which secured the northern kingdom for the Hanoverian succession, was negotiated by the Whig Junto lords ; but only extreme Tories opposed it. The new Toryism of Harley and even of Bolingbroke was in the last resort powerless before the Bank of England, which held the money of many a peer who flirted with the Pretender. ' Those who wanted to restore the Stuarts,' said Sir G. N. Clark, ' were working against the vested interests of the business nation.'

Moreover, if the Whigs had drawn back from popular revolution in 1678-85, how much more should the Tories in 1714-15 ? Their whole ethos was anti-revolutionary. Passive obedience, though focused on the monarchy, meant obedience to the powers that be, including Justices of the Peace and landlords. After 1688 the doctrine had not been abandoned ; but obedience was now no longer due to the King alone but to the whole legislature, to the establishment. Resistance, even to a usurper, therefore, created grave ideological difficulties, in 1714-15 as in 1688-9. Moreover the most enthusiastic anti-Whigs were the London populace (with whom Sacheverell's influence recalled that of Titus Oates), Derbyshire miners (who had been Levellers in the fifties), and the lower orders in general. Some former Monmouthites like Ferguson the Plotter and perhaps even the Leveller Wildman had decided that they were Jacobites. The Tory gentry were therefore chary of following Bolingbroke ; indeed, he avoided committing himself to Jacobitism until every other possibility had been tried.

Once the Tories had accepted 1688, in fact, they faced an inescapable dilemma. Swift and Sacheverell on their behalf vigorously denounced the dissenters and republicans who combined in an unholy alliance with war profiteers and the moneyed interest. But the Tory alternatives were within the system. Backstairs influence and war weariness brought Harley into power in 1710. But Harley himself was an ex-dissenter, an ex-Whig, a moneyed man. The Jacobite gentry were drawn mainly from the heavily indebted backwoods squires of the old Royalist north. The solid mass of the Tory squirearchy, in the last resort, would grumble about stock-jobbers but would not rise in revolt against them. The Tories failed to live up to their non-resistance principles in 1688 ; 1714-15 showed that they had failed to evolve a viable political philosophy. Toryism in the generation after 1715 was a sentimental pose, a nostalgia ; with the new Toryism of the later eighteenth century it had only the name in common.

The contemporary historian, Rapin, saw the political history of England between Restoration and early eighteenth century in the following design :

Cavaliers	Political or state Cavaliers	Arbitrary Tories / Moderate Tories
	Ecclesiastical or Church Cavaliers	Rigid Churchmen / Moderate Churchmen
Parliament-arians	Political or state Parliamentarians	Republican Whigs / Moderate Whigs
	Ecclesiastical or Church Parliamentarians	Rigid Presbyterians / Moderate Presbyterians

After 1688, he thought, neither arbitrary Tories nor republican Whigs had much chance of gaining sole power. At the beginning of Anne's reign, through fear of their own extremists, moderate Tories like Marlborough and Godolphin had joined the moderate Whigs. Nevertheless, the existence of the two violent religious wings kept party strife alive. The Presbyterian Whigs never dared attack the Church of England directly, but their existence prevented complete union between the moderates of the two parties. Moreover, sound Churchmen might be Whigs in point of politics. The element of interest as well as principle entered in, in so far as the ruling party distributed places, honours, and dignities to its members. ' This induced King William to say, that if he had good places enough to bestow, he should soon unite the two parties.'

Some historians, looking exclusively at the House of

Commons, have denied the significance of party divisions and political principles in Anne's reign altogether; and have seen only personal followings of great magnates, similar to those which existed in the reign of George III. It is true there were no party cards, no Whips. There was already in the House a group of the King's or Queen's ' servants ', without whose support no government could carry on. Marlborough and Godolphin were essential to any government so long as Anne continued to back them. Nevertheless, divisions on questions of principle did occur in Parliament. There was already in the Commons a group of independent country gentlemen estimated by Dr Plumb at 200 (out of 513—or 558 after 1707), who opposed the spreading corruption and were a force which had to be reckoned with. And in the country as a whole there were live issues. Not all seats in the Commons were controlled by borough-mongers; the floating vote of the smaller men of property still counted for a great deal. Even Sunderland, virtuoso of Parliamentary management though he was, could not produce docile Parliaments for James II. He was more successful for William, because then he was gliding with the stream. The Sacheverell affair revealed profound divisions in the country. Foreign policy, peace and war, taxation, the succession, were real issues. The state of opinion in the electorate forced Parliament to agree to war in 1701 despite its Tory majority. In 1710 Harley's rise to power owed more to war weariness, expressed in mutinies, riots, and hatred of taxation, than to Dr Sacheverell or Anne's favourite, Abigail Masham. Peace was as popular with squires and populace as it was unpopular in the City. So although the court and the spoils of office exercised a powerful pull on both parties; although fear of popular disturbance inclined sober politicians to shun any step likely to split the propertied classes or to rouse the ' mob '; still within these limits there were lively political disagreements about principles as well as about interests : as Swift's career showed.

In the constituencies a concentration of political power was taking place, strikingly similar to the consolidation of landed property in the hands of an oligarchy. From 1689 the fight for the pocket boroughs is on. Forty per cent of boroughs (returning a third of all members) had less than 100 voters, nearly two-thirds had less than 500, only one-eighth had more than 1,000. Many factors combined to drive up the cost of ' nursing ' a seat : the increasing importance of Parliament ; the Triennial Act and more frequent elections ; brisk competition by members of the rival East India Companies. Gradually the boroughs subsided into the pockets of peers and rich merchants. London had four members ; but forty Londoners sat in the Commons of 1701.[1] It was now the Tories who favoured a wide franchise in the narrow constituencies, the Whigs who supported and profited by the trend towards oligarchy. But the rising cost and frequency of elections helped to destroy party contests in the open constituencies and led to compromises by which seats were shared out between families or interests. As the cost of getting into Parliament rose, so too did the demand for rewards once one had got there : conversely the potential economic advantages of membership of Parliament contributed to enhance the price of seats.

ADMINISTRATIVE CHANGES

The civil service was growing in numbers, especially in the revenue departments, in consequence of the expansion of the armed forces and the abandonment of tax-farming. The Excise Commission had at its disposal inferior places to the value of £100,000 a year. The requirement of security of £200 and upwards from its employees ' effectively closed the door to men without land or connection '. In accounting for the decline of Toryism in the eighteenth century we must not forget how many opportunities were now being offered to the sons of squires in the civil service, the navy, the Army, India. For the many old families which found themselves in financial difficulties, government jobs became a pressing necessity. This tied them to 1688 and the Hanoverian succession no less effectively than the Bank of England tied the moneyed classes.[2] For the lower ranks of the customs administration an entrance examination was introduced ; no qualities except birth were of course required from gentlemen.

[1] R. Walcott, *English Politics in the Early Eighteenth Century* (1956), pp. 23, 26
[2] Hughes, *Studies in Administration and Finance*, pp. 205, 216–19 ; ' The Professions in the Eighteenth Century ', pp. 47–8

As the administration grew more complex, the Interregnum system of rule by committees proved more convenient than the management of departments by a single head. Under William the Treasury was normally thus 'in commission'—a device Clarendon had thought fit only for a republic. Financial business was getting too difficult and too technical to be entrusted to a great magnate. Anne made Godolphin and Harley Lord Treasurers; but after 1714 that office finally disappears. Finance was now so important that the first Lord of the Treasury remained the chief minister of the crown. Simultaneously the Chancellor of the Exchequer emerged from departmental obscurity to become a minister responsible to Parliament. The Admiralty came permanently under a board. Its powers were under effective Parliamentary control. Salaries replaced fees and perquisites in 1694. There was a consequential difference in attitude within the department. Its papers became public, not private, property. The age of Pepys, Mr Ehrman suggests, marks a transition. In one sense Pepys is the first modern civil servant, anxious to promote Commonwealth tarpaulins rather than gentlemen officers; but he also looked back to the age of Buckingham, in which policy and administration were still confused. Similarly the Treasury Office grew between 1660 and 1702 'from something approaching the personal retinue of a magnate into a professional body of civil servants', who were no longer dismissed with their patron. In 1695 it published a fee list.[1]

New departments were similarly run by boards—Committees of Trade and Plantations leading up to the Board of Trade, Commissioners of Customs and Excise. After the Revolution, when revenue was at last raised smoothly and consolidated, Treasury control of departments became effective. The whole administrative system was coming to be based on interlocking committees. It was natural that it should be co-ordinated by a still higher committee, composed of the key individuals in the administrative machine. This is one explanation of the origin of the Cabinet system, which dates from this period. But the Cabinet is a political as well as an administrative body, and its rise was a product of the political struggles

---

[1] Ehrman, *The Navy in the War of William III*, pp. 282–8, 562–4; S. B. Baxter, *The Development of the Treasury, 1660–1702* (1957), pp. 142, 257–62

of the time as well as of administrative evolution. The executive links the political sovereign with the administrative apparatus, and therefore necessarily changes as sovereignty shifts. The personal rule of individual heads of departments had been focused upon the King, so long as he was the real head of his government. The triumph of the new system accompanies the sovereignty of Parliament. To ask whether the administrative changes were cause or consequence of the political changes is to ask whether the chicken preceded the egg. The two inevitably went together.

Under Charles and James the Privy Council had grown too big to be the effective executive, and many of its functions had been delegated to committees of the Council. In addition there had been unofficial groups within the Privy Council, on whose advice the King had especially relied. But now the Privy Council was becoming a merely honorific body, so much so that Anne did not even bother to remove dismissed ministers from it. William III's absences abroad necessitated the appointment of Lords Justices, who for all practical purposes administered the country under Queen Mary. The Whig Junto, with their secure majority in the Commons, began to meet independently of the King even when he was in England. The process continued under Anne, who played a much smaller part than her predecessor. She still attended Cabinet meetings, though often only to ratify decisions taken in informal committees. Not until well on into the next reign did the sovereign cease to attend. By the end of our period the Cabinet, still a body unknown to the law, was formalised to the extent that leading ministers were assumed to have a right to attend, and were therefore held responsible for government policy. The principle of joint Cabinet responsibility, however, was not yet fully established, nor was there any minister who could be called a Prime Minister.

The Cabinet was viewed with suspicion by the House of Commons, especially the Tories. A clause in the Act of Settlement tried to revive the Privy Council as the effective executive, and to insist that Privy Councillors should sign all resolutions to which they had agreed. But it was repealed in 1706. Another clause, also soon repealed, tried to remove all placemen from the House of Commons. We may regard place-

men either as honest civil servants trying to carry on the
administration, or as venal tools of corrupt politicians, according to taste ; but they were a necessary part of the post-
Revolution system.   No government could have retained a
majority in the Commons without this solid block of interested
supporters.

During the seventeenth century personal monarchy had
been undermined in all sorts of ways.   Following the twenty
years of the Interregnum, two Convention Parliaments had
decided the affairs of the country and selected a king.   Parliament drew its significance not from the monarch but from
those whom it represented.   Statutes of 1696 and 1707 provided
that Parliament should continue to sit on the death of the
sovereign and that the Privy Council and all civil and military
officers should continue in place for six months unless dismissed
by his successor.   Under the early Stuarts the phrase ' The
King can do no wrong ' had been used to justify arbitrary royal
actions.   What had then been a revolutionary interpretation
of the phrase was now generally accepted : if wrong was done,
some minister must have done it.   So it was twisted to become
a doctrine of the responsibility, not the irresponsibility, of the
executive.   The Whigs who impeached Danby in 1678, the
Tories who impeached the Junto in 1701, each asserted this
doctrine.

The concept of treason underwent a similar change.   In
medieval thought, treason was a violation of personal loyalties.
There was petty treason, breach of loyalty to an immediate
lord, and high treason, breach of loyalty to our sovereign
lord the King.   In 1629 members of Parliament differentiated
between treason to the King and treason to the Commonwealth.   This had already been described as ' dangerous ' by
Lord Chancellor Ellesmere, but in 1640 the Commons
impeached Lord Chief Justice Finch ' for treason as well
against the King as against the kingdom, for whatsoever is
against the whole is undoubtedly against the head '.   Eight
years later the King himself was condemned for high treason
by Parliament's High Court of Justice, in the name of the
people of England.   This was revolutionary doctrine.   But
1688 was a revolution too.   William announced that members
of the royal navy who resisted him on James's behalf would

be treated as enemies of the kingdom of Great Britain.   Indeed
the beauty of 1688 was that kings had been changed without the
state collapsing, in refutation of Hobbes.   The state was now
different from, and more important than, the monarch.

THE LAW

The Revolution set the lawyers free, Roger North says.   Since
the Act of Settlement judges no longer hold office *durante bene
placito domini regis* (during the King's pleasure) but *quamdiu se
bene gesserint* (as long as they give satisfactory service).   This
had been the Commonwealth principle.   Henceforth judges
were removable only upon address of both Houses.   In 1691
the judges insisted that they had a freehold right to sell subordinate posts in the judicial administration.

'What signify all our laws if we have no estates?' a member
of Parliament asked in 1693.   There was a tendency in William's
reign for the law to be made more savage in protection of
private property.   Statutes made shoplifting and the stealing
of furniture by lodgers punishable by death.   Changes in the
harsh debtors' law were aimed only at assisting creditors.   In
1701 peers' immunity from arrest for debt was ended.   A few
years later, Mandeville wrote of Justice :

> Yet, it was thought, the sword she bore
> Checked but the desperate and the poor,
> That, urged by mere necessity,
> Were tied up to the wretched tree
> For crimes which not deserved that fate
> But to secure the rich and great.

But where property was not concerned there was a reaction
against the methods of James II and Jeffreys : the modification
in the harshness of legal procedure, which had begun in 1640,
was resumed.   The Act of 1653 against burning women had
lapsed after 1660 ; Elizabeth Gaunt was so put to death after
Sedgemoor.   But no more women were burnt alive for political
offences after 1688.   The clause in the Declaration of Rights
against cruel and unusual punishments stopped men being
flogged to death, as Dangerfield (one of the many informers
during the Popish Plot) had been in 1685.   From 1689 the
Quakers' principled objection to judicial oaths was recognised,

and they were allowed to make a 'statutory declaration' instead. Litigation was simplified by the abandonment of the old system of original writs ; and so the revolution in the content of law was accompanied by a procedural revolution which one authority describes as containing 'almost the difference between medieval and modern', between reliance on precedents and authorities and on the core of reason within legal procedure. So it ran parallel to the development of political theory.[1]

After 1696 two witnesses had to be produced against the accused in treason trials ; the accused were entitled to full use of counsel, and to a copy of the indictment, together with a list of crown witnesses and of the jury. In 1697 the last Act of Attainder in English history was passed against Sir John Fenwick, implicated in a plot to assassinate the King. But the most significant changes in procedure, Sir William Holdsworth tells us, were the result of the improved character of judges once the Stuarts had been got rid of. Judges began to protect even Quakers against the Church courts. Holt 'laid the foundations of modern commercial law' by deciding cases 'in the light of mercantile custom instead of by the strict rules of the common law'. On one occasion he invited 'all the eminent merchants of London' to discuss a point of commercial law with him. The inadmissibility of hearsay evidence, on which Coke had insisted, at last won general acceptance after 1688. But proposals for full modernisation of the law still suffered from their association with the radicals of the Interregnum and the Rye House plotters of 1683. So the lawyers were able to thwart attempts in the nineties to reform Chancery and the debtors' law, and to prevent perjury being declared a felony in cases where it led to a man's being sentenced to death. The common law retained many medieval features until the nineteenth-century reforms.

[1] S. Rezneck, 'The Statute of 1696', *Journal of Modern History*, **2**, 13

19   Religion and Ideas, 1688-1714

Whig and Tory, High and Low Church, are names : Hanover
and St Germains are things. . . .   By Whigs we mean those
that are most zealous for the protestant succession.

Dr W. Wootton to William Wake,
Bishop of Lincoln, *c.*1712–13

An entire liberty must be allowed in our inquiries, that
natural philosophy may become subservient to the most
valuable purposes.

Sir Isaac Newton

THE ANGLICAN CHURCH

'THE persecuting prelate and the backstairs priest,' wrote
Mr Ogg, ' were now things of the past.   Here was the essence,
many may think the justification, of the English Revolution.
. . .   Christianity and Sovereignty ceased to be dependent,
for their validity, on the hangman.'   After 1688 the Church
of England had perforce to abandon any thought of recovering
its monopoly.   The political services of dissenters had been
too great to go unrewarded.   As in 1660, the possibility of
comprehending Presbyterians within the Church was mooted.
This time the high-flying Anglicans supported it, in the hope
of avoiding the toleration which they saw would otherwise be
inevitable.   Defeated in this, they continued to hope that the
Toleration Act would be only a temporary concession, which
could soon be withdrawn.   But in fact not even the government
of 1710–14, which passed the Occasional Conformity and
Schism Acts, dared to repeal the Toleration Act.

Henceforth the Church of England was rent by divisions.
A small group of Non-Jurors (including five of the Seven
Bishops) felt that, having sworn allegiance to James, they
could not conscientiously accept William and Mary as
sovereigns.   But few Anglican ministers followed them into the

wilderness for long. This is the age of the Vicar of Bray.
By the end of Anne's reign the Non-Juror schism was virtually
over. More serious were the divisions between those who
remained within the Church. Many rank-and-file parsons
admired, if they would not imitate, the courage and con-
sistency of the Non-Jurors. Inevitably Bishops who resigned
in 1689 or died later were replaced by men who accepted the
Revolution Settlement, including Latitudinarians like Tillotson,
Sancroft's successor at Canterbury, and a radical Whig like
Burnet. Even Anne, despite her personal predilections, had
sometimes to appoint Whig Bishops when her ministers
insisted : Tory propagandists like Sacheverell and Swift never
became Bishops. So the higher clergy were predominantly
Whig or moderate Tory, whilst the mass of the lower clergy
tended to be high-flyers. This division was similar to that
between Whig lords and Tory gentry. The split made
Convocation unworkable as an organ of self-government for
the Church, and led to its falling into disuse. Convocation
failed to agree on revision of the liturgy and canons in 1689,
and the Toleration Act passed through Parliament. An
attempt by Convocation to suppress the deist John Toland's
book, *Christianity Not Mysterious*, also failed ; the Church had
lost its power in the judicial as well as the legislative sphere.

The alliance of parson and squire, however, remained,
and with it thought-control in the villages. A squire believed
in 1706 that all he needed to bring ' these poor deluded
people to their senses again ', and cure them of Jacobitism,
was ' to get an honest parson in '. Parson and squire hated the
Toleration Act almost as much, and for the same reasons, as
they had hated the Major-Generals and James II. The
Toleration Act, Archdeacon Prideaux wrote in 1701, enabled
men to avoid going to church at all.

The Union with Scotland further weakened the Church's
position. Since 1689 the English sovereign had been head
of the Presbyterian Kirk as well as of the Anglican Church,
a theologically athletic position. Now the Act of Union
allowed Presbyterians to sit in Parliament, and guaranteed
the existence of Presbyterian universities in Scotland. It was
the more difficult to treat toleration in England as a temporary
concession when Presbyterianism was legally established across

the Border. Dissenters excluded from English universities could send their sons to study sound theology in Scotland.

Before 1640 there had been Royalist Bishops and Puritan clergy ; after 1688 there were Whig Bishops and Tory clergy. The constant factor is that the higher clergy were rich and the lesser poor. In 1704 Anne surrendered First Fruits and Tenths, taxes on the clergy inherited by the crown from the Pope. With them a fund was formed, Queen Anne's Bounty, from which lower stipends could be augmented. (Under Charles II, First Fruits and Tenths had been used in part for pensions to royal mistresses and bastards ; under William III the Earl of Sunderland drew £2,000 a year from this highly inappropriate source. Burnet, to whom much of the credit for Queen Anne's Bounty is due, remarked that it was odd that the clergy never protested against these acts of sacrilege.) Thanks to the Bounty, but still more to agricultural prosperity, the economic status of the clergy rose in the eighteenth century : the Church became a respectable and remunerative career for younger sons of the aristocracy.

DISSENTERS AND LATITUDINARIANS

Although legally free to worship as they wished, dissenters remained, until the nineteenth century, excluded from the universities, and from bodies like the Royal College of Physicians. But Dissenting Academies, able to come into the open after 1689, multiplied rapidly. They trained men for business and the professions with a far wider and more up-to-date curriculum than that of grammar schools and universities: it included mathematics and science. In the academies the realistic theories of the educational reformers of the Interregnum were put into practice for the first time. Ironically, Harley and St John, who led the Church party, had been educated at Dissenting Academies. They provided the best training for lower grades in the civil service. When scientific invention revived in the eighteenth century, the impetus came from the Dissenting Academies and from individual craftsmen, not from the universities or the Royal Society.

Toleration thus hardened a rift in English society. Nonconformists had their own more utilitarian, more critical, more democratic culture; but it was stunted and provincial, cut off from the great world of affairs. Meanwhile the Grand Tour of the Continent was becoming normal for young men of the upper class. Their horizons were being widened by first-hand knowledge of all things foreign, which partially compensated for time wasted at Oxford or Cambridge. From all this nonconformists were excluded. The cultural split between Anglican universities and middle-class Dissenting Academies extended to a rigid distinction between the arts and the sciences. An assumption that the former were more 'gentlemanly' and superior because of no practical application has survived to bedevil the English educational system ever since. A classical education became the hall-mark of a gentleman and was thought to fit him for public life.

Persecution had hitherto ensured that only those fittest to survive elected to be nonconformists. After 1689 dissenters had to face the perils of worldly prosperity, to which their higher code of business ethics and their more single-minded application both contributed. 'Religion is a natural cause of riches,' observed Bishop Wilkins; but as men prospered they lost some of their earlier enthusiasm. All the sects entered on a period of spiritual decline. The Calvinist faith of the early seventeenth-century revolutionaries was in full disintegration. Presbyterianism collapsed into Unitarianism, and there was a general tendency towards deism—in which, significantly enough, the lead was taken by laymen. The dominant Latitudinarian school of Restoration theologians, no less than Hobbes, was sceptical of any claim to inspiration. 'Reason,' said Locke, 'must be our judge and guide in everything.' By reason he meant what seemed reasonable to the men of his own social class. Christianity was too difficult for 'the day-labourers and tradesmen, the spinsters and dairy-maids', who must be told what to think. 'The greatest part cannot know, and therefore they must believe.' Toleration should not be extended to fanatics who 'upon pretence of religion' claim special authority in civil affairs, nor to atheists (who were thought not to respect oaths and other bonds of society) nor to Papists (who owed allegiance to a foreign power).

Locke's philosophy was a workaday synthesis of the ideas

of the more creative, more revolutionary thinkers of the earlier seventeenth century. Locke was a Christian, and he favoured religious toleration ; but his Christianity was shorn of everything that had made Puritanism revolutionary—of direct contact with God, of enthusiasm—and his tolerance was the rational calculation of the Toleration Act rather than the humanist idealism of a Milton. Locke began as a political supporter of Shaftesbury, and followed him into political exile. Yet he was no democrat, and happily accepted 1688 as the revolution to end revolutions. He and Sir Isaac Newton were the backroom boys of the Whig Junto. Locke associated with the scientists, and attempted, in his *Essay concerning Human Understanding,* to establish a materialist psychology that would reconcile science and Christianity. His historical importance lies in these contradictions. He wrote in a lucid unadorned style, persuasive both because it addressed itself to the man of common sense, and because it side-stepped difficulties that have worried more profound thinkers. Because Locke was a synthesiser, obscuring contradictions between the ideas he brought together, he won universal acceptance for a scientific, materialist approach. For the same reason, his followers diverged into Lockeans of the right and of the left, according as they stressed one or other side of the compromise—for example, either the rights of property or the origin of such rights in labour—that had done duty in the exceptional social circumstances after 1688.

Locke's *Reasonableness of Christianity* was followed by a series of books showing that Christianity was not mysterious. The religious approach to politics ceased to predominate : by the time of the Popish Plot it had degenerated into a stunt manipulated by cynical politicians. Pilgrims who had set out for the Celestial City found themselves lingering in Vanity Fair, or the nearby village of Occasional Conformity. In 1693 a clergyman who proclaimed that the Second Coming was imminent was regarded as a psychological case, and not as a heretic or a political subversive. The last English witch trial took place in 1712. As Calvinism declined there was a new emphasis on works rather than faith, on moral conduct rather than enthusiasm or sacramentalism. Discipline, and especially labour discipline, was felt by the non-working classes to be a national necessity, preached now by economists with the same zest as by theologians. ' 'Tis for want of discipline that any poverty appears in England,' cried Petty. Increased unemployment, Locke thought in 1697, was caused by ' nothing else but the relaxation of discipline and corruption of manners '.

REFORMING MANNERS

The theological trend away from Calvinism thus fitted in with the arguments of the economists. From the nineties Latitudinarians and dissenters co-operated in voluntary societies for the reformation of manners. Their object was to give effect to laws against Sabbath-breaking, drunkenness, swearing, etc. put on the statute book by earlier Puritan and Whig Parliaments. Now that the highly placed protectors of Popery and sin had been driven out, the laws could be enforced, and England swiftly made a virtuous country. Defoe in *The Poor Man's Plea* protested against the class basis of the vice laws. ' The man with a gold ring and gay clothes may swear before the justice or at the justice ; may reel home through the open streets and no man take any notice of him ; but if a poor man gets drunk or swears an oath, he must to the stocks without remedy.'

Inevitably these voluntary societies got involved in politics. Reformation of manners had been one of Oliver Cromwell's aims. The alliance of Low Church and dissent to promote godliness had a Whiggish look. ' Discipline ' still had too many Presbyterian overtones. And could ' discipline ' be limited to the lower orders ? Might not some earnest but misguided reformers seek to curtail the harmless pleasures of the rich, as during the dreadful years of revolution ? Could an Englishman's house really be his castle if busybodies were always peeping through his windows ? Informing had been an unpopular trade since the days of the early Stuarts, yet the societies employed paid informers to denounce vice. This gave a pretext for Tories to leap in with some pleasure to defend the liberties of Englishmen against canting Whigs. One reason for the popularity of Sacheverell was his pose as defender of popular rights against the reformers. There was thus some sense in the Toryism of the lower classes. By the end of our period the societies for the reformation of manners were in decline : what survived was the charity-school movement and the Society for Promoting Christian Knowledge. In the long run, gin (a Dutch drink whose consumption began to expand rapidly under the Dutch King) may have provided more consolation for the miserable urban poor than the well-meant efforts of the voluntary societies.

The word ' mob ' first appears in this period. There were political as well as economic reasons for this. The nonconformist congregations had abandoned politics, had become narrow, sectarian, and respectable. They do not seem to have attracted the urban poor. 1688 brought no widening of the franchise, even in corporations where it had been narrowed by Charles II and James II. There was thus no political outlet for the passions and resentments of those whom their betters expected to work hard for low wages in deplorable living conditions. The ' mob ' might express its feelings in the form of Jacobitism, but it was anti-government rather than pro anything else. Hence its reputation for political instability. Its existence set limits to popular agitation by the official Whig and Tory parties, and was one of the main reasons for their solidarity in and after 1688. Sacheverell was felt by many to have gone too far in his appeal to the rabble. ' The reason . . . for which all government was at first appointed,' Defoe thought, ' was . . . to prevent mobs and rabbles in the world.' [1]

POLITICAL IDEAS

This period saw decisive changes in political thinking. Filmer's divine-right non-resistance theories had been exposed as irrelevant. In his *First Treatise on Civil Government* (not published

[1] Defoe's attitude to the mob is particularly interesting because of its ambivalence. Luther and Calvin, Knox and Cranmer, were sons of the mob.

> Our mobs the reformation still pursue,
> And seldom have been in the wrong till now.

But now a sovereign Parliament exists to express the wishes of the people. The mob has lost its creative power : it has become fickle, purposeless, destructive, and can only serve the interests of the Jacobites. So ' these new dictators of the streets ' must be controlled—' and if persuasion won't the gallows will ', *Hymn to the Mob* (1708) ; cf. Alick West, *The Mountain in the Sunlight* (1958), pp. 67-73.

till 1690 but written long before), Locke performed the easy task of demolishing them. From Hobbes, whom he did not attack, Locke took over much—his utilitarianism, his scientific spirit, his emphasis on the necessity of government. Only by Locke's time the fear of revolt by the many-headed monster which underlay *Leviathan* had diminished : the mob could only riot destructively. So Locke argued, in contrast with Hobbes, that the executive may forfeit its rights if it endangers the stability of property, maintenance of which is the reason for the existence of the state. Hobbes thought that any revolution against the authority of the sovereign must dissolve society into anarchy. Locke held that society could continue to exist even if the men of property found it necessary to change the sovereign. 1688 proved him right.

In that year Archbishop Sancroft pointed out, as Cavaliers and Levellers had done forty years earlier, that the forty-shilling freeholders who possessed the vote were not the people of England. But this fact seemed less relevant in Locke's world than it had been in Lilburne's. Locke talked ambiguously of government deriving from and being responsible to ' the people ', but it was perfectly clear that by ' the people ' he meant the propertied class. Their control of society had been established against monarchical absolutism by the abolition of the prerogative courts, and confirmed by the expulsion of James II. It had been established against the lower orders by the defeat of the radicals during the Interregnum, and confirmed by the defeat of Monmouth's rebellion. Economic tendencies were on their side, fortifying the men of big property, disintegrating the class of small proprietors. Defoe in 1706 could state as an obvious truism that :

> There can be no pretence of government
> Till they that have the property consent. . . .
> For laws are reason's outworks to enclose
> And fortify the man against his foes ;
> Built from immediate dictate from on high
> To strengthen and defend his property.

Freeholders own England, Defoe thought, and have the sole right to govern it. Other inhabitants are ' but sojourners . . . subject to such laws as freeholders impose upon them '. In *Ashby versus White*, Chief Justice Holt insisted that the vote was a species of property of which the owner cannot be deprived ; and the House of Lords maintained this view. Harrington in 1656 had generalised the political experience of his generation in the maxim that political power follows possession of land. Swift in 1710 saw that ' power, which according to the old maxim was used to follow land, is now gone over to money '.

In the course of the century all efforts to strengthen the central administrative machinery had been defeated. The state which Thomas Cromwell reorganised in the sixteenth century was broken in the sixteen-forties. In the fifties, and again after 1688, the English state had exceptionally powerful military and naval forces which protected foreign trade ; but memories of Strafford, the Major-Generals, and James II kept the internal aspect of the state relatively weak until the nineteenth century. Justices of the Peace and the militia maintained local law and order, and protected property ; but the central power exercised little control over them. The sixteenth-century Reformation produced a cheap Church ; the seventeenth-century revolution a strong state, which was cheap in relation to the functions it performed. Local government was still run by unpaid officials, rewarded by prestige and influence ; central government was still financed in large part by fees and perquisites rather than by salaries. Thus whilst most European populations groaned under vastly expensive bureaucracies, far the heaviest English government expenditure was on the armed forces which fought off trade rivals. It was a *laissez-faire* state, whose chief internal function was to hinder hindrances to the sway of the ' natural rulers ', just as in the economy there was internal free trade and external protection.

So the English conception of liberty came to be a negative one : the Englishman's freedom means being left alone, being free from arbitrary arrest, from taxation which he has not voted, from conscription, from government interference with his economic activity, from religious persecution. The Englishman's house is his castle, a ' liberty ' in the feudal sense, from which state power is excluded. Legislative and executive are separated ' powers ', with the judiciary a third independent power balancing the other two. Locke's state is a limited liability company, the ringholder in a *laissez-faire* business community. The antithesis of individual and state looks back to the struggles against Laud, the Major-Generals, and James II and also to the dissenters' struggles against religious intolerance. In France, Germany, or Russia, the relation of individual to state has been conceived in very different terms, because of their very different history. Deliberate circumscription of state action and of the coercive power of the Church in England naturally led to an expansion of the type of voluntary effort conducted by the societies for the reformation of manners, henceforth so characteristic of the English tradition.

THE ARTS AND SCIENCE

Milton's political writings were more influential in this period than in his lifetime. After 1695 the Stationers' Company's monopoly of printing came to an end. Printing was no longer criminal simply because unauthorised. The Act of 1696 for regulating treason trials made executions for seditious printing (such as had occurred in 1664 and 1693) much more difficult ; there was only one in the eighteenth century. Scores of newspapers came into existence, including regular dailies. Until the Tory government's stamp duty of 1712 killed about half of them the press played a very important part in politics and elections. Journalism established itself as a social force ; Charles II had thought it worth personally wooing Dryden as a propagandist—and how right he was in his choice ! But now men of letters did not need to turn their coats as often or as humiliatingly as Dryden had done. Addison's poem on Blenheim was solicited by Godolphin, and helped its author into the House of Commons and state office ; Swift's powerful pen gained him the friendship of the great even if not the bishopric he so much desired. Defoe probably helped to bring England into the War of Spanish Succession : Swift's *Conduct of the Allies* certainly stimulated the demand for the war to be ended.

Addison and Steele sought to end ' the long divorce of wit from virtue ', to civilise the nonconformist *bourgeoisie*, to pietise the backwoods gentry—and their wives and daughters. Their success testifies to the existence of a steady reading public, outside court, Church, and universities, sufficient to maintain men and women of letters. The rise of this middle-class reading public, combined with the decline in the importance of the court, reduced the dependence of men of letters on patrons. Defoe sold 80,000 copies of *The True-Born Englishman*. Whereas Milton had received only £10 for *Paradise Lost*, Archbishop Tillotson's sermons sold for 2,500 guineas in 1694, and Matthew Prior received 4,000 guineas for a collection of his poems. When an attempt was made in 1703 ' to restrain the licentiousness of the press ', London's seventy printing and publishing shops successfully lobbied the House of Commons against it. Printing was already too important an industry to be lightly interfered with. In 1711 authors, for the first time, were granted copyright in their works.

A new popular Toryism rose as Whiggery became associated with the City and an aristocratic oligarchy. A similar ' Tory democracy ' can be seen in literature. Under Charles II Otway had managed in *Venice Preserved* (1682) to combine a topical criticism of corrupt and demagogical Parliamentarians with a passionate radical libertarianism ; and Dryden's savage satires against the Whigs had political humbug as a principal target. Mrs Aphra Behn, one of the first women to live by the pen, joined Toryism with denunciation of slavery and a cult of the noble savage, which in *Oroonoko* (1688) started a new fashion. Both Defoe and Swift began as Whigs, but neither found eighteenth-century Whiggery attractive, and Swift wrote his ferocious attacks on war, war-profiteers, and stock-jobbers in the interests of the Tory party. It is after 1688 that poets feel most out of sympathy with the accepted values of society, that the poet as outsider replaces the poet as public functionary. This was made possible by the poet's newly won economic independence, but it was also due to the contrast between the values and the realities of his society. Nathaniel Lee, Tory son of a Puritan divine, was one of the first poets to go mad ; but in the eighteenth century the greatest poets were more often mad than sane.

The period after 1688 looks forward to the Augustan age of English literature. The ubiquitous rhymed couplet and the gentlemanly elegant prose of Addison and Steele mark the triumph of the new manner. With Defoe the novel came of age, though it still bore traces of the guides to godliness from

which it derived. But the new age killed Restoration comedy.
The Restoration theatre had combined an aristocratic monar-
chism in politics with Hobbist scepticism. It attacked religious
humbug in what Jeremy Collier, in his *Short View of the
Immorality and Prophaneness of the English Stage* (1688), called
' down-right porter's rhetoric ', reminding him of Interregnum
republicanism. Opposition to the alleged licentiousness of the
theatre now came not only from Puritans—Collier was a Non-
Juror—but from those who felt that the sceptical libertinism
of the dramatists endangered the social order. ' If eternity was
out of the case,' observed Collier, ' general advantage and
public reason and secular policy would oblige us to be just
to the priesthood. For . . . religion is the basis of government.'
Collier had the same horror for witticisms about the nobility
as for witticisms about God. ' What necessity is there to kick
the coronets about the stage, and to make a man a lord only in
order to make him a coxcomb ? I hope the poets don't intend
to revive the old project of levelling, and vote down the House
of Peers.'

Restoration comedy had reflected the hostility of the
sceptical courtiers to the society into which they had been
restored, and so was necessarily transitional. By 1688 the
aristocracy had adapted itself to the new world. The monarchy
had been adapted to it : the ' family on the throne ' (William
and Mary, Prince George of Denmark and Anne) contrasted
markedly with the atmosphere of Charles's and James's courts.
The improvement in moral tone (and deterioration in quality)
of eighteenth-century drama was the result not of Collier's
book but of social changes of which that book was a symptom.
Sentimentalism replaced wit. Dryden accepted Collier's
criticisms, Congreve ceased to write, Vanbrugh abandoned
drama for architecture. Thomas Rymer invented poetic
justice, the theme-phrase of the reconciliation between Puritanism and the drama. ' Every tragedy,' wrote John Dennis in
1701, ' ought to be a very solemn lecture, inculcating a particular providence, and showing it plainly protecting the good
and chastising the bad, or at least the violent : . . . otherwise
it is either an empty amusement, or a scandalous and pernicious libel upon the government of the world.' Or as Collier
put it, ' The business of plays is to recommend virtue and

discourage vice.' It is of course nothing of the sort ; but that seemed a very desirable role for the drama in the eighteenth century.

Nor was it Puritanism that led to the ' dissociation of sensibility ',[1] to the decline of English music, to the divorce between the literature and art of the few and of the many. These disasters resulted rather from changes affecting the whole of society, which dried up the springs of natural poetry, and also drained Puritanism itself of its revolutionary fervour, leaving only a secular utilitarianism. Locke, like the early scientists, favoured a language stripped of its poetical connotations. He urged parents whose children showed a taste for poetry to have it ' stifled and suppressed as much as may be '. An ability to play musical instruments was no less harmful, he thought, since it ' wastes so much of a young man's time, to give him but a moderate skill in it, and engages him in such odd company '. Music should be left to women as an ' accomplishment ' for the recreation of their menfolk ; or, in this society of division of labour, should be a commodity produced by specialists for sale to those who could afford to buy. Family chamber music decreased ; the habit of passive listening increased. From the sixteen-seventies there was a large enough public in London for performances to be organised on commercial lines. The violin, which gave greater scope to individual virtuosity, replaced the viol, more suited to private performances. Foreign virtuosi, being more expensive, tended to be preferred to English. Since these developments coincided in time with the break-up of the village community, with its songs and dances, a catastrophic decline in English music set in. Purcell, who died in 1696 at the tragically early age of thirty-six, was the last great English composer for two centuries. He was also the last great English composer of public, ceremonial music, the last great English court composer, and the first great English composer of music for the theatre and opera.[2]

'The full Baroque style,' it has been said, ' was pre-eminently suited for the service of absolute monarchies ' or the Roman Catholic Church. This is the main reason why it never triumphed in England. Baroque's most ' unequivocal

[1] See above, p. 4
[2] Meyer, *English Chamber Music* ; A. K. Holland, *Henry Purcell* (1948)

statement ' in painting was made in the inner chambers of
Windsor Castle which the Papist Antonio Verrio decorated
for Charles II.   After 1688 court and high aristocracy ceased
to be sole patrons.   In the early nineties there was a boom in
picture sales, some 24,000 being sold in London in 1691 alone.
This may have been due to snob buying, the new bourgeoisie
aping the culture of its betters ; but it led to a great increase
in the number of professional painters working in England,
including some women.   Foreigners like Verrio and Sir Godfrey
Kneller continued to be patronised by the very rich, and it
was still the foreigners who were knighted ; but a reaction
against court taste, together with a possibly narrow patriotism,
contributed to a revival of the native tradition.   John Riley,
whose reputation had been won among the middle-class public,
was sworn chief painter together with Godfrey Kneller in
December 1688.   At the end of the century Sir Christopher
Wren observed that English artists ' want not a genius, but an
education in . . . practice in designing or drawing '.   They
failed to get this education so long as their highest hope was to
be a hack copyist in the mass-production studios of a Lely or a
Kneller.   Only after our period did the native tradition come
to full fruition, with Hogarth, Reynolds, Gainsborough, and
Blake.[1]

In architecture patronage was necessarily more restricted :
it passed from the court to Whig aristocrats and municipalities.
London was rebuilt after the Great Fire of 1666 in the plain
brick style copied from the Dutch burghers, which by then had
become the English vernacular.   The Fire of London gave
Wren the opportunity for rebuilding many City churches,
including St Paul's, his masterpiece.   ' Neither the society in
which Wren lived . . . nor the scientific temper of his own
mind made it possible for him to create a wholeheartedly
Baroque architecture.'   ' The English Church and the English
monarchy were, during his lifetime, working out a compromise
solution of their relations to Parliament.   Wren's architecture
reflects that compromise.'   As the demand for country houses
expanded, architecture ceased to be the pastime of a gentleman

[1] Whinney and Millar, *English Art, 1625–1714*, esp. pp. 285, 297, 319 ;
H. V. S. and M. S. Ogden, *English Taste in Landscape in the Seventeenth Century*
(1955), esp. pp. 88–9, 163

like Pratt or Vanbrugh, the part-time occupation of a scientific virtuoso like Wren or Robert Hooke : it became the job of professionals like Nicholas Hawksmoor, who collaborated with Vanbrugh in building Marlborough's palace of Blenheim. These professional architects inherited the anonymous craft tradition of masons and joiners as well as an awareness of foreign and classical models. Extension of the market had led to specialised division of labour in the arts as in other sectors of the economy.[1]

Finally, this period saw the emergence of a series of assumptions about society and the universe which point far into the future. Newton's theory of universal gravitation, like Locke's philosophy, brought into a single system a mass of complex phenomena and the contributions of the scientists of a creative century and a half. Newton depicted the universe as a self-moving machine. It had needed a creator, but since the act of creation it was governed by physical laws of motion. By the end of our period the categories of time, space, matter, and motion, within which science operated down to the present century, had been set up. Newton was a Unitarian, who denied the divinity of Christ, the mystery of the Incarnation. His principles made intolerance and dogmatism impossible. His great synthesis seemed to establish law and order in the universe, as 1688 did in society. God was no longer an arbitrary monarch : He was bound by His own laws, which were those of reason. The universe ceased to be mysterious : God the great watchmaker had set the machine going and was unlikely to intervene in future. Meanwhile men could with profit study the predictable workings of the machine.

Locke established equally consoling truths for society : not only that property did rule, as had long been accepted, but that the men of property ought to rule ; that the sovereignty of Parliament was the sovereignty of the people ; that the right of revolt exercised in 1688, though theoretically still in existence, need in future never be used again. The state was accepted as a human contrivance, politics as a rational science. In the last resort Locke's state rested on divine law ; but the

[1] Whinney and Millar, *op. cit.*, p. 333 ; Summerson, *Architecture in Britain, 1530-1840*, pp. 148, 169

interference of priests or of other would-be interpreters of God's will was as alien to Locke's mode of thought as the direct intervention of God would have been in Newton's universe. The earth had ceased to be the centre of the physical universe, but man had become the centre of this world. ' The proper study of mankind is man.' This emphasis on reason in religion witnesses to a growing confidence in human powers. By 1691 Robert Boyle thought it necessary to endow a series of lectures whose object was to defend the truths of Christianity against unbelievers. For the first time for a thousand years Christianity was on the defensive. We may regret the loss of some poetic insights in this mechanical universe. But the society which took it for granted was more tolerant, kinder, more urbane, at least to those whose poverty did not put them beyond its pale.

20 Conclusion, 1660-1714

> In commending or disallowing the actions of men, it is a
> course very requisite to consider the beginning, the proceeding
> and the end : so shall we see the reasons and causes of things
> and not their bare events only, which for the most part are
> governed by fortune.
>
> Sir Walter Ralegh, *The Cabinet Council*

THE England around which Daniel Defoe was beginning to
tour at the end of our period was very different from that
through which James I rode in 1603. We are already in the
modern world—the world of banks and cheques, budgets, the
stock exchange, the periodical press, coffee-houses, clubs,
coffins, microscopes, shorthand, actresses, and umbrellas. It
is a world in which governments put first the promotion of
production, for policy is no longer determined by aristocrats
whose main economic activity is consumption. Defoe's eye
was always wide open for ways in which the national wealth
could be increased : he knew this would interest his readers.
The country as a whole has become far richer. The amount
raised in taxes has multiplied by twenty-five. The system of
taxation has been reorganised so that a higher proportion of the
burden falls on landowners and the poor, less on industrialists.
The great agricultural boom has begun. Casual labour has
replaced vagabondage. Political institutions have adapted
themselves to this new society. The men of property are
secure and unfettered in their control of local government ;
as taxpayers they determine government policy. Anyone rich
enough can buy himself into Parliament, and once there he
has good chances of winning returns on his investment. Government patronage is now dispensed by ministers responsible to
the House of Commons, and has become a system of outdoor
relief for far more of the ruling class than the fortunate few

who profited under James I's favourites.   Money talks, at
Westminster no less than in the City.

In other words, the three-handed fight has ended in
victory for those whom the House of Commons represented.
They consolidated their power after the Civil War by allying
with their defeated adversaries against the many-headed
monster ;   and this alliance was strengthened after 1688.
The old régime was fatally compromised when Charles II and
James II put themselves under the protection of Louis XIV,
the personification of absolutism as well as England's chief
trade rival.   It was finally discredited when James threatened
to use the unfree against the free, and when some of the unfree
rallied to Jacobitism.   James also associated himself with
England's victims in Ireland ;   the reconquest of Ireland by
foreign mercenaries finally ensured English domination there,
just as the Union of 1707 secured the businessmen of the
Lowlands against the depredations of the barbarous High-
landers, alliance with whom in 1715 was to drive the last
nail into the Stuart coffin.   All but an ineffective group of
sentimental squires deserted Divine Right monarchy and put
their money in the Bank of England.

The compromise of 1660 was directed against the lower
classes.   The world of 1714 was one in which, Dr Plumb says,
' without protection, the poor, the weak, and the sick went
under ;   the rich and the strong prospered '.   The yeomanry
was disappearing, the independent artisans were entering
upon their long agony in competition with bigger economic
units.   The close-knit patriarchal household community was
being undermined in the same decades as the patriarchal
theory of monarchy collapsed.   The wives of the poor were
becoming domestic drudges for their absent husbands rather
than partners in a family workshop ;   higher in the social scale,
the ideal of the lady of leisure, white-handed and delicate,
spread down into the middle, novel-reading classes.

Recorded history is like a photograph of an iceberg :   it
deals only with what is visible above the surface.   Yet below
the surface is the vast mass of the population, surviving sometimes in records when they are born, married, accused of
crime, or buried, but otherwise leaving no trace.   Through
all the far-reaching changes of this century which affected

the upper classes, the labour of peasants, craftsmen, mariners went on relatively unchanged. We can trace the humblest of the propertied classes in their wills : but at least fifty per cent of the population had nothing to leave. We know far too little about those who lived in mud houses, ate rye and bran bread, and got a high proportion of their calories (if they were lucky) from home-brewed beer. Even at the end of our period, Roger North tells us, the common people walked barefoot ' all over the north '. Children of the poor, Locke observed, seldom got more than bread and water up to the age of three years, and little enough of that. Rickets was known as ' the English disease ', though this may be only because it was first seriously studied (from the sixteen-forties) in England, where it had long existed but was made more noticeable by rising middle-class standards of living. Three out of every four Englishmen, the Quaker philanthropist John Bellers wrote in the last year of our period, could not afford medical advice or treatment. Three out of every four babies born in one London parish died almost immediately.

The ' unfree ' probably seldom went to church in what we traditionally regard as a very religious century : their clothes were not good enough for them to be seen in God's house. Husbandmen ' are usually so poor ', Baxter wrote in 1691, ' that they cannot have time to read a chapter in the Bible or to pray in their families. They come in weary from their labour, so that they are fitter to sleep than to read or pray. . . . They dare not displease them [their landlords] but they turn them out of their houses ; or increase their rents. I believe that their great landlords have more command of them than the King hath.' Yet, as Dean Hickes put it in 1684, ' the poor are the hands and feet of the body politic, . . . who hew the wood and draw the water of the rich. They plough our lands, and dig our quarries, and cleanse our streets. . . . No commonweal can subsist without poor.' To the preacher this seemed ' necessary for the establishment of superiority and subjection in human society ', a *reductio ad absurdum* of demands for civil equality. But within the memories of many of his congregation the iceberg had turned over ; and in the year after his sermon a survivor of those days, defeated in a last attempt at revolt, died on the scaffold proclaiming human equality in traditional Leveller phrases that live better than those of the Dean of Worcester : ' I am sure there was no man born marked of God above another ; for none comes into the world with a saddle on his back, neither any booted and spurred to ride him.'

The struggle for freedom, then, in the seventeenth century, was a more complex story than the books sometimes suggest. The men of property won freedom—freedom from arbitrary taxation and arbitrary arrest, freedom from religious persecution, freedom to control the destinies of their country through their elected representatives, freedom to buy and sell. They also won freedom to evict copyholders and cottagers, to tyrannise over their villages, to hire unprotected labour in the open market. The ' unfree ' had always been press-ganged into army or navy whenever their betters decided to have a war. But regular conscription dates from Anne's reign. The Act of 1708 made it clear that only those with ' no lawful calling or employment '—and no Parliamentary vote—were to be conscripted. Through Justices of the Peace, employers used the threat of call-up against recalcitrant workers. The smaller men failed in all spheres to get their freedom recognised, failed to win either the vote or economic security. ' The poorer and meaner people,' wrote the self-made Duke of Albemarle in 1671, ' have no interest in the commonweal but the use of breath.' When these poorer and meaner people broke through into literature with Bunyan, their symbol was a man with a burden on his back ; and Bunyan, former Parliamentarian soldier though he was, no longer thought it possible to shake off the burden by political action.

Freedom is not something abstract. It is the right of certain men to do certain things. Wildman had hoped that the Agreement of the People would ' lay down the foundations of freedom for all manner of people ' ; but the freedom that emerged was more circumscribed. The efforts of Levellers, Diggers, and others failed to create a homogeneous popular party in the forties : the last fling of Monmouth's revolt was as localised and hopelessly defeated as the risings of 1607 and 1628-31. The century which began with the many-headed monster ended with the mob. Only very slowly and late have men come to understand that unless freedom is universal it is only extended privilege. 'If the common people have no more freedom in England,' Winstanley asked, 'but only to live among their elder brothers and work for them for hire, what freedom then have they in England more than we have in Turkey or France?' By the end of our period the Good Old Cause was dead; the organisation of trade unions was just beginning.

Following Ralegh's advice quoted in the epigraph to this chapter, we have now considered the beginning, the proceeding, and the end of the great conflicts of our period. But in commending the actions of the men of the seventeenth century, as we should, in noting the very real constitutional, economic, and intellectual advances, let us also remember how much of the lives of how many men and women is utterly unknown to us.

21 Epilogue

> There is nothing either good or bad, but thinking makes it so.
>
> Shakespeare, *Hamlet* II, ii

> All, all of a piece throughout,
> The chase had a beast in view;
> The wars brought nothing about;
> The lovers were all untrue.
> 　　'Tis well an old age is out,
> 　　And time to begin a new.
>
> Dryden, *Secular Masque* (1700)

THE proverbial phrase, ' Queen Anne is dead ', came to mean that something had disappeared finally and irrevocably. If the age of faith ever existed, it was over by 1714. Witches and parsons, so powerful in 1603, counted for little in the world of rationalism, materialism, science, toleration. The most anachronistic thing about James II was his fanatical religious conviction. The Stuarts' decision that London was not worth a Holy Communion made them finally impossible even for the Tories. It did not matter what religion, if any, George I believed in, so long as it was not Popery. Latitudinarianism had triumphed in the upper ranks of the Church of England, moderation had replaced enthusiasm among the sects. Even the Quakers were remarkable now only for their quaint clothes and their business acumen. Charles II had ' touched ' nearly 100,000 people who believed he could cure them of scrofula. Queen Anne ' touched ' Samuel Johnson in 1712 (unsuccessfully), but she was the last English sovereign to try this magical cure. The age of reason is upon us. The eternal truths of 1603 have been abandoned, for ever. New and— men thought—more eternal truths had replaced them. ' Whatever is, is right,' sang Pope.

Yet was the universe as stable as it appeared to the unsophisticated observer ' when George in pudding time came o'er ' ? The South Sea Bubble is only six years ahead ; but society survived that crisis. The new economic order had sixty successful years before Adam Smith challenged it. In politics too, although the historical scholarship of the Tory Dr Brady had demolished Whig myths about the origin of Parliament, Whig and Parliamentary sovereignty was so firmly established that history seemed not to matter. It was again some sixty years before radicalism arose to rally the unfree once more. When it did, historical memories of the seventeenth century played their part, just as they were to do in the American and French Revolutions. But already by 1714 a different kind of subversive force was at work in the minds of men. Acquaintance with the exquisite art of the ancient civilisations of India, China, and Japan was beginning to shake European complacency. The worship of wild nature was coming into fashion in England, and reveals a quite new dissatisfaction with urban society and its self-conscious art. The eighteenth-century age of reason, in which only poets went mad, was ushered in to the savage irony of Mandeville and Swift. Another Irish cleric, George Berkeley, was beginning to wonder whether this solid material universe of Newton and Locke really existed at all outside men's minds. Already these isolated voices were suggesting that nothing is eternal, neither Whiggery nor Reason nor the mechanical universe, nor even perhaps the Bank of England.

Certainties come, certainties go ; history alone remains, because history changes with the events it records. So we can look back at this brilliant, bewildering century of change and try to assess ' what happened ', where contemporaries saw only events governed by fortune.

Appendix A

RULERS AND PARLIAMENTS

James I   1603-25

1604-10	First Parliament
1614	Addled Parliament
1621	Business Parliament
1624	Fourth Parliament

Charles I   1625-49

1625	First Parliament
1626	Second Parliament
1628-9	Third Parliament
April 1640	Short Parliament
Nov. 1640-9	Long Parliament

Republic   1649-53

1649-April 1653	Rump of Long Parliament
July-Dec. 1653	Barebones Parliament

Protectorate of Oliver Cromwell   1653-8

1654-5	First Parliament
1656-8	Second Parliament

Protectorate of Richard Cromwell   1658-9

Jan.-April 1659	Parliament

Republic   1659-60

May-Oct. 1659	Restored Rump
Oct.-Dec. 1659	Army Rule
Dec. 1659-Feb. 1660	Rerestored Rump
Feb.-March 1660	Secluded members added to Rump
April-May 1660	Convention Parliament : recalls Charles II

Charles II   1660-85

May-Dec. 1660	Convention Parliament
1661-79	Cavalier or Pensioner Parliament
March-July 1679	Third Parliament
1679-81	Fourth Parliament
April-May 1681	Oxford Parliament

James II   1685–8

1685–7   Parliament

Interregnum   Dec. 1688–Feb. 1689

Jan.–Feb. 1689   Convention Parliament : declares William and
                               Mary sovereigns

William III and Mary II   1689–94

Feb. 1689–Feb. 1690   Convention Parliament
1690–5   Second Parliament

William III   1694–1702

1695–8   Third Parliament
1698–9   Fourth Parliament
Feb.–July 1701   Fifth Parliament
1701–2   Sixth Parliament

Anne   1702–14

1702–5   First Parliament
1705–8   Second Parliament
1708–10   Third Parliament
1710–13   Fourth Parliament
1713–14   Fifth Parliament

Appendix B

ARCHBISHOPS OF CANTERBURY

1583–1604   John Whitgift
1604–10   Richard Bancroft
1611–33   George Abbott
1633–45   William Laud
1645–60   Episcopacy abolished
1660–3   William Juxon
1663–77   Gilbert Sheldon
1677–90   William Sancroft
1691–4   John Tillotson
1694–1714   Thomas Tenison

Appendix C

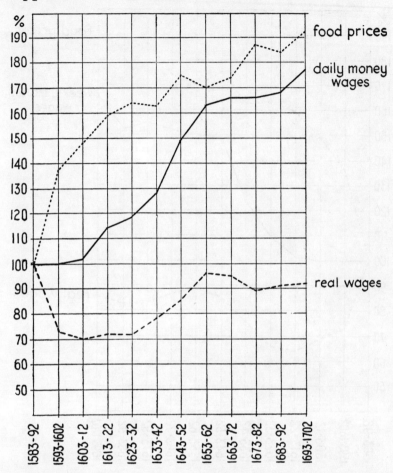

DIAGRAM 1

Real wages of skilled labourer (mason), 1583–1702

Figures (averages over ten-year periods) are taken from D. Knoop and
G. P. Jones, *The Medieval Mason* (1949), pp. 237–8. Prices are calculated
from twelve articles of food—wheat, beans, barley malt, cheese, butter,
oxen or beef, sheep, pigs, hens, pigeons, eggs, herrings. Money wages are
based on those prevailing at Oxford, Cambridge, and London Bridge.

The graph is shown in percentages, 1583–92 being taken as 100. In
that decade food prices were already over three times what they had been in
1501–10, money wages not quite twice what they had been in 1501–10. Cf. a
graph covering the same period in *Economica* (New Ser.), **24** (1957), p. 291.

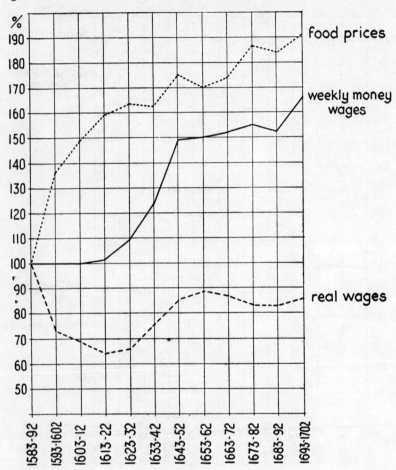

DIAGRAM 2

Real wages of unskilled labourer, 1583–1702

Figures for wages (averages over ten-year periods) are taken from Thorold Rogers, *A History of Agriculture and Prices in England* (1887), v, pp. 664–71. Prices as in Diagram 1.

The graph is again shown in percentages, 1583–92 being taken as 100.

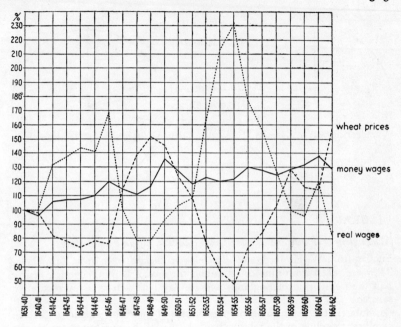

DIAGRAM 3

Wages and prices, 1639–62

Figures from Thorold Rogers, *op. cit.*, pp. 825–7.

The decennial averages in Diagrams 1 and 2 conceal the very considerable fluctuations which occurred from year to year. Diagram 3 shows wages in relation to wheat prices (only) ; wages are an average of skilled and unskilled. The graph again shows percentages, the decennial averages for 1631–40 being taken as 100.

Note that the periods when real wages were lowest coincide with those of most acute political discontent among the lower classes. The fact that the purchasing power of wages rose so steeply in the early fifties, culminating in the two most prosperous years of the century (1653–5), may help to explain the decline of popular agitation under the Protectorate.

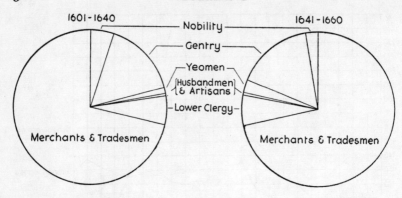

DIAGRAM 4

Money given to charity and charitable endowments by different social classes

Figures from W. K. Jordan, *Philanthropy in England, 1480–1660*, pp. 385–7.
They are taken from nine counties and the city of Bristol, covering nearly
half the population of England, and so may be taken as a representative
sample.

Note (i) the astonishing preponderance of merchant charity ; (ii) the
significant decline in the relative contribution of the nobility in the second
period, and the equally significant rise in the contribution of yeomen.

	(a) 1601–40	(b) 1641–60
Nobility	£55,078 — 5·17 %	£10,588 — 2·74 %
Gentry	£164,502 — 15·46 %	£62,786 — 16·23 %
Yeomen	£15,495 — 1·45 %	£10,442 — 2·70 %
Husbandmen and artisans	£4,063 — 0·39 %	£2,103 — 0·54 %
Lower clergy	£62,589 — 5·88 %	£24,034 — 6·22 %
Merchants and tradesmen	£762,339 — 71·65 %	£276,829 — 71·57 %
Total	£1,064,066 — 100 %	£386,782 — 100 %

Appendix D

ECONOMIC FLUCTUATIONS

1603	Plague. 33,500 deaths in London
1604–14	Revival of trade after depression. Prosperity
1615–17	Cokayne Project. Slump
1618–19	Partial recovery
1620–4	Catastrophic depression, bankruptcies, riots
1621–3	Bad harvests
1625	Plague. 35,500 deaths in London
1625–31	Slight recovery, then renewed depression
1629–31	Bad harvests
1632–7	Slight recovery, then stagnation
1636	Plague. 10,500 deaths in London, 5,500 on Tyneside
1638–50	Political and economic crisis
1646–51	Bad harvests
1651–8	Recovery and prosperity
1653–4	Excellent harvests
1659–60	Economic and political crisis
1658–61	Bad harvests
1661–5	Recovery
1665–6	Great Plague (the last plague—69,000 deaths in London, 5,000 in Colchester); and Fire of London
1667	Dutch Fleet in the Medway. Financial panic
1668–71	Building boom in London and partial recovery
1672–4	Stop of Exchequer, bankruptcies, depression
1673–4	Bad harvests
1674–86	Recovery and boom, with recession in 1678
1686	Recession
1687–95	Recovery and boom
1693–9	'Seven ill years'. Bad harvests 1693, 1697–8; 1696 distress among poor caused by calling in debased coinage
1696–7	Recession
1699–1709	Recovery and general prosperity, with recessions in 1701, 1706, 1708
1710	Recession
1711–14	Recovery and boom

Books for Further Reading

The seventeenth century is the greatest age in English literature. Far more than from any textbook, the student will learn about the period by reading the plays of Shakespeare, Jonson, Middleton, Wycherley, Congreve ; the poems of Donne, Herbert, Milton, Marvell, Dryden ; the essays of Bacon, Addison, and Steele ; the letters of Dorothy Osborne ; the works of Winstanley, Bunyan, Defoe, Swift.

It is also a great age of diarists, memoir writers, and historians. The student who wants to get below the surface of events will soon find himself reading Ludlow's *Memoirs*, George Fox's *Journal*, Pepys's *Diary*, Baxter's and Reresby's *Autobiographies* ; *Lives* of their husbands by Mrs. Hutchinson and the Duchess of Newcastle; Clarendon's *History of the Rebellion*, Burnet's *History of My Own Time*, and a host of others.

Anyone seriously interested in the period will one day have to read S. R. Gardiner's great *History of England, 1603–56* (18 vols.) and Sir C. H. Firth's continuation, *The Last Years of the Protectorate* (2 vols.), as well as Lord Macaulay's *History of England*, especially the incomparable Chapter 3 describing England in 1685.

Here are some further suggestions. (For List of Abbreviations, see page x.)

1 GENERAL

(a) Books

Clark, Sir G. N., *The Seventeenth Century* (2nd ed., 1950) ; *The Later Stuarts* (2nd ed., 1955)

Hill, C., *Puritanism and Revolution* (1958)

Hill, C., and Dell, E. (Editors), *The Good Old Cause* (1949)

Holdsworth, Sir W., *A History of English Law* (1924), vols. IV and VI

James, M., *Social Policy during the Puritan Revolution* (1930)

Ogg, D., *England in the Reign of Charles II*, 2 vols. (2nd ed., 1955) ; *England in the Reigns of James II and William III* (1955)

Oxford Book of Seventeenth Century Verse, The (as a start)

Notestein, W., *The English People on the Eve of Colonisation, 1603–30* (1954)

Slater, M., *Englishmen with Swords* (1949)—a novel

Trevelyan, G. M., *England under Queen Anne*, 3 vols. (1930–4)

Trevor-Roper, H. R., *Historical Essays* (1957)

(b) Articles

Hobsbawm, E. J., ' The Crisis of the Seventeenth Century ', *P. and P.*, **5** and **6**
Tawney, R. H., ' The Rise of the Gentry ', *Econ. H.R.*, **11**, 1
Trevor-Roper, H. R., *The Gentry, 1540–1640*, Econ. H.R. Supplement, 1 ;
   ' The General Crisis of the Seventeenth Century ', *P. and P.*, **16**

2 ECONOMIC

(a) Books

Albion, R. G., *Forests and Sea-Power* (1926)
Beer, M., *Early British Economics* (1938)
Clark, Sir G. N., *The Wealth of England, 1496–1760* (Home University Library)
Court, W. H. B., *The Rise of the Midland Industries, 1600–1838* (1938)
Davies, K. G., *The Royal African Company* (1957)
Dobb, M. H., *Studies in the Development of Capitalism* (1946)
Fuz, J. K., *Welfare Economics in English Utopias* (The Hague, 1952)
Hill, C., *Economic Problems of the Church* (1956)
Hoskins, W. G., *The Midland Peasant* (1957)
Johnson, A. H., *The Disappearance of the Small Landowner* (1909)
Kennedy, W., *English Taxation, 1640–1799* (1913)
Lipson, E., *The Economic History of England*, vols. II and III (3rd ed., 1943)
Nef, J. U., *The Rise of the British Coal Industry*, 2 vols. (1932) ; *Industry and Government in France and England, 1540–1640* (1940)
Newton, A. P., *Colonising Activities of the Early Puritans* (1913)
Ramsay, G. D., *English Overseas Trade during the Centuries of Emergence* (1957)
Roll, E., *A History of Economic Thought* (1938)
Tawney, R. H., *Religion and the Rise of Capitalism* (Pelican ed.) ; *Business and Politics under James I* (1958)
Unwin, G., *Industrial Organisation in the Sixteenth and Seventeenth Centuries* (1904)
Williamson, J. A., *A Short History of British Expansion*, vol. I (3rd ed., 1945)

(b) Articles

Coleman, D. C., ' Labour in the English Economy ', *Econ. H.R.* (2nd Ser.), **8**, 3
Davis, R., ' English Foreign Trade, 1660–1700 ', *Econ. H.R.* (2nd Ser.), **7**, 2 ; ' Merchant Shipping in the Economy of the Late Seventeenth Century ', *Econ. H.R.* (2nd Ser.), **9**, 1
Fisher, F. J., ' The Development of the London Food Market ', *Econ. H.R.*, **5**, 2 ; ' London's Export Trade in the Early Seventeenth Century ', *Econ. H.R.* (2nd Ser.), **3**, 2
Habakkuk, H. J., ' English Landownership, 1680–1740 ', *Econ. H.R.*, **10**, 1

Hoskins, W. G., 'The Rebuilding of Rural England, 1570–1640', *P. and P.*, **4**

Kerridge, E., ' The Movement of Rent, 1540–1640 ', *Econ. H.R.* (2nd Ser.), **6**, 1

Nef, J. U., ' The Progress of Technology and the Growth of Large-scale Industry in Great Britain, 1540–1640 ', *Econ. H.R.*, **5**, 1

Stone, L., ' The Nobility in Business ', in *The Entrepreneur*, Papers presented at the Annual Conference of the Economic History Society, April 1957

3 POLITICAL AND CONSTITUTIONAL

(a) Books

Abbott, W. C., *The Writings and Speeches of Oliver Cromwell*, 4 vols. (Harvard University Press, 1937–47)

Brailsford, H. N., *The Levellers* (1961)

Feiling, Sir K. G., *A History of the Tory Party, 1640–1714* (1924)

Firth, Sir C. H., *Cromwell's Army* (1902) ; *Oliver Cromwell* (World's Classics)

Foot, M., *The Pen and the Sword* (1957)

Foxcroft, H. C., *A Character of the Trimmer* (1946)

Haller, W. (Editor), *Tracts on Liberty in the Puritan Revolution*, 3 vols. (Columbia University Press, 1934)

Haller, W. and Davies, G. (Editors), *The Leveller Tracts, 1647–53* (Columbia University Press, 1944)

Hexter, J. H., *The Reign of King Pym* (Harvard University Press, 1941)

Hill, C., *Oliver Cromwell* (Historical Association Pamphlet, 1958)

Judson, M. A., *The Crisis of the Constitution* (Rutgers University Press, 1949)

Kemp, Betty, *King and Commons, 1660–1832* (1957)

Kenyon, J. P., *Robert Spencer, Earl of Sunderland, 1641–1702* (1958)

Mathew, D., *The Jacobean Age* (1938)

Morley, Iris, *A Thousand Lives* (1954)

Notestein, W., *The Winning of the Initiative by the House of Commons* (1924)

Petegorsky, D. W., *Left-Wing Democracy in the English Civil War* (1940)

Plumb, J. H., *Sir Robert Walpole*, vol. 1 (1956)

Tanner, J. R., *English Constitutional Conflicts of the Seventeenth Century* (1928)

Trevor-Roper, H. R., *Archbishop Laud* (1940)

Turner, F. C., *James II* (1948)

Willson, D. H., *James VI and I* (1956)

Wolfe, D. M. (Editor), *Leveller Manifestoes of the Puritan Revolution* (New York, 1944)

Wormuth, F. D., *The Royal Prerogative, 1603–49* (New York, 1939)

(b) Articles

Aylmer, G. E., ' Office-holding as a Factor in English History, 1625–42 ', *History*, **44**

Hexter, J. H., ' The Problem of the Presbyterian Independents ', *American Historical Review*, **44**

Manning, B. S., ' The Nobles, the People and the Constitution ', *P. and P.*, **9**

Stone, L., ' The Inflation of Honours ', *P. and P.*, **14**

Trevor-Roper, H. R., ' Oliver Cromwell and his Parliaments ', in *Essays Presented to Sir Lewis Namier* (ed. R. Pares and A. J. P. Taylor, 1956)

Wagner, D. O., ' Coke and the Rise of Economic Liberalism ', *Econ. H.R.*, **6**, 1

4 RELIGION AND IDEAS

(a) Books

Allen, J. W., *English Political Thought, 1603–44* (1938)

Bahlman, D. W. R., *The Moral Revolution of 1688* (Yale, 1957)

Bush, D., *English Literature in the Earlier Seventeenth Century* (1945)

Butterfield, H., *The Origins of Modern Science, 1300–1800* (1949)

Carritt, E. F., *A Calendar of British Taste, from 1600 to 1800* (n.d., 1948–9)

Caudwell, C., *The Crisis in Physics* (1939)

Clark, Sir G. N., *Science and Social Welfare in the Age of Newton* (1937)

Cragg, G. R., *From Puritanism to the Age of Reason* (1950) ; *Puritanism in the Period of the Great Persecution* (1957)

Cruttwell, P., *The Shakespearean Moment and its Place in the Poetry of the Seventeenth Century* (1954)

Douglas, D. C., *English Scholars* (2nd ed., 1951)

'Espinasse, M., *Robert Hooke* (1956)

Farrington, B., *Francis Bacon* (1951)

Gooch, G. P., and Laski, H. J., *The History of English Democratic Ideas in the Seventeenth Century* (1927)

Haller, W., *The Rise of Puritanism* (Columbia University Press, 1938) ; *Liberty and Reformation in the Puritan Revolution* (Columbia University Press, 1955)

Harbage, A., *Shakespeare and the Rival Traditions* (New York, 1952)

Jones, R. F., *Ancients and Moderns* (Washington University Press, 1936)

Jordan, W. K., *The Development of Religious Toleration in England*, 4 vols. (1932–40) ; *Men of Substance : Henry Parker and Henry Robinson* (Chicago University Press, 1942) ; *Philanthropy in England, 1480–1660* (1959)

Knights, L. C., *Drama and Society in the Age of Jonson* (1937)

Laski, H. J., *The Rise of European Liberalism* (1936)

Laslett, P. (Editor), *Patriarcha and other Political Works of Sir Robert Filmer* (1949)

Marlowe, J., *The Puritan Tradition in English Life* (1956)

Mason, S. F., *A History of the Sciences* (1953)

Miller, P., *The New England Mind : the Seventeenth Century* (New York, 1939)

Morton, A. L., *The English Utopia* (1952)

Notestein, W., *History of Witchcraft in England from 1558 to 1718* (Washington, 1911)

Schlatter, R. B., *The Social Ideas of Religious Leaders, 1660–88* (1940)

Scholes, P. A., *The Puritans and Music in England and New England* (1934)

Tawney, R. H., *Harrington's Interpretation of his Age* (1941)

Wedgwood, C. V., *Poetry and Politics under the Stuarts* (1960)

West, A., *The Mountain in the Sunlight* (1958)

Westfall, R. S., *Science and Religion in Seventeenth Century England* (Yale University Press, 1958)

Willey, B., *The Seventeenth Century Background* (1934)

Winstanley, G., *Selected Writings* (ed. L. D. Hamilton, 1944)

Wolfe, D. M., *Milton in the Puritan Revolution* (New York, 1941)

Woodhouse, A. S. P. (Editor), *Puritanism and Liberty* (1938)

Wright, L. B., *Middle-Class Culture in Elizabethan England* (North Carolina University Press, 1935)

Zagorin, P., *A History of Political Thought in the English Revolution* (1954)

(b) Articles

Cole, A., ' The Quakers and the English Revolution ', *P. and P.*, **10**

George, C. H., ' A Social Interpretation of English Puritanism ', *Journal of Modern History*, **25**, 4

James, M., ' The Political Importance of the Tithes Controversy in the Puritan Revolution ', *History* (New Ser.), **26**

Macpherson, C. B., ' The Social Bearings of Locke's Political Theory ', *Western Political Quarterly*, **7**, 1 ; ' Harrington's " Opportunity State " ', *P. and P.*, **17**

Mason, S. F., ' Science and Religion in Seventeenth Century England ', *P. and P.*, **3**

Mercer, E., ' The Houses of the Gentry ', *P. and P.*, **4**

Merton, R. K., ' Science and Technology and Society in Seventeenth Century England ', *Osiris*, **4**

Thomas, K. V., ' Women and the Civil War Sects ', *P. and P.*, **13**

Whitman, A. O., ' The Re-establishment of the Church of England ', *T.R.H.S.*, 1955

Index

Black figures refer to main entries